D1134934

SHAKEDOWN

SHAKEDOWN

HOW THE NEW ECONOMY
IS CHANGING OUR LIVES

Angus Reid

Doubleday Canada Limited

Canadian Cataloguing in Publication Data

Reid, Angus
    Shakedown: how the new economy is changing our lives

ISBN 0-385-25610-8

1. Canada – Economic conditions 1991–
2. Economic forecasting – Canada. I. Title.

HC115.R15 1996   330.971'0648   C96-930583-4

Jacket illustration by Paul Watson
Jacket design by Kevin Connolly
Text design by Heidy Lawrance Associates
Printed and bound in the USA

Published in Canada by
Doubleday Canada Limited
105 Bond Street
Toronto, Ontario
M5B 1Y3

For Margaret,

Jennifer and

Andrew

CONTENTS

PREFACE

The only time I was punched in the nose for asking too many questions was when I was 15. It happened in 1963, in the stock room of a Safeway store on the corner of River and Osborne in Winnipeg. My assailant was a tall 19-year-old named Bob, who thought I was a bit too curious about the details of his private life. Luckily, nobody has assaulted me since, although I am pretty sure that at least a few politicians have been tempted.

I was raised in an Irish Catholic family – one of eight children – so I guess I'm used to hearing opinions and offering some of my own. My mother grew up in rural Saskatchewan, where the most popular entertainment was listening in on endless debates that would take place on long winter nights over the telephone party line. "When I was a child," she would tell us children, "I could pick up the phone and hear as many as a dozen of my neighbours arguing about politics. It was magic." That magic is my inheritance, since I have spent most of my adult life using telephones to find out what people are thinking.

I founded the Angus Reid Group above a 7-Eleven store in Winnipeg in the late 1970s. Since then, I like to think that my colleagues and I have put some important questions on the Canadian table. We aim for questions designed to get to the nub of issues and to produce scientifically credible pictures of how people think and feel about various issues. My guess is that we have asked about 50 million questions over the past two decades. These have run a wide gamut, touching on the political, social, cultural and commercial life of Canadians as well as people around the world. We have queried Canadians about the big issues and the not so big – everything from belief in God (82% say yes) to whether they own a garlic press (38% own at least one).[1]

Inevitably, perhaps, I have learned quite a bit during these exchanges. The first thing I have learned is that "the common man" doesn't exist. Elsewhere in this book, I talk about the needs of "ordinary "or "average" Canadians, mainly because my faith lies not so much with the elite but with the ordinary and in some cases, exceptional, Canadians that are the marrow and sinew of this country. That said, I don't really think there is any such thing as an average Canadian. Everyone knows that Canada has a unique cultural mosaic – it is a place where people of all backgrounds can live in peace as long as they respect the rights of their neighbours. But what my colleagues and I keep discovering is that there is also an attitudinal mosaic. For a country with such a placid reputation, differences of opinion abound, and you will find them wherever people gather, including the offices, living rooms, kitchens and bedrooms of the nation.

Second, while not every Canadian has an opinion about breakfast cereal, most have a deep interest in their country and the issues that confront it. Again, there is considerable disagreement about these issues. But you do not find many people wary about saying exactly what's on their minds.

That frankness is not by any means universal. In some countries, people are afraid to speak up. In others, they just don't care. When we poll in the United States, we are always surprised at how many Americans have no opinion on even the most important political questions. Indeed, the subject of voter alienation is one of the most critical issues in American polling today. In Japan, people may care, but they are reluctant to reveal their opinions. In

Britain, survey respondents are invariably polite, but class differences make upper-class Britons less cooperative than those in the working class.

Canadians, regardless of income, age or position, do care, and they are usually more than ready to verbalize their sentiments – regardless of whether they agree with what their neighbours think. Canadians make good citizens because they want to get involved. Americans may have a brasher, more gregarious image, but a smaller proportion of them wants to be bothered with concerns that affect people at large. That is why Canadians have a high voter turnout. It is also part of the reason why it is so much fun being a pollster in this country. It's like sitting in the front seat of the great Canadian rollercoaster. At times, such as during the 1995 Quebec referendum, it can even get scary.

During the past two decades, it has become increasingly clear that our national well-being is ultimately measured by the attitudes, opinions and feelings of Canadians about themselves and the broader communities of which they are a part. Economic measures, such as gross domestic product, competitiveness, productivity and price stability, though useful indicators of our material progress, fail to penetrate the real soul of Canada – the dreams and aspirations of its people and the sense of trust and mutual support they display to one another.

Of course, everyone, in every country, wants economic security. But if that's as far as it goes – if there is no more imagination in the air about how much better life could be if we showed due concern for all those other things that matter to us – then we might as well forget elections. We might as well call in the accountants and tell them to run the place.

Those 50 million questions and answers tell me that Canada is about far more than numbers on a balance sheet. There are flashier places in the world, no doubt, but none whose existence has been defined by the collective decision to carve a unique social space out of a hostile environment, using principles that celebrate rather than constrain cultural and linguistic differences, principles that promote a far different mix of private initiative and public responsibility than we see in our neighbours to the south.

The 1990s have witnessed a great stirring of the Canadian soul. Issues of national unity, anxiety over jobs, the emerging global economy, the changing role of government, new technologies and fundamentally different demographic forces are rapidly changing our social space. Many Canadians feel marooned on what seems an alien landscape, confronted by seemingly contradictory paths to the future. I wrote this book because I'm convinced that the concerns and anxieties about the future expressed in recent polls need to be addressed. Canadians sense that *something* is happening – that powerful changes are coursing through their lives. And they're right.

Over the past two decades, more than two million ordinary Canadians have shared their opinions, perceptions and aspirations with the Angus Reid Group. Without their cooperation, this book and the work that we do would not be possible.

I would also like to thank my friends and associates at the Angus Reid Group whose enthusiasm for this undertaking and patience during my leave of absence to write this book is gratefully appreciated. During the course of researching and writing this book I received helpful advice and assistance from a number of people whose contribution I wish to acknowledge: Gary Bennewies, David Bond, Darrell Bricker, John and Heather Brown, Chris Bunting, Mag

Burns, Bruce Cameron, David Fish, Cathy Heatherington, John Horne, Marie-Louise Huot, Andrew Grenville, Jake MacDonald, Paul and Dianne McGeachie, Doug Mazur, Jim Morakis, Angela Muzzo, Katja Panzar, Liz Poyser, Bob Richardson, Terry Roberge, Gus Schattenberg, Jim Travers, Jeff Vidler and John Wright. I owe a special debt of gratitude to Jane Dyson who conducted much of the documentation research, prepared the index and offered helpful comments and criticisms on earlier drafts.

I also wish to thank Dan Turner for his considerable contribution. Dan demanded an accessible, readable style, something that doesn't come easily to one trained as a sociologist. In addition to serving as a writing coach and editor, Dan provided many helpful insights and suggestions that improved the content and flow of the manuscript.

Thanks also to John Pearce, associate publisher at Doubleday Canada, whose enthusiastic support for *Shakedown* began the day I first met him in the fall of 1994 and never wavered. I am particularly appreciative that John had the wisdom to appoint fellow former Manitoban Michael Posner as my editor. Michael's insights into the mind of the reader gave this book its final form.

Finally, I wish to thank my family who have been forced to contend with a somewhat distracted writer over the past year. No acknowledgment can do proper justice to the support, guidance and encouragement I have received from my closest and dearest friend – my wife, Margaret.

INTRODUCTION

" Everything now lies in the balance
between catastrophe or creation
as possible human destinies."
Arthur Kroker, "THE ECLIPSE OF CULTURE"

When massive ice floes collide in the high Arctic, they create tower-
ing pressure ridges, a source of considerable frustration to adventur-
ers and Inuit alike. Often impenetrable, these ridges obscure the
horizon and delay a traveler's progress. Crossing them can be
exceedingly dangerous, requiring reserves of patience and skill, and
a lot of teamwork. The reward, on the other side, is a vast expanse
of packed snow, limitless horizons and easy sledding – or, I should
say, *easier* sledding, since very little comes easy in the Arctic.

This book is about a different kind of dangerous crossing, one
that Canadians are now making as they navigate the social,
economic and political pressure ridges that have formed at the inter-
section of two great eras in our history. It's about the frustration,
anxiety and anger most Canadians feel over a journey delayed; the
bickering among our leaders and experts over which route we
should take; the casualties and triumphs that have occurred in the
private and public lives of Canadians; and the future that awaits us

if we can stay together, remain calm and summon our reserves of energy and creativity.

The 1990s have confronted Canadians with enormous challenges. Our pressure ridges seem insurmountable – massive debt at every level, from households to the federal government; restructuring of the labour force, with lower wages and increased insecurity; stagnant consumer spending, which is depressing housing values and killing jobs; and fragmentation in the Canadian political system, which threatens the very existence of the country. Most of us weren't ready for this.

To traverse these obstacles and to secure the future, we must grasp two fundamental truths. The first is that the forces that have sustained us for nearly two generations have lost their momentum. A unique era, which began in the mid-1960s, has ended. The second truth is a corollary of the first: a new set of forces is moving swiftly into place – forces that will create challenges and opportunities we couldn't have dreamed of a decade ago. These forces include the accelerating use of dazzling new technology by Canadian businesses and households, the growing influence of global economics and the impending movement of more than five million Canadians into an age group characterized by pre-retirement values.

There's a shakedown coming in Canada. In fact, it's already begun. Consider the following.

- In the 1993 federal election campaign, more parties ran for office than at any time in our history.
- In 1995, more personal computers than televisions were purchased for use in Canadian homes.
- For the first time since the early 1960s, self-employed entrepreneurs outnumber government workers.

- For the first time ever, there are more Canadians over 55 than under 15.[1]

As we struggle to adapt to new social and economic realities, long-established practices, principles and values are being questioned and in many cases abandoned. Everyone – companies, households and governments – is engaged in a frantic process of cost containment, reengineering, delayering and downsizing. The dominant ethos of the new era – do more, better, for less – has gripped Canadians in all walks of life. Whether the future will bring progress and hope or decline and despair is the central question of our age. There is, for now, no strong consensus among either experts or average Canadians on this issue. But few doubt that this decade is producing a level of dislocation and gut-wrenching change the likes of which haven't been seen in 50 years.

Only a few years ago, in *MegaTrends 2000,* John Naisbitt and Patricia Aburdene glowingly predicted that "in the decade of the 1990s the world is entering a period of economic prosperity."[2] Two years after that grand pronouncement, the G7 leaders met in an atmosphere of alarm. The developed world was caught in the grip of a major recession, as the global unemployment rate hurtled toward the one billion mark. Since that summit, France has been rocked by terrorist attacks and massive demonstrations staged by farmers and civil servants. Germany has been confronted with the rise of the far right and the economic pain of absorbing East Germany. The once invulnerable Japanese have suffered through recession and have been forced to rethink the sacred principle of lifetime job security. The United States has been faced with domestic terrorism, legislative deadlock over the federal debt and growing concerns about a shrinking middle class.

As for Canada, after 10 years of smiling, sonorous optimism, Brian Mulroney finally got out in 1993 when the getting was good. He did not leave a happy nation in his wake. While Canada remained a rosy place for investors, with a buoyant stock market, healthy corporate profits, stable prices and declining interest rates, it was hardly business as usual for most Canadians. At work, increasing job insecurity and declining wages became the rule rather than the exception. At home, declining disposable income and higher debt levels began to exact their toll on consumer spending. In the polling booth, a revolution of sorts was in the making, with the surprising victory of hard-line politicians such as Mike Harris in Ontario and the unprecedented support for cost-cutting measures by politicians of all stripes, including Roy Romanow in Saskatchewan, Paul Martin in Ottawa and Ralph Klein in Alberta.

Many economists, lulled by 25 years of marketplace optimism and strong consumer demand, were caught completely off guard. Take economist Jeffrey Rubin, who declared in 1992 that Canadians would be "shocked" by the strength of the economy's recovery.[3] Canadians were shocked all right, but the shock was over the sputtering weakness of the so-called recovery. A year earlier, federal finance department economists forecast that the unemployment rate would be 7.5% by 1996. They missed the mark – by about 300,000 very distressed workers.

If the experts keep getting it wrong, who can blame Canadians for being confused? In the morning papers, we read articles about record profits. On the evening news, we saw 15,000 people line up for jobs at a General Motors plant in Pickering, Ontario. And while the papers were reporting record highs on the stock market, they also carried polls showing widespread pessimism and insecurity among ordinary Canadians.

Imagine the confusion of a middle manager living in Calgary who reads both the *Calgary Herald* and the *Globe and Mail*. In June 1994, the *Globe* reported that middle managers were making a comeback following the recession of the early 1990s, a recession that was unusually hard on managers and supervisors. In April 1995, the *Herald* ran a piece suggesting that middle managers were going to be replaced by self-managed work teams. A month later, the *Globe* declared that middle-management jobs were safe, then reversed itself 10 months later in a story headlined "One Day You're Family; the Next Day You're Fired."[4] The theme of this last piece was how quickly companies were jettisoning middle managers.

In any month during the 1990s, it was possible to read that we were going through an economic boom or an economic bust, that the job market was bad or the job market was good, that competition from the United States was helping or that it was hurting. In any given week, we were likely to hear that the worst was behind us or ahead of us, that the future for young people was awful or wonderful, that our health-care system was terrific or falling apart, that Quebec was staying or that it was leaving. The media trumpeted technology as the saviour of the economy while thousands of full-time jobs were lost because of technology. We read about the benefits of trade liberalization on page 1, but on page 3 we discovered that huge swings in exchange rates had wiped out the gains of 30 years of negotiations overnight. Excuse me, does anybody know what's going on out there?

I don't pretend to have all the answers to the surprising and largely unexpected events that have occurred in this decade. Reading the mood of the country is never easy, but it's impossible to ignore the sense of frustration and anxiety evident across Canada. At the end of 1995, almost 60% of Canadians described the overall state of the economy as "poor" or "very poor."[5] When Canadians look back over the last seven years, most feel that their standard of living has declined, the security of their jobs has decreased and the unity of the country is threatened as never before. When they look to the future, a growing number worry about how best to react to the forces of change that are battering their lives and their society.

In recent years, I have spoken to hundreds of gatherings across Canada, talking about these unprecedented changes. What I have learned in this process has meshed with our findings from scientific polling: Canadians are almost dizzy from the events swirling around them and are anxious to understand why they are occurring and where we are heading.

We have to understand that the chaos we're seeing isn't attributable to any one simple factor – too much debt, too many immigrants, too many people on welfare, too much concern about Quebec, too much government, too many timid politicians, or whatever other pat explanation is making the rounds. What is taking place isn't a quick response to superficial problems. What is taking place is a much broader transformation of Canadian society, bringing fundamentally new economic, technological and demographic forces that will permanently change the lives of millions of Canadians.

The sooner that we accept this reality, the better able we will be to consider the social and personal adjustments that will be required if we are to survive, adapt and succeed. The risk of failing to confront the scope and intensity of the changes taking place involves far more than our national competitiveness – which, to hear some analysts talk, is all that matters. At stake are a number of equally important considerations, including the social and cultural heritage of our country and our ability to maintain some control over the way our lives unfold. To some degree, these are universal themes. Nations everywhere are struggling to adjust to the new realities. That said, every country will not respond in the same way. The new era must be evaluated in the context of each nation's unique historical, geographic and cultural circumstances.

Despite unmistakable similarities, Canada and the United States remain societies with enough fundamental differences to justify a border. Different geography, institutions, populations and histories have produced sharply different values and beliefs. Many Americans, for example, are zealous minimalists when it comes to government. Canadians, at least until recently, have respected the notion of good and strong government. Although these values may be shifting, the differences between Americans and Canadians have not disappeared.

Ponder an electorate that has always provided at least some encouragement for socialist parties at both the federal and provincial levels. Recall 11 legislatures that stepped over a political land-mine into the world of medicare, which remains an institution of pride to most Canadians and still can't be sold in the U.S. How right-wing – and how libertarian – a population do you have when a majority of Canadians don't think gun registration will work but *two-thirds of them want it anyway?* Canadians are unique, and we need to understand our own circumstances if we are going to successfully adapt to the new realities we face.

This book begins with a review of the often contradictory events and trends that distinguish the first half of the 1990s from the decades that came before. These changes have not only affected the economic and political life of Canadians; they have fundamentally altered the signposts and beacons that define our present position and illuminate the path to the future. The time for mourning what we have lost is over. The time for understanding what we're up against has begun. Looking back will provide a baseline for determining the dimension of change, and it will help us plot a new direction.

Most of the events that govern our lives rarely make headlines, yet they are much more powerful than the myths we live by. The conventional wisdom is that the 1980s were the money years. The decade seemed to drip with power and dollar bills. But Canadians' real wages actually increased by only 2% – the lowest rate of growth since the beginning of the Second World War.

Then there's the Myth of the Baby Boom. Everyone knows the mammoth effect the boomers have had on Canadian society. A huge population bulge produced a big economy, right? There is truth there, but it's a half-truth at best. The real effect wasn't so much a product of the baby boom generation as a whole as of the female boomers, whose behavior helped ignite one of the most important social transformations in our history.

One of the prevailing myths involves excessive government spending. It's true that not every government has always spent our money wisely over the past 25 years. It's not true, however, that government is the ogre it's made out to be. Nor is Adam Smith the saviour his disciples insist he is. Government spending ran into new circumstances that politicians were slow to comprehend. In the years to come, we must take an unemotional look at what we're going to need from governments, rather than trying to put them in shackles and escort them to the executioner.

There is also the Myth of Leadership, otherwise known as the

Myth of Political Saviours. If observers from some distant land were to examine our newspapers and video files for the story of Canada over the past three decades, they would be justified in thinking that almost everything that happened here was the result of the actions of Pierre Elliott Trudeau and Brian Mulroney. The truth is that they did matter, but only marginally.

To understand *why* Canada has been transformed over the past 30 years we must look beyond our politicians, for the most part, and study ourselves. We must exorcise, once and for all, the demons of an era that has now ended. The values that defined Canadian society from the 1960s to the late 1980s – unbounded confidence in government, the sexual revolution, a lust for material possessions and soaring optimism about the future – are museum pieces. The seminal forces of that era – a rapidly growing labour force, voracious levels of consumer spending, mushrooming government programs and a booming services industry – are now spent.

It is vital to understand that the recession of the early 1990s was not the typical cyclical downturn, the momentary pause that allows us to catch our breath before we returned to business as usual. In fact, this recession turned out to be not a recession at all but a social and economic chasm the size of the Fraser River Canyon. Deep and rocky waters flow through it. It is no place to try to tread water. It is a place to sink or swim. And it marked a distinct turning point in Canadian history: the end of one era and the dawn of another.

The new era is being shaped by changing technology, globalization and the ageing of our population. These are not only powerful new forces; they are fascinating. The technological breakthroughs, of course, are amazing. Who, even a decade ago, would have guessed how rapidly technology would reshape our lives, both at home and in the workplace? Who would have suspected, in the mid-1980s, that the cold war would end and the world would come charging at us as though borders no longer existed? True, the ageing of the population was predictable enough, but are we ready for the changing values and consumer spending patterns that will follow in its wake?

That all three trends are converging at the same time adds an apocalyptic dimension to the future. Although some Canadians are clearly benefiting from these new realities, many are fearful, about their own futures, the future of their children and the future of the country. Are these fears justified or are they simply an understandable but groundless psychological response to rapid change?

Nowhere has this transformation been felt more acutely than in the workplace. The picture is not pretty. Millions of Canadians are working harder than ever, yet feel their wages and job security slipping backwards. And the unemployment rate, while depressingly high, tells only a small part of the current job crisis. The bigger story concerns the restructuring of the workplace – huge reductions in full-time paid jobs and equally significant increases in the number of Canadians working in part-time and temporary jobs and as self-employed entrepreneurs. It also concerns the growing employment anxiety recorded in our polls. There is, as we'll see, good reason to be worried.

The transformation of work is being matched by equally important shifts at home and in public life. Declining take-home income and rising personal debt are changing patterns of consumption and producing new consumer values. Collective institutions, ranging from local schools and hospitals to giant Crown corporations, are experiencing sweeping changes in response to new fiscal pressures and altered public expectations. At the same time, the family and immediate community are re-emerging as pivotal sources of material support and emotional security.

The risks of failing to confront the future, of pretending that nothing has really changed, are enormous. I conclude this book by stepping out of my role as pollster and observer and offering suggestions about how Canadians should adapt to the new forces changing their lives. We must recognize that Canada has deep reserves of social resources that give us a competitive edge in the new economy. These resources, matched with the energy and creativity of individual Canadians, are our best hope for the future. The new era will offer access to resources and information on an unprecedented scale. We must use them to our advantage. We don't have much time.

One

A PATH OBSCURED

*"We are entering a tricky,
contradictory zone, full of paradoxes and blind alleys."*
Salman Rushdie, "IN GOD WE TRUST"

Forget for a moment that you are a Canadian. Imagine that you are a nomad somewhere on the Sahara. You are piloting a camel caravan across the shifting sands. You travel at night to escape the heat of the desert sun. You move under a dome of stars that have guided you for many years. These stars are old allies. They have lent comfort to your journeys since childhood. They were friends and guardians to your parents and, long after you are gone, they will be friends and guardians to your children and grandchildren. Then, one night, some of the very biggest and most trusted of stars suddenly disappear. The next night, they do not reappear. Every member of the caravan, from the oldest and wisest to the youngest and most innocent, feels lost.

This is, of course, a remote and melodramatic image for Canadians. We have always known our way, even if the climate, major historic events and our own idiosyncrasies have occasionally created stumbling blocks. The settling of the land, the First World War, the

Great Depression, the Second World War – all caused hardship and confusion to our parents and ancestors. But most of us have heard of these events second-hand. For the vast majority of us, the road to prosperity has been smooth and well lit for as long as we can remember. That was the case right up until the end of the 1980s, when some of our own stars began to flicker and disappear and others started to move in new and confusing patterns.

Since then, many Canadians began to feel disoriented about the present and anxious about the future. Institutions that were our beacons of safety and security during the past 50 years – governments, large corporations and the professions – are not offering us what they once did. The Canadian marketplace, once a warm and cozy haven, stands naked against the blizzard of international competition. Political parties that inspired loyal followings for decades have been all but obliterated overnight. The basic rules and patterns that made our lives predictable, that imposed a sense of order and continuity, no longer seem to apply. The Canadian economy has supposedly climbed out of the trough it fell into during the early 1990s, but who can tell, other than Bay Street? The unemployment rate remains high, and when jobs do open up, many of them are minimum wage. The most obvious unemployment problems are in the shrinking resource sectors, such as fisheries. But every sector has been victimized. The professions and upper management, for instance, used to be sacrosanct. Not any more. Today, while leaders in business and politics lionize the virtues of knowledge and education, graduate lawyers, nurses, teachers, engineers and architects are competing for fewer jobs.

This age of discontinuity involves a far different dynamic between elements of the economic and social order. Productivity and wages, which used to increase arm in arm, are no longer linked. There has also been a separation of production and consumption. The principles of Henry Ford, who insisted on paying his workers enough so they could afford the cars they were producing (thereby generating more consumption), have been reversed. Now, a new discipline that tries to extract more for less is depressing consumption and killing even more jobs. Finally, in politics, we have witnessed the delinking of ideology and identity. The left-right continuum that defined our public life has been replaced by culture, regionalism and tribalism as the most important sources of political identity.

In recent years, Canada has ranked first or second in just about every international poll measuring prosperity or quality of life. Yet when my firm interviewed citizens of several nations about their confidence in the future, Canadians emerged at the gloomy end of the spectrum. For many of us, the path to the future has turned as treacherous as a sidewalk during freezing rain. We inch along, never quite sure of our footing, half expecting our world to turn upside down at any moment. What makes our journey even more frustrating is all the chirping we get from the experts about how nice the weather is and how the universe is unfolding just as it should.

"Not to worry," prattle the economists. "The heavens aren't really falling. There's just a bit of restructuring going on."

"Not to worry," jabber the politicians. "We'll just shrink government and everything will brighten up in no time."

"Not to worry," intone the entrepreneurs. "This may seem like Hell, but it's really Heaven. It's a brand-new kind of Heaven, and a heck of a lot more efficient than the old one."

All of these reassurances are starting to sound a little hollow. This decade, which began with the fall of the Berlin Wall and the Canada-U.S. Free Trade Agreement, was supposed to bring increased security and improved prosperity to all Canadians. Instead, it has brought a general decline in our standard of living and a heightened sense of anxiety about the future. Some of this, of course, has to do with money. Falling incomes and increased debt are bound to make people uncomfortable. But money is only part of the story. In many respects, the more important reality in Canada today is the declining relevance of a broad constellation of rules that illuminated the world around us. If we now feel lost, it is not just because there are fewer coins in our pockets. It is because the beacons that have guided us have started to flicker and fade. Here are 10 that are now starting to look more like myths.

MYTH NO. I – BIG IS SAFE

The most enduring image of my early school days in Nanaimo, B.C. is the map of the world that seemed to cover the entire front wall of my classroom. There was Canada, this strange jigsaw of shapes and colours, an ocean of pink surrounded by blue seas, poised powerfully above a noticeably smaller U.S.A. In this child's world of the early 1950s, a frightening world of air-raid drills and fallout shelters, there was special comfort and security knowing that I lived in one of the biggest countries in the world. Big mattered. Big meant safety. Big meant prosperity. If you played your cards right, when you grew up you'd be able to buy a big car with a big engine and big fins. The bigger the better.

Most of the pointers in our lives have emphasized that there is safety and security in size. These pointers have guided us as workers, consumers and citizens. Want a safe job? Find a big employer. The biggest and safest is government. Want to find the best selection of products at the best prices? Go to the biggest department store. Who deserves your vote in an election? Choose between the big, established political parties. Otherwise, your vote won't count.

Size has been worshipped in the Western marketplace for most of this century. Henry Ford set the tone in the 1920s, with mass production of Tin Lizzies. Corporations built huge factories all over North America because "economies of scale" allowed fixed costs to be spread out over more production, lowering per-unit prices. Corporate leaders became addicted to bigness; witness all those mergers in the '80s, many of which made little business sense.

Canadians emerged from the Second World War wanting more of what governments had to offer. They had served us well during the Great Depression and led us to victory in the war. Now they would help us build upon our sacrifices, giving us a larger, more secure safety net and new economic opportunities. And we loved this wonderful combination that became the Canadian way. But in 1989, the Canadian way began to unravel. Everything suddenly started to shrink – governments, corporations, nongovernmental institutions, labour unions, paycheques, job opportunities. Even the globe seemed smaller, with borders no longer barriers and information moving at the speed of light. As the computer chip shrunk, so did we. We entered what philosopher Arthur Kroker calls an era of grim consolidation. Decision-makers began to think not about expansion but retraction. Visions of growth were replaced with a new ethic: downsize, outsource – get small, fast.

The '90s have been filled with surprises, but none has been more unexpected – or more troubling – than this: big is no longer safe. Ask the hundreds of thousands of employees who got severance slips or were forced to take early retirement from such institutional giants as Ontario Hydro, the CBC, Petro-Canada, Bell Canada, IBM, CIBC and CN. Talk to anyone who invested in Campeau, Bramalea, Woodwards or Confederation Life. Ask civil servants what happened to those guarantees of job security that once went hand in hand with working in the public sector.

Not long ago, Statistics Canada reported that during the first half of the 1990s, the number of commercial enterprises with fewer than five employees grew by 3.5%, while the number with more than 100 employees dropped by nearly 7%. That may not seem a dramatic reduction, but it comes in a country that regarded growth as a sign of prosperity. And it's a clear indication that corporations and governments have turned their backs on bigness. One of the most important touchstones in the lives of Canadians has been turned upside down.

MYTH NO. 2 – GROWTH IS GOOD FOR EVERYONE

There's a cartoon that I can't get out of my mind. In it, an affluent businessman is making a speech at a banquet; a waiter is walking by. "Last year," intones the businessman, "thousands of new jobs were created in this country." There is a thought balloon over the waiter's head, which says: "Yeah, and I've got three of them."

Almost 25 years ago, when I was a young sociologist and university professor, I experienced an epiphany of sorts when I read a seminal article by economist Grant Reuber on the effect of economic growth on poverty levels in Canada during the 1960s and early '70s. Reuber demonstrated that during this period the proportion of Canadians living below the poverty line decreased, the result, he claimed, of improving economic conditions, not government transfer programs.[1] Though unpopular among some of my more socialist-inclined colleagues, the Reuber piece made a lasting impression on me. It underscored a rule that guided business leaders and politicians throughout the postwar era: growth is good for everyone.

This rule united the objectives of the business community with the aspirations of workers: become more productive and wages will increase; if companies become more profitable, your jobs will become more secure. Everyone will benefit from a growing, more productive economy.

Well, epiphanies come and go. You wouldn't call me a socialist; I remain very much an entrepreneur. But I'm not nearly as sure as I used to be that growth spells happiness for all concerned. Increasingly, it seems that economic growth is good only for some people. Since 1990, the Canadian economy has grown, on average, by just over 2% per year. Over this same period, the wages of the average worker have dropped by about 5% when inflation is taken into consideration. For workers in the bottom 20% of the economy, the decline was 19%.

Historical comparisons of the salaries of Canadian CEOs are hard to come by, largely because Canadian regulators have only recently begun to require disclosure. But top Canadian salaries tend to follow a North American pattern, and in the United States figures show the folks at the top have been doing increasingly well, while the folks at the bottom have not. In 1972, the average American corporate executive made 44 times as much as the average corporate worker. That's a wide gap, but wide isn't the same as breathtaking: by 1992, the gap was a stunning 222 to 1.[2]

Everywhere I look, there is a discontinuity between economic growth and the welfare of ordinary Canadians. In February 1996, when newspapers reported that the TSE 300 index had surged for the first time above the 5000 mark, they also carried stories showing consumer confidence *dropping*. And while the five largest banks in Canada recorded a combined profit of more than $5 billion, their employment levels *decreased*. In 1994 and 1995, Statistics Canada reported modest gains in worker productivity and modest declines in wages.

The Canadian elite – politicians and business leaders – would have us believe that the decade has seen significant job creation. These new jobs, they maintain, are the evidence that growth and progress are working for everyone. What they neglect to point out is that most of the new jobs fall into a category Statistics Canada refers to as "non-standard" work: part-time or temporary jobs, and the fastest-growing category of all, self-employed workers with no employees.

In fact, the number of full-time jobs (with all those benefits and pension plans) has decreased by about 130,000 since 1989, even though the population of the country has continued to increase. Some self-employed individuals are doing okay. But most of them have become "just-in-time" workers, used when they're needed and then discarded, perfect tools for the efficient just-in-time economy. Once they were parts of teams designed to make corporations more competitive. They're still competing, only now they compete against each other.

MYTH NO. 3 – SCIENCE AND TECHNOLOGY WILL SAVE US

North Americans have always been dazzled by technology. We have learned to love what it can do for us, and with good reason. For the past several centuries, scientists have been finding ways to improve our lives, serving up such innovations as the electric refrigerator, the internal combustion engine, hydroelectric power, jet propulsion, the telephone, radio, television, the green revolution in agriculture, miracle drugs and space travel. Even when these advances were used for destructive purposes, they left most of us in awe. During the Gulf War, we watched U.S. planes shoot smart bombs through minuscule air vents in buildings many kilometres away. Reporters couldn't believe their eyes when they saw cruise missiles turn corners in pursuit of their targets.

All the better when science was used to save rather than destroy. The postwar generation had a huge burden lifted off its back with the triumph of the Salk vaccine over poliomyelitis in the 1950s. Today, doctors perform delicate operations on babies in the womb, and use magnetic resonance imaging technology to detect problems in the human body with an accuracy that once required surgery. Almost every month, scientists make genetic discoveries that provide clues to some of humankind's worst diseases. In the field of communications, the miniaturization of computer circuits and the development of fibreoptics cable have made network capacity a concern of the past. Digital data transfer now permits the contents of a 400-page book to be transmitted from one computer to another in less than a minute.

The stunning technological leaps should have served as clear evidence of our ability to eventually conquer all problems – other than death and taxes. Science stood for progress and, whatever problems we humans caused, scientists could somehow make the world a better place. And yet ... more and more problems seem to be cropping up, some with the science itself, some with human failures in applying it and some perhaps, with our over-confidence that science is omnipotent.

The suspicion that we have paid too little attention to the proper application of scientific advances is not new, but has started to grow. Fear about the threat of nuclear war has turned into concern about troubled reactors like Chernobyl and its nuclear cousins around the world. Some of the fear is close to home: recent investigations into operations at the nuclear plant at Pickering, Ontario, revealed that what we had always been told was safe was no longer safe. There is also a growing concern that ideological and religious warriors will soon find a way of turning humanity's destructive inventions – not only conventional arms but biological and chemical weapons – against their inventors. The Unabomber and others have demonstrated that deadly bombs can be built in anybody's rec room. The Unabomber's protest was particularly ironic, for he used technology to protest "the destructive tyranny" of modern-day technology. His point? That technocrats and efficiency experts have been allowed to direct the future of humanity, treating human needs and the human spirit as little more than impedimenta to good circuitry. Is technology serving humanity well? The new communications technology has been particularly useful to financiers, providing them with a breathtaking capacity to move data and money. Then again, that same technology almost led to the destruction of the Mexican economy overnight.

The Third World provides some instructive lessons about technology. In fact, in some of this planet's poorest countries, billions of dollars in aid has been wasted trying to prove that Western technology can be pasted onto developing nations. Most experts now believe that technology cannot take root unless there is an indigenous component to its development; the application must reflect the needs of the society. The lesson: technology is often useless when abstracted from human values. There may be lessons for the industrialized world here as well. Robots and circuit boards have replaced all kinds of drudgery in the workplace. But not since the emergence of the nineteenth-century Luddites has there been so much concern that technology may be consigning hundreds of millions of people to the marketplace's scrap heap.

As for the global ecology, critics have complained since Rachel Carson's *The Silent Spring* (1962) that technology primarily used to enhance economic efficiency is despoiling the planet. Carson was seen as an alarmist, but with some 11 billion people expected to inhabit Earth by the middle of the next century, and with hectares of rain forest and entire species disappearing every hour, the threat has become far more real. Electric refrigerators, air conditioning and aerosol cans were undisputed marvels when they were introduced. Only when we started noticing large holes in the ozone layer did it become clear that there is a price to be paid for "progress."

And are we ready for the torrent of questions that the mapping of the human genome is about to raise? From this information, we will be able to determine whether a person is likely to die young of an untreatable disease, or is predisposed to mental illness, certain personality traits and intelligence. Pregnancy could become a kind of lottery, parents forced to decide whether to bet on a particular set of genomes or hope that a subsequent fetus might be an improvement.

It could be argued that all this reflects badly not on science but on humans, who seem so incapable of using science in the service of humanity. When couples use ultrasound to determine whether to abort if they don't like the sex of their future baby, perhaps we should blame the parents and not the technology. If we could ever get our moral and social act together, science might still prove a saviour. But in the '90s, science has shown a suspiciously vulnerable side. Diseases once thought to have been eliminated have started to reappear. New strains are resistant to the most miraculous set of drugs biologists ever discovered – antibiotics. Increasingly, the bugs appear to be *winning*, science to be *losing*.

MYTH NO. 4 – A GOOD EDUCATION MEANS A GOOD JOB

All of us know stories about the guy who quit high school after Grade 11 and went on to run a hundred-million-dollar company. But these were exceptions that proved the rule. The rule for students was simple, and well understood: get a university degree and your economic future will be secure. Don't get a university degree, and you might not get a good job. Not every student earned a post-secondary degree, of course; about a third of Canadian high-school students went on to university during the 1980s, and only about half of those graduated. But most parents prayed that their children would attend university, and most secondary school boards designed curricula to reflect those aspirations. Community colleges were the back-up choice, or occasionally a first choice when they offered more relevant training for a particular job market.

University and college degrees are still important as predictors of economic achievement. Canadians who have acquired some post-secondary education earned over 30% more than the average Canadian worker during the past few years while those with a university degree earned about 50% more than those with no post-secondary education. But the formula has become much more fallible. What is missing is the presumption that post-secondary graduates will find work in the field in which they have studied. In truth, they may find nothing more than menial jobs when they graduate. The statistics may show that these scholars are still doing considerably better than the general populace once they enter the workforce, but even the well educated are having a tough time finding a good job.

And what about those monumental structures of prosperity, the big and powerful professions, where years of preparatory slogging inevitably led to financial relief at the top? Why are there suddenly too many doctors, lawyers, architects, dentists? Why can't nurses get jobs, when everyone knows the baby boomers will soon be entering old age? Why are there so many unemployed teachers, when knowledge and education are the keys to everything? We all have relatives or friends who graduated in respectable fields but who are now putting in time as security guards, hamburger flippers, taxi drivers or couriers, until one of hundreds of job applications leads (they pray) to something more rewarding.

There is, of course, the question of pursuing the *right* kind of post-secondary education. It's become fashionable to question the judgment of a student foolish enough to pursue a degree in English literature or anthropology rather than computer engineering. But the truth is that there are no "safe" fields of study any more. Commerce and computer courses are predictably glutted, so institutions can be very selective about whom they admit. An oversupply of physicians has led medical schools to trim their enrollments by 6%; others have simply closed down. Oversupply has also resulted in closures of dental schools. Dentists, who could once expect six-figure incomes within five years of graduation now struggle to find work; in 1995 more Toronto dentists went bankrupt than in the previous 10 years. The 2,500 lawyers who enter the profession each year are finding law firms are not hiring: at least

20% of the University of Windsor law school's class of '93 had, by all accounts, failed to obtain work as lawyers three years later. Architects are not faring much better. Alberta's architects, faced with a stagnant market, are increasingly having to work outside the country.[3]

In the late 1960s and early '70s, virtually every institution in Canada, from huge corporations to tiny school boards, sent recruiters to university campuses to beg even students with indifferent grades to work for them, all benefits included. Few employers go begging any more. More skills are needed to create a more efficient workplace, and more students are acquiring those skills, but the push for efficiency has meant fewer jobs. There are fewer positions and more demanding work, at all levels.

The skills required by the information age pose a huge challenge to Canada's economy, and students are rising to it. Many university graduates are flocking to community colleges, upgrading themselves by acquiring practical skills in areas like graphic design, hotel management, home appliance repair and television production. In 1986, Canadians were pretty well divided on whether it was best for young people to learn a skilled trade or get a general university education (39% vs 31% with 30% unsure). By October 1995, those favouring a skilled trade had increased to 56% while supporters of general university education were unchanged at 32%.[4]

The point is, there is no longer any surefire formula for translating education and training into the kind of rewarding jobs baby boomers once had for the asking. In the '90s education is regarded as an even more magical wand than it used to be. Unfortunately, as Canadians are discovering, the magic wand often doesn't work.

MYTH NO. 5 – LOYALTY IS ALL

Along with competence and trustworthiness, loyalty has always ranked high on the pedestal of great corporate virtues. In fact, if you happen to be buying from corporations, rather than working for them, loyalty is just about the only thing that matters. Today, however, loyalty isn't the wonderful two-way street it used to be. After managing the Los Angeles Dodgers for 25 years, Tommy Lasorda may be the last loyal person in professional baseball – he says he bleeds "Dodger blue." So many players and other personnel skip back and forth among major league teams these days that you need a scorecard to keep track.

Of course, loyalty has always been a watchword in the workplace. Unless something went terribly wrong with the company's bottom line, if you were a loyal employee – a team player, doing things management's way – a place would invariably be found for you, even if you weren't quite as productive as some other employees. Now, team players right up to the senior-management level often arrive at their desks to find files missing and a note to report to personnel. Those with offices frequently find a new lock on the door. Loyalty has been replaced by new, more functional values – competitiveness and productivity. "We live in a time of monetarization of the social order," *Globe and Mail* columnist Michael Valpy wrote in 1996, "when the liquidity and mobility of relationships are chiefly governed by money."[5]

A friend of mine in the newspaper business, a man who has survived a number of newsroom contractions over the past few years, recently got a new boss. He was surprised that the new man seemed so brusque and unfriendly, especially since managers and reporters had always tried to create an atmosphere of camaraderie, and new bosses had traditionally eased into their jobs with a modicum of good will. It took a few days to dawn on him: new bosses always have to do something to make their mark. But in the modern workplace, the most common way to score points is to please the accountants and shareholders by cutting staff. Why be congenial with someone, even someone clearly quite friendly and competent, when you may decide to trim them from the payroll in a few weeks? Not even the "Judas goat" managers responsible for firing fellow employees now have any longevity guarantees. In early 1995, the *Financial Post* reported that Jim Tennant spent six months handing out pink slips to redundant managers at Air Canada. His reward: a meeting with his managers to inform him that he was no longer needed.

In 1993, Ontario Hydro eliminated 5,000 jobs through a combination of buyouts and early-retirement incentives. What was lost, however, according to Dane MacCarthy, then human resources VP, was more than the jobs. "The psychological contract for many Hydro employees was: 'I will give you loyalty and you will give me security.'" But now, because of changing economic circumstances, this contract between loyalty and security "is no longer viable," MacCarthy says.[6] Indeed, the Angus Reid Group found in October 1995 that 53% of working Canadians feel their current employer "values its employees less today compared with a few years ago."[7]

If corporations are retreating from the concept of loyalty they held so dear, their customers are retaliating by showing less brand loyalty. Television advertising persuaded people to adopt emotional attachments to the brands they selected, and most of us fell for it. Now, in many product lines, the average consumer is as likely to switch from a brand as to stick with it. Retailers still talk about their "customers" – derived from the Greek word meaning habit or custom – but "shoppers" is about as far as it goes these days.

Loyalty is equally out of fashion in politics. Ontarians in particular seem to enjoy tasting a new flavour at virtually every election. Nor can the traditional churches, hit hard by a decline in worshippers over the past three decades, count on churchgoers to stay with the denomination they grew up in. Many Canadians are experimenting with nontraditional alternatives and not coming back. The *Ottawa Citizen* told of one Catholic couple who auditioned six churches in three years before finally settling on the Pentecostals.

Despite this erosion of traditional loyalties – or perhaps because of it – Canadians appear to be showing more loyalty in the home. More young people in their early 20s are living with their parents, more elderly people are being cared for in the home, and the divorce rate has stopped climbing. In a world in which the permanence of just about every other relationship can't be taken for granted, family and friends seem to matter more than ever.

MYTH NO. 6 – LOCATION, LOCATION, LOCATION

Several years ago, I was invited to give a speech at Queen's University in Kingston, Ontario. After the lecture, my hosts gave me a tour of the campus, proud of the historic buildings and idyllic setting that have made Queen's such a special place. I remembered this tour when I read recently that the university now offers an executive MBA, available across Canada via video-conferencing. It struck me as odd that it's possible to earn a degree from Queen's without ever visiting it. For these students at least, Queen's is less a physical place than a brand name in educational cyberspace.

Ask successful retailers what the key to winning was in the 1980s and the odds are they will answer with one word: location. Ask any librarian about the most important rule in running a library: know the location of the books. Ask anyone who has played Monopoly how to win: buy the right properties. Location, location, location. In the early 1990s, some of our largest corporations played monopoly and lost. Canada's chartered banks are among the pre-eminent retailers in the country, but most of them now fear that their billions in real estate may not matter in a world in which you can shop at a bank and never visit a branch. Librarians? Who needs to worry about the location of books when everything can be retrieved from a laptop? Chartered banks, librarians, Monopoly players, universities like Queen's (and many other organizations that invested heavily in bricks and mortar) have found themselves on a collision course with a basic new reality: location matters less and less. Overnight, it seems, the spatial dynamics that have defined our lives for generations are obsolete.

The separation of work and home has been one of the most important by-products of the industrial revolution. These spaces are fundamental to our definition of work and leisure. But lately, it is increasingly hard to find the line that divides work from home. Telecommuting is growing rapidly across North America. The home-based business is the fastest growing category of employment. Some companies, like IBM, now allot fewer offices than they have employees, to encourage staff to work from home. Others load employees up with virtual offices in their cars. Cell phones, laptops and fax machines are the new tools for these nomadic workers, for whom location is kinetic, always in motion. According to one estimate, 10 million Americans were working from their cars in 1994.

The declining importance of location is, of course, not all bad. Places that have for decades been considered economic backwaters suddenly have new promise. Consider New Brunswick, written off by many as a chronic have-not province. Its decision to invest heavily in telecommunications infrastructure has given it a significant toehold in the new economy. When it comes to the growing demand for telemarketing services, New Brunswick, with its comparatively cheap, bilingual labour force, becomes, as economist Thomas Courchene has observed, "a business solution rather than a location."[8]

Our rules about physical space – how to value it and what it means in our lives – have changed dramatically in the shadow of the new millennium. In the early 1990s, the Canadian-invented board game Trivial Pursuit sold more copies in Canada than the old standard Monopoly. Is there a lesson here?

MYTH NO. 7 – TIME IS LINEAR

Time has been a constant in our lives. Just as we know *where* we are by looking at a map, we know *when* we are by looking at a calendar or a clock. In the industrialized world, we have come to treasure our chronographic fastidiousness. It's a sign of an advanced civilization; only ski bums and Stone-Age tribes remain free of the regime of the clock. We may dread the inevitable conclusion, but the constancy of time's relentless march provides order and meaning to our lives. And throughout human history, the accuracy of our time-keeping and our sense of time have been inextricably intertwined.

About 800 years ago, according to German social historian Adolf Holl, "people in some European cities began to feel a strong and previously unheard-of desire: They wanted to know the time."[9]

These early stirrings, though linked most directly to the needs of traders, were a harbinger of a shift in how people thought about time, a shift in orientation from the past to the future. At the core of the Age of Enlightenment was the concept of progress, the idea of a better future created through human intervention in the forces of nature. This intervention increasingly relied on the accurate measurement of time. As the early explorers discovered, the more precise their timepieces, the more exact their navigation. Industrial production also required punctuality, the ordering and sequencing of hundreds or thousands of workers. In fact, the frustration of English industrial workers with the indignities of factory work were as likely to lead to smashed clocks as to smashed machines.

No one smashes clocks any more. Two hundred and fifty years after the industrial revolution, punctuality is no longer a virtue but the basic price of admission to most forms of collective life in developed societies. The accurate measurement of time has become a science of pulsing electrons, cesium atomic clocks and humming crystals. Time has become an exact science and a universal constant, with the Bureau International de l'Heure in Paris declaring leap seconds every few years just to keep everyone in line.

But just as we have honed our measurement of time to an incredible precision, our sense of time has begun to shift. Ironically, two technologies that wouldn't exist without exact timekeeping – the computer and digital communications – lie at the heart of this shift. Both have increased the volume of sensory inputs and accelerated the rate of change. As a result, the world of the "now" is rapidly growing, and the future has suddenly jumped into our laps. We are living, says American social commentator Don Gifford, in "the expanding present tense."

In other words, we have become removed from the cycles of time. There is now an immediately accessible "present" of global proportions, in which it is always daytime and nighttime. Stock markets and currency trading never stop – there is always a market open somewhere in the world. Stores are always open. The 24-hour clock has become irrelevant to many global companies that operate in a continuous present – real time. No one wants to miss anything, and something is always happening. The sheer *mass* of present events presses in on us, creating a sense of urgency and a feeling that there is never enough time. British psychologists have recently coined the term *presenteeism* to describe a condition in which workers stay at work long past their scheduled hours, struggling to cope with the huge volume of information that assaults them every day in the digital age. Polls in Canada show that one of the chief complaints about daily life for a growing number of Canadians is "not having enough time."

In this expanded present, our sense of the past is unraveling like a baseball with broken seams. Almost 60% of Americans under 30 do not know that the Soviet Union and the U.S. were allies in the Second World War. In Canada, 43% of all adults asked to name our first prime minister either didn't know or gave the wrong name. As for the future – who has time to think ahead? The flux and change that characterizes contemporary life has transformed the future from a distant place where we focus our hopes and dreams to one with a chilling immediacy. Flexibility is everything. Moving thoughtfully and deliberately is now passé; to delay is to lose.

Historians know the folly of humankind repeating the errors of their past. Philosophers know the folly of living lives with no sense of consequences. But historians and philosophers are considered almost irrelevant in the world of today. Financiers and corporate managers clearly have the upper hand. Time no longer marches on. Instead, time has started chasing its own tail, and we humans are caught up in the pursuit.

MYTH NO. 8 – WHAT YOU SEE IS WHAT YOU GET

In 1966, the People's Republic of China, desperate to show that its ailing leader, Mao Tse Tung, was in good health, distributed a photograph of him swimming in the Yangtze River. The ruse didn't work. We *knew*. The photo looked so superimposed that it only confirmed our convictions that Mao's days would soon be over (although he managed to hang on for several more years). But generally, when we looked at a picture of someone or something, we were looking at a genuine image. When Betty Crocker smiled at us from a box of cake mix, we could be pretty sure that what we were looking at was a portrait of a real person.

Today, on the other hand, nothing is for sure. *The Crying Game* showed us that, underlining the extreme uncertainty of certainty. We live in the Age of Virtual Reality. While this is fascinating, it is also unsettling. Consider that any photograph, in any newspaper or magazine, can now be doctored to show anybody doing anything, compromising or otherwise, without any hint that there is trickery afoot. Sometimes the changes are innocuous, such as when the *Globe and Mail* digitally removed a *Toronto Star* newspaper box outside the courtroom in which Paul Bernardo was being tried; the box appeared as a blue blotch. Other manipulations have been more controversial, such as the digitally rearranged mug shot of O.J. Simpson that appeared on the cover of *Time*. (Readers felt the photograph had intentionally been changed to make O.J. look like a criminal.)

Your local photofinishing shop can now extricate a divorced spouse from family photos without anybody being the wiser. The Betty Crocker image that began appearing on grocery shelves in 1996 was no longer based on a single person, but was a composite portrait produced by digitally morphing pictures of more than fifty "real" American women. Surreal cakemixes. TV commercials for Diet Coke feature long-dead artists such as Louis Armstrong, James Cagney and Humphrey Bogart interacting with living performers. In the movie *Forrest Gump*, Tom Hanks conversed with every American president who has died during the past quarter century: Kennedy, Nixon and LBJ.

Mickey Mantle's 1952 Topps baseball card, which cost a penny new, is now valued at more than $30,000. What card dealers won't tell you, however, is that it can be counterfeited by any 12-year-old using simple technology. It would take a forensic expert considerable effort to identify a fake.

The virtual world extends beyond photography. A decade ago, most of us, I think, had a pretty firm grip on reality. Today, mood-altering drugs like Prozac not only counter the serious medical condition of depression; they help take the rough edges off life. Their users may seem more pleasant and capable of coping with stress. But sometimes you feel like whispering in their ear: "Harry, is that *really* you?"

Almost daily, modern technology plays tricks on our senses, and perhaps our increasing inability to distinguish what is real from what is "virtually" real is responsible for the rising cynicism among consumers. The luster of the Rolex watch has long since lost its cachet because it's hard to spot the difference between the real one and the fake. Magic used to be fun – we all knew when the magician was on stage. Now, it's hard to tell.

MYTH NO. 9 – CANADIAN CULTURE IS A SACRED TRUST

In the United States, culture seems to be just one more commodity to be bought and sold. The Americans have never had to be particularly concerned about the erosion of their beliefs and traditions: as in nature, it's the gazelles who do the fretting, not the lions. Hollywood and the American television industry have saturated the world. We in Canada have been particularly susceptible to the flood and, since Confederation, Canadians and their leaders – with the possible exception of Brian Mulroney – have generally fought hard to protect Canadian culture.

The Trudeau Liberals, for example, demonstrated a keen interest in defending our culture, going so far as to outlaw TV satellite dishes. At one point, when the U.S.-based World Football League was considering moving a team to Toronto, the Liberals threatened to pass legislation to protect the Canadian Football League. Defending Canadian cultural institutions was part of an overall effort to prevent assimilation into the American way of life. Foreign companies planning to invest in Canada were forced to show evidence that their investments would benefit Canada, rather than their own country.

That all seems like a long time ago. The Mulroney government's successful campaign to create the Canada-U.S. Free Trade Agreement may only have recognized the inevitability of the fall of tariff barriers around the world, following from the General Agreement on Tariffs and Trade. But it was also symbolic of a waning interest, at least at the political level, in defending Canadian culture against the Philistines. The CBC, whose mandate once was to protect and promote Canadian culture, saw its budget slashed in a series of Tory blood-lettings. The Chrétien Liberals have shown no signs that they intend to reverse the trend. The most potent Canadian image in the world – the RCMP – is now being marketed by Disney. The Canadian Radio-Television and Telecommunications Commission (CRTC), established in the late 1960s to regulate and defend Canadian broadcasting, has become little more than an arbiter between powerful communications empires seeking bigger pieces of the marketplace. Our polls show that Canadians no longer regard the CRTC as a guardian of Canadian culture, but as a protector of corporate interests.

Perhaps the decline was inevitable. Philosopher George Grant predicted it in his 1965 book, *Lament for a Nation*. However, as Mathew Horsman and Andrew Marshall note in *After the Nation State*, governments around the world are losing power more quickly than their constituents are losing their nationalistic feelings: "The strong sense of allegiance to the nation-state borne by its citizens, and developed over the past two hundred years, has not yet weakened in line with the diminution of the autonomy of national governments."[10] In other words, while many of us still feel patriotic, we believe our politicians have lost the capacity to sustain a distinctly Canadian vision. As inevitable as this may have been, it is bound to feel a bit like waking up one morning and finding that someone has dismantled – brick by brick – the walls of your house.

MYTH NO.10 – THE PUBLIC INTEREST STILL COUNTS

In 1988, we asked Canadians what they felt was the most important aspect of their national identity. Germans point to their machines, French to their food and wine, Italians to their design, and Americans to their entertainment industry. In Canada, medicare topped a long list of public institutions that Canadians pointed to as their most potent symbols of national identity.

For most of this century, the best way for governments to serve the public good was for them to create public institutions. This rule, used to form the Canadian National Railways at the start of the century, has since been applied to everything from gas stations and car insurance to hockey teams and liquor stores. So pervasive was this pattern that by 1990, more than 200,000 Canadians were employed by Crown corporations and not-for-profit organizations owned or directly supported by one or more levels of government.[11] And then something happened. Mounting concerns about public debt coupled with growing cynicism about government began to change Canadian public opinion. Almost overnight, public was out and private was in. Public assets were privatized, not just Crown corporations like CN Rail or Petro-Canada, but just about everything that had traditionally been public property. The federal government has privatized most of the country's airports and much of its air traffic control system. In B.C., Ontario and Quebec, several highway megaprojects will be financed by the private sector and paid for at the toll booth. In Ontario and B.C., there are demands from industrial customers and some consumer groups that provincial hydro corporations be privatized. Liquor store privatization is also being considered.

Now, privatization is moving out of the domain of transportation and Crown corporations and into areas traditionally considered fundamentally public, such as education, prisons and social welfare. Alberta has sold its educational broadcaster to private interests; Ontario is considering a similar move. In Surrey, B.C., experimental projects have seen developers build and own school buildings, then lease them back to local school boards. In other jurisdictions, traditional principles of public education are under attack by new so-called charter schools, in which parents become involved in planning the curriculum. Alberta and Ontario are examining proposals to have prisons operated by the private sector and allow private contractors to administer welfare payments.

Even medicare has begun to feel the tug of privatization. Private clinics that offer specialty services have been sprouting up across the country. Although former federal health minister Diane Marleau threatened in 1995 to reduce Ottawa's transfer payments to Alberta, alleging that the province had violated the Canada Health Act by allowing private clinics to charge patients a facility fee, other facilities found ways to impose user fees without drawing attention. For example, Shouldice Hospital in Thornhill, Ontario, charges an additional fee for all semi-private rooms. But all rooms at Shouldice are semi-private and all patients are required to stay at least three days. The daily room fee is $60, so Shouldice collects at least $180 in room fees per patient. The Ontario medical insurance plan covers operations performed at Shouldice, but not the room surcharge. Magnetic resonance imaging (MRI) is another focus of the growing conflict between public and private. MRI machines produce three-dimensional pictures of the inside of the human body and are far more useful for diagnosis than x-rays or even CAT scans. Hospitals in some provinces are suffering from a shortage of these extremely expensive machines. The waiting list for a scan can be up to six months. But private MRI clinics offer the same procedures, without the wait; for a tidy $575 to $1,000, patients can have the scans performed immediately.

In less than a decade, fiscal constraints and changing public attitudes have created a tidal wave in the direction of privatization. The most visible manifestations involve the great public enterprises and programs of this century. Like the trend toward cocooning – private boxes in hockey arenas and tinted windows in autos – this transformation marks a fundamental retreat from a model of shared experience and common purpose that has guided our lives.

Noam Chomsky once said that if you want to understand a society, you should begin with its language. Look at the new words or definitions creeping into our vocabularies – digitization, jobless recovery, virtual reality, McJobs, convergence, delayering – words that define an age of contradiction and discontinuity. We thought we knew the rules, but increasingly they no longer apply. And with this transformation, our path to the future has become obscured.

Did Ontarians really elect the New Democrats in 1990 and then the arch-Conservatives in 1995? Is it an illusion – or have both these governments made us more dizzy instead of less? How about Quebec? How, in the midst of all this anarchy, can this society want to create *more* turmoil? Or am I missing something? Could it be that all this flux has made the Québécois determined to have at least one anchor to steady themselves, one touchstone that nobody can take away, no matter how bad things get? And if self-determination is that totem, what about the rest of the country? What do we have to hold on to? Are we following Ralph Klein and Mike Harris towards what our ancestors tried so desperately to keep at arm's length – the American way?

Now, a surreal kind of street scene stretches before us. There are three categories of pedestrians in the picture. The first group still bounces along the sidewalk with a spring in its step. It constitutes what U.S. Secretary of Labour Robert Reich calls "the fortunate fifth" of the population – those people who still have a handle on their destinies. They were either born rich or are sufficiently specialized to stay on top of things, for now. The second group no longer has any bounce; in fact, they're lying in the gutter, with passersby telling them what a burden they're imposing on society. Some of these people – construction workers, fishermen, factory workers, labourers, even welfare recipients – lived relatively decent lives not long ago, but the sidewalk simply isn't big enough for them any more. The third, and by far the biggest group, is still up on the sidewalk – just. These people once strode confidently down the middle of the boulevard. Now they teeter. Many of them are falling off the curb, or worrying that it won't be long before they do. They're not numb, like the folks in the gutter: they're just dizzy. So dizzy that they have to think about how they walk. "Put one foot in front of the other. Listen to the rules. Make sure you've got a good résumé. Be *flexible*, for God's sake." But as much as they keep reassuring themselves, somehow these people, or their spouses, children or friends, can't help wobbling toward the curb.

Scary? You bet. Surely there must be some trick to staying on the sidewalk that the rule-makers forgot to tell us. Who ever had to think about *walking* in the good old days? We Canadians were so sure of ourselves, marching along the sunny side of the street, humming the catechism that had worked since the end of the war. Now, the ground beneath our feet always seems to be shifting. Perhaps it might be a good idea to stop our uncertain journey for a moment and see if we can't retrace our steps.

Two

THE REAL SIXTIES

"Imagine yourselves backward to the year 1963.
How much culture shock would
you experience in the early sixties?"
Robert Theobald, AVOIDING 1984:
MOVING TOWARD INTERDEPENDENCE

I was born in 1947, right at the start of the baby boom. Like many people my age, I have some powerful memories of the 1960s. At the beginning of the decade, my dad was transferred from Nanaimo to Winnipeg. I remember our trip across the prairies and gazing out the window of our '58 Chevy at a horizon that offered limitless possibilities. Although I wasn't quite prepared for the stark contrast between the beaches of Departure Bay and the blizzards on Portage and Main, this was to become a decade full of contrasts. My images of the sixties form a moving collage that dissolves from black and white to colour: from Tommy Dorsey to the Beatles, from Mass in Latin to Mass in English, from John Diefenbaker to Pierre Trudeau, from the old to the new. Of course all of these images are now old, not quite ancient history, but distant enough that some readers may think it a strange place to start my story about what's happening in the nineties. I do so because a major part of the crisis we're facing today is the result of events that trail all the way back to that legendary decade. In a sense, the sixties ended not in 1969 but 20 years later.

We all remember the sixties. Let me put that another way: we all *think* we remember the sixties. Even many people born in the 1970s and '80s worship the mythology of that magical era. It was a time when the young truly believed they could have a powerful influence on the way people thought, felt and behaved. And they did. But it wasn't anything like the change many of them expected to make. And it had little to do with the mythology that sprang out of Woodstock. The wellspring of values that gushed out of the sixties was far more complicated than flashing the peace sign – and a lot more powerful. The decade was supposedly marked by a breakdown of communication between older Canadians, who had endured the Great Depression and the war, and younger Canadians, who had not. In many families there was indeed a breakdown; Bob Dylan warned people over 30 not to criticize "what you can't understand." But for all that lack of understanding, the yearnings of younger and older Canadians actually came together in that time and helped create forces that dramatically changed both the Canadian economy and Canadian society over the next 25 years.

And contrary to conventional wisdom, it was the parents – themselves finally liberated from the anxieties of the Great Depression – that led the way. They created the economic conditions from which the *real* revolution of the sixties emerged. That's not to say that the spirit of youthful independence wasn't part of the value shifts that would subsequently transform Canada. It's just that the independent spirit of these young Canadians got its directions mixed up. It set out on a path that was supposed to lead to love-ins and communal living, but before you knew it, it had drifted off in search of the two-car garage.

In 1965, Winston Churchill's funeral flotilla drifted down the
Thames River past Westminster. He had been Britain's prime minister and the free world's most inspiring leader during the Second
World War. The war had been over for 20 years, but so profound had
its anxieties been – on top of the anxieties that still clung from the
Great Depression before it – that most adult Canadians were only
finally beginning to shake them. In the 1950s, everyone knew that
life was improving, but people still looked over their shoulders,
remembering when times were tough and security had been a far-
off dream. Rarely a week went by when you wouldn't hear someone
remind you that "a penny saved is a penny earned," or "a bird in the
hand is worth two in the bush." Canadians of the '50s were an
accountant's dream: increasingly prosperous, but still quite
cautious; hard-working, but frugal; dreamers, but wary realists. They
spent *some* money, because they were earning more than they ever
had. But few people were foolhardy enough to spend more than
they earned. It wasn't until the early 1960s that Americans and
Canadians alike realized that this new period of uninterrupted peace
and prosperity was for real.

In the fall of 1965, *Maclean's* sent reporters to find out what was
on Canadians' minds. Though hardly scientific, this poll provided a
unique snapshot of the mood of the country. Essentially, *Maclean's*
found a contented population, not terribly concerned about
anything. The issue of Canada possessing nuclear weapons, which
had dominated the 1963 election campaign, attracted little pubic
interest. The debate over the new flag was over. Foreign policy
inspired neither fear nor panic. Canadians didn't like what they saw
in Viet Nam, but they were willing to go along – within limits. They
weren't overly excited about their Liberal government and they were
equally unenthused about the opposition parties. U.S. ownership of

our resources was a source of irritation, but it was balanced by a belief that Canada needed more outside investment. The only real areas of concern, it is worth noting, were vague misgivings about the effect of automation on jobs and a sense that authorities were dragging their feet in the areas of training for youth and retraining for displaced workers. There was not much hand-wringing about poverty, although that fall, Lester Pearson took a page from Lyndon Johnson's domestic social program and declared Canada's own "war on poverty." While Canadians were generally sympathetic toward their less-fortunate neighbours, these worries had been eased by substantial improvements in the general well-being.

Even the Quiet Revolution in Quebec attracted only muted concern. Some heads of Canadian companies with operations in Quebec mused about having more of their Quebec-based employees learn to speak French. To be sure, there was a genuine revolution under way in Quebec, but for many Canadians, it seemed to be largely a parochial affair, with the Catholic Church at the center. During the 1960s, church attendance in Quebec dropped from 80% to 20% and the birth rate plunged from one of the highest to one of the lowest in the developed world. Mailbox bombings were a source of concern, but support for separation as recorded in published polls stood at less than 10%.

The postwar years had been marked by unprecedented economic growth and the meteoric rise in average incomes. In fact, the average wage for Canadian workers had more than doubled. This was accomplished with negligible inflation, interest rates below 5% and minimal unemployment. At the same time, the federal government's war debt had been paid down and was virtually eliminated. The portrait of the average Canadian household in 1965 shows a reasonably contented family, with a husband, wife, and two children. Most dads worked, and most moms stayed home, taking care of the kids. Almost every family had made material progress since the war. Those with jobs had grown accustomed to modest but regular increases in their salaries. Those at home were able to enjoy new labour-saving devices, symbols of their increased freedom from the drudgery of housework.

Consumer goods that had once been the privilege of the well-to-do were suddenly within the grasp of nearly everyone. For example, the percentage of households with a gas or electric stove increased from 48% in 1948 to 94% by 1968. Those with refrigerators soared from 29% to 97%, electric washing machines from 59% to 83%, and vacuum cleaners from 32% to 72%.[1] Almost 75% of Canadian households owned at least one car,[2] and owning a second car was rapidly becoming the badge of admission to the middle class. Canada had become a land of affluence. Canadians didn't need statistics to know that this was a better life than the vast majority had been used to. Hundreds of thousands were living seemingly idyllic lives in modern bungalows and split-levels neatly organized in suburban communities. And there were children everywhere.

Canadian maternity wards overflowed between the war and the mid-1960s. The men (and some women) who had been overseas during the war were making up for lost time in populating what had suddenly become a much more hospitable world. At the end of the war, there were about 12 million Canadians. During the 1946-65 baby boom, nearly nine million newcomers arrived on the scene, a ripe market for advertisers using new media to sell new products as fast as producers could get them to the shelves.

By 1965, the fastest-growing segment of the Canadian population was 15 to 25 years old, and the median age was 25. (Today the median is slightly over 35.) Parents watched this new generation with a mixture of amusement, confusion and concern. On the one hand, traditional values of romantic idealism and the family seemed intact. Young people married in record numbers and at an earlier average age (21) than at any time since the 1920s. Maudlin boy-girl love songs were still in vogue: Sonny and Cher led the year's charts with *"I Got You, Babe."* On the other hand, this appeared to be a generation with an overt libido. Bikinis were the rage in the summer of '65. The first co-ed residences came into vogue at universities. *The Pawnbroker* was released, not the most memorable movie ever made, but the first major studio film to contain frontal nudity. The birth control pill and the increasingly popular IUD were gratefully received. The argument was less about whether young women should use them than about which was the most effective.

In 1959, looking forward to the coming decade, *Maclean's* had confidently predicted that "conformity will continue to be a cherished goal." But the conformity of the 1960s didn't turn out to be anything like the conformity of the '50s. Two groups emerged to challenge the Ozzie-and-Harriet values that North Americans had settled into: the outspokenly passive hippies, and the outspokenly active student movement.

Jon Ruddy, writing in *Maclean's* in 1965, portrayed hippies as people who had withdrawn from "comfort, security, property, politicians, the Mass media, martinis, cars, social graces, hockey, the profit motive, char-broiled steaks, urban renewal, golf, houses, children, dogs, cats, budgerigars, Juliet, slum clearance, rush-hour traffic, laws, lawnmowers, Christmas and the clock." They had replaced these bourgeois afflictions, he said, with heartfelt concerns for "marijuana, other kicks, the Bomb, each other, chess, Zen Buddhism, We Shall Overcome, passivism, Bob Dylan, psychiatry,

LSD and psychedelic experience, sex, poetry, pickets, police, sit-ins, minorities, crafts, travel, art, brotherhood and guitars."[3] There are no reliable estimates of how many young Canadians bought into this lifestyle. The number was by no means huge, but many dabbled on the fringes. The hippies were symbols. They stood for rejection of both authority and conformity. They wanted to liberate the "self" from society's traps, materialism included. Materialism, of course, fought back.

The student movement also featured long hair, unconventional clothes and a fondness for sex and drugs, but it was more attuned to Chairman Mao than to Mahatma Gandhi. Although much of its rhetoric was imported from America, the Canadian student movement didn't have the same angry edge. For example, in early 1970, American activist and radical icon Abby Hoffman spoke at the University of Alberta in Edmonton. He began by thrusting his clenched fist into the air and shouting "Fuck Canada." South of the border these words (substituting *America* for *Canada*, of course) were guaranteed to bring U.S. college audiences to their feet, chanting approval. In Edmonton, Hoffman was booed. Despite the revolutionary tone that prevailed in both countries, the sixties were different for Canadians because we thought about our societies in fundamentally different ways.

In the U.S., the decade was dominated by domestic and international conflict: race wars at home and Viet Nam abroad. The New Left rose to challenge the establishment. Radical groups like the Symbionese Liberation Army and the Weathermen flourished. Students for a Democratic Society attracted hundreds of thousands of followers. But by the end of the decade, the New Left was in disarray. The helium started leaking from the balloon when Washington ended the draft. No draft, no burned draft cards. Older American voters turned cranky and in 1969 elected Richard Nixon, bringing the Democrats' "war on poverty," to an untimely end. Nixon preferred Old Testament righteousness to compassion, family values to reform. "Benign neglect" replaced inner-city self-help programs.

For young people who continued to believe if not in revolution at least in reform, the Canadian establishment was slightly more palatable. Certainly Trudeau, who affected fringe jackets and side-burns, looked like a better bet than Nixon. Young Canadians had shared the era's climate of rebellion with one clear advantage over their American cousins – they didn't have to wonder whether they would end up in a body bag. It may have been annoying when Canadian politicians mouthed words of support for the U.S. war effort, but at least Canada offered safe haven to deserters and draft dodgers. Canada even had socialists in Parliament, even if they were from the old school. Indeed, the New Democratic Party, founded in 1961 from the remnants of the Co-operative Commonwealth Feder-ation, used the left-wing fervour of the 1960s to emerge as a signif-icant force in Canadian politics.

Part of the reason that the student protest movement was more restrained in Canada was because Parliament was quite a progressive place. Major social programs, such as the Canada Pension Plan and medicare, introduced during the Pearson era (1963-68), were still being bolstered. Trudeau took the government out of "the bedrooms of the nation," decriminalizing homosexuality. Abortions became more readily available as a result of amendments to the law. The Company of Young Canadians was founded to redirect some of the immense energy reserves of young people toward community devel-opment. Rather than battle the tide of change sweeping the country, Ottawa decided to study it, appointing royal commissions on the changing role of women, the future of bilingualism and the use of illegal drugs.

The hippies of Yorkville ... the Chicago 7 ... mail box bombings in Quebec ... Germaine Greer... John and Yoko lying in revolutionary splendour on their Montreal hotel bed ... Pierre Vallières' *White Niggers of America*. Everyone who lived during the 1960s nurtures memories of a unique time. Change was everywhere. The Catholic Church abandoned the Latin mass. Astronauts walked in space. Nuclear generating plants spewed out power. New plastics and synthetic compounds created disposable packaging, creaseless garments and garbage bags. Corner grocery stores with carbon-paper account books gave way to supermarkets like Loblaws and Dominion, which created huge shopping "environments." Downtown stores began to atrophy; everyone headed for the suburban mall, where the shopping hours were less restrictive and there were acres of free parking. And if a certain sameness was starting to creep into all this change, there was always Trudeau.

Behind these images, however, behind all the love beads, protest marches and the rose in Trudeau's lapel, a revolution was awakening. This revolution flowed not from the writings of Karl Marx but from the works of John Maynard Keynes. It was ignited not by machines that changed the means of production but by television, which transformed our patterns of consumption. And at its vanguard there were no hordes of dispossessed workers, but a young, confident and growing middle class. It was a revolution involving four core values that dramatically rearranged the Canadian economy and Canadian society.

CHANGING GENDER ROLES

The most important change in core values that occurred in the 1960s involved the role of women. Like their counterparts around the world, Canadian women had long been involved in struggles to win the most elementary of social equalities. By the 1920s, Canadian women everywhere but in Quebec had finally gained the right to vote. During the Second World War, Canadian women had been active on the home front, filling what were considered "male" jobs while the men were overseas. These women enjoyed their new lives in the workplace and the financial independence it brought, and some found it difficult to return to their traditional role as homemakers.

In the postwar years, the lingering effect of working outside the home changed women's sense of themselves. By the 1960s, a revolution was occurring in women's values. Its most essential element involved neither legal nor social equality rights so much as a basic shift in attitude toward work. Although this attitude had begun to change during the war, it was the women born in the Baby Boom – particularly those born between 1946 and 1956 – who really questioned the prevailing mores of the time. As a 1994 Statistics Canada report by Diane Galarneau points out, these women were to display "the most radical break" with earlier generations of Canadians.[4]

A few of their mothers may have worked outside the home, but certainly not most. There was usually a pattern if they had: they tended to marry young, work briefly until the first child was born, then leave the workforce, probably forever, but at least until the children were out of the nest. The baby boomers were a different crew entirely. They went to work in record numbers, delayed having children, had fewer of them and returned to work soon after the children were born. Female boomers were disinclined to accept the gender stereotypes of wife and mother that existed up to that point.

This transformation in the self-image and roles of women sprang from a convergence of several technological, demographic and sociological factors. First, there was the birth control pill, an invention of the late 1950s. In 1960, Enovid became the first such pill to gain approval from the Department of National Health and Welfare. Although later experience would question the safety of birth control pills, leading many women to consider other options, the Pill gave Canadian women a significant degree of control over their reproductive choices. It did not force them into the workplace, but it certainly gave them the option.

There were other factors in the mix. The 1970 Royal Commission on the Status of Women pinpointed two. The first was the increasingly urbanized world in which women lived. In the 20 years since the end of the Second World War, the epicenter of Canadian life had shifted from small communities and farms to the cities. During this period, the percentage of Canadians living in cities with populations of more than 30,000 almost doubled, from 30% to about 55%.[5]

In rural Canada, the line between home and work was always fuzzy at best. While there was usually little question about who the head of the household was, a woman's economic contribution on a farm was hard to miss. In the suburbs and urban centers, on the other hand, the dividing line between those who went to work and those who stayed home was clear. Those at work (the men) were the producers; those who worked at home (the women) were the consumers. And, according to the theory of the times, not having to be the bread-winner meant that life was a piece of cake.

Betty Friedan didn't agree. Her book, *The Feminine Mystique*, published in 1963, became an instant best-seller. Her core argument resonated with millions of women, the message being that the seemingly idyllic life of puttering around the home in a subservient role in the suburbs was more likely to induce a feeling of loneliness and low self-esteem than joy and contentment. Friedan argued that, while the modern suburban family might be materially much better off than it had ever been, it was also often what sociologist Jackson Toby called "an island of intimacy in a sea of strangers."[6] Many readers were quick to agree that being stranded in suburbia often produced a pressure-cooker environment, leading to strained marriages and frayed nerves.

The urban economy, in conjunction with the Pill, offered alternatives. The booming services sector had begun to provide plentiful job opportunities in social, health and business services and in retailing. The pay was rarely comparable to what men earned, but women grabbed the opportunities nonetheless. Traditionalists warned that there would be social implications, but the sense of liberation that came from earning a salary and participating in the workforce made other considerations seem secondary.

The Status of Women report pinpointed a second factor that helped encourage women to adopt less-traditional roles: television. When we look back to the 1950s, we remember all those stay-at-home female roles: Lucy Ricardo stayed home, Ricky went to work; June Cleaver stayed home, Ward went to work; Harriet Nelson stayed home, Ozzie went to work (or at least left the house for a while). Women watching afternoon television in the 1950s tuned **to** programs such as the American classic *Queen for a Day*, in which women contestants described how terrible their lives were. The "winner," chosen by the studio audience (via **an** applause meter) was the person with the worst life. This program sent a simple but politically powerful message to the millions of women tuning in: no matter how tough you think your life is, it is not as bad as this. As Linda and S. Robert Lichter and Stanley Rothman have demonstrated in their extensive review of the history of television, the medium in the 1950s was more an agent of social control than of social change.[7]

Television in the 1960s didn't exactly overthrow all those old stereotypes, but women's roles started to be projected in less-restrictive ways. Shows like *Mission Impossible, The Avengers*, and *That Girl* at least depicted women as something other than housewives, however subservient they usually remained. By the 1970s, Mary Tyler Moore, her friend Rhoda, and Cloris Leachman were allowed to have their own apartments, their own careers and their own love lives. It may not have been a call to the barricades, but it wasn't June Cleaver's lifestyle either.

A third factor that helps explain the changing self-concept of women is education. In 1961, 24% of all full-time university undergraduates in Canada were women; by the end of the decade, this figure had increased to 37%. In the 1971-72 academic year, more than 55% of education degrees and 64% of social work degrees were earned by women.[8] While women would continue to be underrepresented in such "masculine" fields as medicine and engineering, their increasing levels of education – and the professional achievements that resulted – clearly played a crucial role in the transformation of their self-identity. As sociologist Jill Vickers commented in 1976, young women at the time were "increasingly aware of the value of higher education from the point of view of personal development and self-esteem."[9]

The shift of women into the workforce did not happen overnight. Indeed, it was not until the end of the 1970s that a majority of Canadian women were working full time. But the female participation rate kept climbing throughout the late 1960s and the '70s. The impact was incredible. Over the past quarter century, no other single event has had such a dramatic effect on the consumer and employment markets at the heart of the Canadian economy.

A NEW MATERIALISM

After 20 years of prudence, older Canadians were ready for a fling, and neither romanticized poverty nor revolutionary wars were what they had in mind. They had suffered more than their share of poverty and more than their share of war. Now, they wanted something more consistent with the dreams that had sustained them through all the hard times. And young people, who had placed such a premium on freedom of expression and individuality, were beginning to discover that *consumption* could satisfy both needs. As Eric Hobsbawm has noted, "Paradoxically, the rebels against the conventions and restrictions shared the assumptions on which mass consumer society was built."[10] In the lingo of the truly committed, it was called selling out. And it was happening everywhere. By the early 1970s, the hippies had disappeared from Toronto's run-down Yorkville district. In their place stood fashionable boutiques.

Once Canadians let go, there was no holding back. In Canada, as in the United States and other Western industrialized countries, the 1960s witnessed the emergence of new attitudes toward affluence and materialism. Daniel Yankelovich, the American pollster and social commentator, has remarked on this phenomenon: "The depression may have ended with World War II, but it was not until the late 1960s that Americans who had lived through the depression were able to put their depression psychology, and the fear, insecurity and outlook it engendered, behind them."[11] Later, some of us would occasionally stop to wonder whether we hadn't become slaves to materialism, but in the late '60s, earning and spending money had an incredibly emancipating appeal. It offered a new freedom of choice in lifestyles. Dual incomes meant more material possessions. And more material possessions meant more status, a niftier identity. As Neil Postman has observed, once the "god of Consumerism" takes over, the basic moral axiom becomes "Whoever dies with the most toys wins."[12]

Immediate gratification was clearly a lot more fun than deferred gratification, and inflation gave the habit of indulging our appetites a rational base. Spending started to make more sense than saving. Function became less important than status. A sustained market-place demand emerged, bankrolled by better salaries gushing from the pockets of a swollen new labour force. It was demand that would translate into years of great joy – and profit – for Canadian manu-facturers and retailers.

Entrepreneurs had new tools to help stoke that demand. Manu-facturers and retailers learned that the combination of television and urbanization created opportunities to "engineer" what people wanted from life. Television began to realize its potential as one of the greatest persuaders of all time. Marshall McLuhan, a University of Toronto professor who turned into a communications guru, was the first to articulate the profound emotional nature of television. "The medium is the message" was his well-known mantra, and it conveyed the novel idea that TV allowed advertisers to connect directly to the audience's central nervous system. As long as adver-tisers understood that this was not a logical process, that they were actually better off *circumventing* logic, they could connect and score. "Advertising creates environments," McLuhan wrote, "and these are very effective as long as they are invisible. Some think that an ad is good if it is noticed. This is quite mistaken. The work of an ad is totally subconscious. As soon as you realize it is an ad, it is not serving its function."[13]

Television advertising soon proved its genius at making a direct link between products on the screen and the personalities of viewers. At one time advertising had been concerned almost totally with promoting the benefits of products – "*Ipana cleans your teeth whiter.*" Now, TV ads made you feel better about identifying yourself with a particular brand, *your* brand. It didn't matter whether Pepsi tasted better than Coke. What mattered was that drinking Pepsi made you part of a new and exciting generation, and Coke didn't.

John Kenneth Galbraith, the Harvard economist born and raised on a farm in southwestern Ontario, was interested less in the mechanism by which television gained its power over people than in the power itself. In *The New Industrial State*, Galbraith stated flatly that television had become "the prime instrument for the management of consumer demand."[14] It was clear to Galbraith and others that television added a new excitement to consumption. Choosing a car, a soft drink or a toothpaste was no longer simply a matter of balancing price and quality. Different brands now conveyed different images that triggered a variety of emotional responses.

The second new weapon in the hands of the marketers was the shopping center. Like television, the shopping center created an emotional environment that encouraged consumption. Hundreds of malls began to appear on the outskirts of Canadian cities, where parking was plentiful, taxes were cheaper and freshly built suburbs created vast new demand. The shopping center slaked this thirst by offering consumers a wide range of retail shops in one location. Collectively, they offered a cornucopia of goods that had never been available in such close proximity.

Television made consumer goods a lot more appealing. The shopping center had made them marginally more appealing but a lot more accessible. Malls were strategically placed: North York, in Toronto; New Westminster, in Vancouver; St. James, in Winnipeg. Outside one's place of work, two new centers of attention had emerged for Canadians. Inside the home, the focus was no longer the kitchen or the living room, it was the TV set. Outside the home, it was no longer downtown or the drive-in movie, it was the shopping centre. Needless to say, marketers recognized a formidable combination when they saw one. The credit card, which had first appeared in the 1950s, became commonplace. Goodbye to messy carbon copies, now it was click-click, and a bill in the mail every month. Inevitably, money became easier to spend. Just about the only thing you couldn't buy with a credit card was a house, but mortgages were plentiful, and people were willing to buy into them even when interest rates were high.

For nearly a hundred years following Confederation, Canadians had been perceived as cautious and prudent, especially when it came to their pocketbooks. But things were changing, fast. Take lotteries. In the early 1960s, anyone caught selling Irish Sweepstakes lottery tickets on behalf of Irish hospitals was fined. People who bought them had to use a nom de plume; fictitious names were published in newspapers so that winners would not be arrested. But by the end of the decade, governments were seriously in the lottery business, making money in an industry they had outlawed for years. On Sundays, Canadians in some parts of the country were even starting to go to the movies and sporting events. Charles Dickens was said to have branded Canada "the sanctimonious icebox." It's a pity he didn't live longer. By the mid 1960s, the weather was still lousy, but Canadians were loosening up.

A NEW CONFIDENCE IN GOVERNMENTS

The third significant value shift of the decade was an increasing confidence in government to serve as an engine of economic progress and as a protector of the collective security of individual Canadians. Canadian governments already had some reasonably good credentials. The federal government had, for instance, presided over Canada's contribution to the winning of the Second World War, and had managed to pay back its war debt without disrupting the smooth performance of the economy. Canadians had been getting good value from their governments and by the mid-1960s had begun to expect more of them. Those who now blame politicians for expanding the role of government err grievously. Canadians *wanted* more from governments. Even Conservative governments – such as those that presided over Ontario into the eighties – believed in big government: Ontario Hydro, after all, burgeoned under the Tories.

This confidence was rooted in a quarter century of economic success, which had involved varying degrees of government intervention in the economy. It had been reinforced by the emergence of "image" politics, which saw political leaders transformed into television personalities. These leaders vied for the attention of a new generation of Canadian voters who distrusted the private sector and who looked to government as the repository of solutions to the social and economic problems confronting the country. From the Great Depression on, governments had become more involved in the economic well-being of their citizens. In the 1960s, the role of the Canadian government began to expand in areas ranging from medical care and pensions to job training and post-secondary education. Strictly speaking, many of the jurisdictions were provincial. But because there was a clear public demand for a "Canadian" approach to problems in these areas, and because the provinces welcomed federal funding, many overlapping programs were developed. Medicare was the most visible initiative, yet a great many other programs were on the planning board.

There were plans to encourage investment in Canadian stocks, to discourage foreign ownership, to encourage Canadian culture, to encourage investment in the Atlantic provinces, to discourage pollution of the Great Lakes, to encourage participation in sports, to discourage smoking, to encourage cross-cultural exchanges with Quebec, to discourage hateful attitudes toward minority ethnic groups, to encourage the development of nations on the other side of the world. Everywhere you looked, it seemed, another federal department had drafted another ambitious program.

Of course, all these plans required platoons of bureaucrats to implement them. In later years, this enthusiasm for planning would be judged excessive, but in the 1960s, government offices were the place to be. Sharp young bureaucrats always knew they had a good chance of getting funding if they came up with ideas to wrap the taxpayers' money around. And it was all for the benefit of the public. A new sense of mission fueled the partnership between Canadians and their governments, a revival of the "can do" attitude that had brought Canada through the depression and the war. Now Canadians had the money to do it. To build a "special" kind of country. The spirit had always been there.

This partnership wasn't just a romantic fling; it had economic theory behind it. That was the influence of John Maynard Keynes, a brilliant British economist who held that governments should use their taxing and spending powers to lessen the negative effects of business cycles, which tended to produce periods of high inflation followed by periods of high unemployment. "We are all Keynesians now," declared *Time* in its 1965 cover story on Keynes. In fact, he was *Time*'s "Man of the Year," a remarkable honour to bestow, given that Keynes had died in 1946. "The U.S. right now is closer to Keynes's cherished goal of full employment of its resources during peacetime than it has ever been," crowed *Time*. That year, U.S. unemployment melted from 4.8% to 4.2%. There were labour shortages in many industries, including aerospace, construction and shipbuilding. Manufacturing was pumping away at 91% capacity, with some sectors, such as automobile manufacturing, scraping 100%.[15] In Canada, Keynes appeared to be working his magic as well. Unemployment stood at 3.9%. Inflation was less than 3%. Wages were growing at 7%. The economy, experiencing its strongest sustained period of growth in the century, was operating at almost full capacity. Canada was a "mixed" economy of capitalistic venture and government planning – and proud of it.

Keynesian economics was as political as it was economic. It served to reinforce the notion of the centrality of the state. If the fiscal and monetary powers of the state could be used to soften the worst effects of the business cycle, could they not also be used to lessen other hardships? If an activist government could improve the Canadian economy, why not expand the role to deal with other ills – unequal access to health care, poverty and the need for better retirement benefits?

But if Canadians were excited about what governments could do, they had also become fascinated by the people at the controls. The prism through which they witnessed political events had switched from newspapers to television, and TV brought these people alive. In politics, as in consumption, television tugged at people's emotions. Television projected body language, facial tics, perspiring brows, dark circles under the eyes, glints of humour *in* the eyes, nervousness, composure, crankiness – all those tip-offs that we use to judge people. A line of sweat on Richard Nixon's face may have cost him the U.S. presidency in 1960. John Diefenbaker's jowls got in the way of anything he had to say, just as Joe Clark's chin did 15 years later.

Politicians like Trudeau thrived on TV and added excitement about government. In 1968, a Gallup poll found that 55% of Canadians had become more interested in politics during the past five years; for voters in their twenties, increased interest was reported at 69%. Politicians who played well to the cameras became larger than life. The personality and demeanour of the party leader became the image and identity of the party. If Keynesian economics had served to reinforce the centrality of the state, television confirmed the centrality of the party leader. There was less a feeling of danger here than of relief. No longer would Canada be bogged down in the quagmire of compromise and debate that had characterized its politics in the past. Canadians could expect more from government, because the leaders who promised more were now powerful enough to deliver.

A NEW AIR OF OPTIMISM

The fourth and final horseman in the set of values that transformed Canadian society in the 1960s was optimism. Having shaken off the anxieties associated with the Great Depression and the Second World War, Canadians began to radiate a confidence that economic progress and an improved quality of life was now inevitable. Science and technology would deliver continuous improvements in productivity. And, even if these breakthroughs eliminated a few outmoded jobs, so many quality jobs were evolving in the service sector that it didn't matter. The ebullience reflected reality, and reality fed off the ebullience: paycheques were fatter, work weeks were shorter, and there was no reason to believe that the rest of the century didn't belong to any Canadian willing to work hard. A 1969 article in *Maclean's* about graduating high-school students was entitled "These Shall Inherit the Earth," a comment that could have been made at any point during the later 1960s. It certainly wouldn't be made today.

The wonders of technology radiated brightly into the near and distant future. *Gemini* astronauts floated effortlessly in space. An amazing new device was introduced – the computer. By 1965, IBM reported that the number of computers in Canada had increased dramatically, from around 90 in 1960 to around 820. The Iron Ore Company of Canada was at the cutting edge; it announced that after two years of "working out the bugs," a computer at its Quebec pelletizing plant was performing marvelously. Ontario Hydro flipped the switch at its nuclear plant on the Bruce peninsula to the accompaniment of marching bands and speeches about the bright new world of nuclear power. There was not one protest. Air travelers watched in fascination as the Boeing 707 was supplanted by the bigger and faster 727. Designers were already touting the wide-bodied 747 that would be introduced in 1970, able to transport what amounted to whole villages of people at a time. The French and British were working on a supersonic passenger plane, the Concorde, which would make Paris to New York a five-hour jaunt. In 1965, there were no flight attendants, just stewardesses. Being one meant you had a glamorous job, because everyone knew that the skies were filled with excitement. You could even find excitement in Buffalo, New York. Colour televisions were hard to find in Canada – the CBC was still scrambling to convert from black-and-white. But for $700 you could buy one in Buffalo and bring it home, where it fit nicely with the hand-sized transistor radios and other gadgets that were making the depression seem like it must have happened back in the Middle Ages. Even can openers went electric, although nobody has yet been able to figure out why.

On the one hand, the threat of the Bomb had been intensified by the Cuban Missile Crisis of 1962 and the beginning of U.S. involvement in Viet Nam. On the other hand, nuclear weapons reinforced the idea that technology was king. Over the horizon, technology appeared to offer limitless opportunities. In 1961, President John F. Kennedy had promised to put Americans on the Moon. By the end of the decade, moviegoers watched *2001: A Space Odyssey* and emerged half-believing they would be out there some day. Canadians eagerly awaited the opening of the 1967 World's Fair in Montreal; its innovative designs – futuristic domes, monorails and creatively constructed living spaces – captured their imagination and challenged Canada's dowdy image.

This infatuation with the future was contagious. Newspapers and magazines published fanciful descriptions of an age in which clothes would be cleaned by sound waves, the work week would be reduced to 20 hours, and people would inhabit the moon. Colonialism was coming to an end in Africa and Asia, and it was widely assumed that generous transfers of Western technology would transform low-income countries into productive and self-sustaining nations within a few years. Technology was the key to productivity, and jobs went hand in hand with productivity. Canadians could hardly be blamed for believing that jobs would be plentiful, secure and rewarding for as long as people wanted to work.

Gallup Canada captured the era's optimism in a mid-decade poll; it found that Canadians were *five times* more likely to feel that the economy would be better as opposed to worse by 1970. A Centennial-year poll reported that 82% of Canadians believed that the country would experience significant progress over the next 20 years. As the writer and social commentator Myrna Kostash remarked, "Canada's postwar youth were coming to maturity at the conjuncture of several portentous developments . . . [They believed they] were to inherit a rising standard of living, jobs of their choosing, a variety of divertissements, and, more than ever, were to be educated, and liberated from the determinism of class, race and sex."[16]

Together, the four core values of the 1960s produced a unique epoch that would define our collective lives for more than a generation. The Spend-and-Share era had begun. I call it that because, between the mid-1960s and the end of the '80s, we Canadians were able to convince ourselves that we had found a formula for what had never existed before: a society that allowed its citizens to be both selfish and generous at the same time.

The signs of this new era weren't written on Simon and Garfunkel's "tenement walls and subway stalls." Instead they were recorded in brief passages in newspapers and magazines. In 1962, the Roper polling firm reported that for the first time, more Americans were relying on television than newspapers as their primary source of information. In 1965, the French fashion industry produced more women's pants than skirts. A year later, according to a Gallup survey, the percentage of Canadians who believed that employers should treat women the same as men had risen to 39%, up from 19% in 1950. In the space of 13 years – 1955 to 1968 – the percentage of Canadians who thought that religion was exerting an increasing influence on daily life plummeted from 53% to only 12%.

The times were a changin', all right, but not precisely the way Bob Dylan had reckoned.

Three

THE SPEND-AND-SHARE ERA

"Time and the world stretched endlessly then,
before the bad days came and everything shrank."
Rohinton Mistry, SUCH A LONG JOURNEY

Early in 1996, I had the honour of addressing several thousand
students graduating from the University of Manitoba. As I gazed out
at the sea of caps and gowns and the smiling faces of a hopeful new
generation, I was struck by the irony of it all. I had received my
degree on this same platform in '69, and here before me was the
class of '96. Of course it was just a tiny coincidence – the reversal of
numbers – so trivial in ordinary circumstances that it wouldn't have
been worth noting. But there was nothing trivial about how our
fortunes were also reversed.

The year I graduated, corporations, school boards, even government departments dueled on campuses for the available pool of job
seekers. Many who earned degrees in 1996 will have not courters; in
fact, they'll have trouble finding jobs. During the years leading up
to my degree, the most important single piece of legislation passed
was the 1966 Medical Care Act, which created Canada's medicare
system. Medicare was a tribute to the perceived benefits and healing

powers of sharing communal wealth. For the class of '96, the most important piece of legislation during their school years has been the North American Free Trade Agreement, a tribute to the perceived benefits and healing powers of competing for wealth in the international marketplace. In 1969, Canada had no debt and was still basking in the unifying glow of Expo '67. In 1996, the country was crippled with more than a $500-billion debt and still reeling from the aftershock of the latest Quebec referendum. How had it come to pass that the world I faced in 1969 now seemed such a distant memory?

The Spend-and-Share era, featuring a mix of selfishness and generosity few Canadians are likely to witness again, endured for the better part of 25 years. By the time it collapsed, many of the forces that nourished it had eroded to the point of illusion. That does nothing, in my judgment, to diminish them: the strength that was there in the beginning changed our lives. And the events that created that era stemmed from the dreams and appetites of ordinary Canadians, not their legislators. We got what we asked for. There were parts of it that we ultimately decided we didn't much care for, but there is no denying that we asked for it all. And why not? Everything seemed to be working. For the longest time, it seemed that we had created something permanent and good. But this era, too, had its illusions.

Many of these illusions were created by inflation. Oh, we fretted about inflation – polls showed it was an even greater concern than unemployment. But, in a perverse way, inflation also kindled our optimism. Housing prices boomed, so people felt richer; what they owned was worth more than they ever could have imagined. And they were earning more money than they had ever expected to, even if prices were beginning to rise as quickly, or even more quickly, than wages. After all, you didn't *have* to buy all those things. Besides, wages would just keep going up. Could anyone remember when wages went down? It couldn't happen could it? The low-wage 1990s weren't within the realm of most people's possibilities.

Who had time for doubts? Canadians were riding a powerful wave of enthusiasm. The new values combined to create a climate that promoted risk taking, experimentation and bold initiatives. Each value shift tended to reinforce one or more of the others. Optimism about the future both fueled and was fueled by confidence in the public sector. New gender roles that encouraged women to work were reinforced by a new materialism that encouraged them to spend their salaries as quickly as possible. Spending, rather than saving, was encouraged by a new confidence that governments would always provide. Taken together, these values played a critical role in shaping and intensifying the four most important social, economic and political forces that define the Spend-and-Share era: massive labour force growth; voracious patterns of consumption; a burgeoning public sector; and the transition to an economy based on services rather than resources or industry.

These forces produced a monumental transformation in the lives of Canadians, at work and at home. They created huge opportunities, both for individuals and for many of Canada's largest companies. It is not an exaggeration to claim that they effectively altered our national identity. These forces nourished us, sustained us economically, gave our lives meaning. That's why the 1990s have been so difficult for so many. Gone is the presumption of growth. Gone, too, is the feeling that, if we work together, anything is possible. As I will demonstrate, the irony of the Spend-and-Share era is that the transformation of Canada during this period ultimately undermined many of the values that ignited it in the first place. In the end, many of us have been left feeling that the country has lost its bearings, and maybe its soul as well. But if it is too soon to proclaim the demise of Canada's soul, it is high time we acknowledged that the seminal forces that molded it are missing and presumed dead.

LABOUR FORCE GROWTH

To find the most important and direct link between the distant land of the 1960s and the new realities of the 1990s, look at what happened to Canada's labour force during the Spend-and-Share era. The growth in Canada's labour force averaged 3.5% a year between 1965 and 1989. This may not seem like a big number, but it was enough to put us first among the 10 largest economies in the world. And it becomes a *really big* number when we compare it with the paltry 1% growth the labour force has experienced since 1989.

This growth occurred over a period in which Canada's population growth averaged about 1.5% a year; in other words, the labour pool was growing more than twice as fast as the population. Part of the reason for this surge was the coming of age of the Baby Boom, over nine million strong. What really made a difference, however, was the women of the Baby Boom. Here the values of the 1960s set off an explosion, whose shock waves would be felt for the next quarter century.

Compare, for example, the participation rate of women aged 26 to 35 for three different years: 1966, 1976 and 1986. In the 1966 group, according to Statistics Canada, 43% had full- or part-time jobs. A decade later, 65% of this age group were employed. By 1986, the participation rate had hit 78% – nearly double that of the first group. Between 1969 and 1979, the number of women working in

Canada jumped from 2.5 million to 4.9 million. Between 1960 and 1990, in contrast, the male percentage of the labour force dropped from 70% to 54% . Overall, the number of Canadians in the workforce soared 111% over those three decades, compared with 85% in the United States and 5% in Italy. The consequences were immense. Educators knew that the baby boom would require institutional growth. What they couldn't have predicted was the tidal wave of women deciding to pursue post-secondary education for the same reason that men did: to prepare themselves for careers. By 1990, women were awarded 56% of all bachelor's and first professional degrees granted by Canadian universities, up from 25% in 1960.

There were, of course, some sobering side effects. During the 1970s and '80s, the Canadian divorce rate more than doubled. Part of the increase was clearly a function of less-restrictive divorce legislation. There was also a degree of irony inherent in the massive infusion of women into the workplace: while this generation was the output of the fecundity that followed the Second World War, its own level of fecundity was very low. In fact, since 1972, the Canadian fertility rate has never climbed to the replacement level, a trend that led demographers to predict that, without immigration, the country would be vacant by the year 2786.[1] Working women now had the means to support themselves, independent of their husbands. Many of them did just that. Between 1971 and 1991, the number of households with children under 16 headed by a single parent doubled from 500,000 to just under one million. Over 80% of those families were headed by a woman.

Whatever the side effects, the era of the stereotyped mild-mannered Canadian housewife was over. All kinds of men (and some women) continued to doubt that women deserved equal rights, equal pay and equal respect in the marketplace, but former

Ottawa mayor Charlotte Whitton had a clever answer for them: "Whatever she does, a woman must do twice as well as any man to be thought of just half as good. Luckily, that's not difficult."

CONSUMER SPENDING

Inevitably, the changing role of women fed the country's engine of economic growth. The rising number of dual-income families coupled with declining rates of fertility created a generation of flush consumers. In 1958, fewer than 2 in 10 married women were working for wages; by 1990, the number had climbed to almost 6 in 10.

In 1967, only about a third of all families had both spouses working. By 1989, this had increased to more than 60%. The result was the longest sustained period of consumer spending in Canadian history. The spending surge affected all parts of the economy, but the influx of women into the labour force had a particular impact on some, notably the auto sector, the retail sector and the packaged and convenience foods sector.

Two parents working often meant two cars instead of one, creating a 20-year boom in the auto sector. New lifestyles created new pressures, most of which involved time. And new pressures led to new purchases. Working wives demanded more and better labour-saving devices. Department stores flourished. Sears established its first store in Burnaby, B.C., in 1954. In 1960, it had 17 outlets across the country, and by 1980 sales had climbed to $3 billion. Fast food became the rage, the landscape littered with McDonald's, Pizza Hut, Kentucky Fried Chicken and other chains. McDonald's ("We do it all for you") raised its first golden arches on Canadian soil in 1967. By 1989, there were 606 of them.[3]

Fully 60% of the growth in Canada's gross domestic product

between 1965 and 1989 was generated by consumer spending. During this astounding quarter century, real spending growth averaged about 4.3% a year; since 1989, it has averaged about 1%. For anyone providing goods and services to consumers, it was hard to avoid making money. Not only were there more shoppers but their appetites were voracious. The new materialism that had swamped the hippie movement just kept feeding on itself.

The demands of the young led to a nation-wide surge in housing prices that added to the wealth not only of their parents but of anyone who got into the real-estate market early. The quest for housing was almost unprecedented. On two occasions, the demand became so heated in Toronto that potential buyers would show up at homes and start outbidding one another, as though they were at an auction. It was a feeding frenzy that sent real-estate agents dancing to the banks. Nor was housing the only industry affected. In 1972, when shoppers began hoarding meat because prices were rising so quickly, some Toronto appliance stores announced that they had run out of freezers. Canadian banks introduced Visa and Mastercard, fueling the flames of consumption. Nor were consumers deterred by the combination of high interest rates and high inflation rates they often confronted. On the contrary, high inflation rates created an urgency to buy now, before prices went up more.

It was truly a grand time to be in retail sales. If you bought the right model car, you could put 40,000 kilometers on the odometer, then sell it for more than you had paid. Consumer spending was briefly slowed by 20% interest rates in the early '80s – but surged again during the last half of the decade. Wage increases, some of them whopping, had become so automatic that people factored them into what they could afford. The increase in "real" wages (after inflation had been taken into account) had all but evaporated by the late 1970's, but even then, consumer momentum was maintained. The 1980's gave rise to the "me" generation, which meant only one thing: *indulge*. On second thought, it meant something else: *debt*.

GROWTH OF GOVERNMENT

Canadians have expressed increased cynicism toward government in recent years, but hostility toward the *concept* of government has never caught on in Canada. Call us naive, but we tend to think of governments as useful mechanisms that allow citizens to come together in common cause. As clumsy, over-formalized and expensive as that assembly can be, Canadians in the Spend-and-Share era believed in government. Consider this: in the mid-1950s, about 30 cents of every dollar spent was shelled out by government. By the early 1990s, that had increased to slightly more than 50 cents – over half the economic activity in the country.[2]

Inevitably, the number of people employed by the federal government soared during this period, from 124,580 in 1951, to 202,807 in 1961, and to more than 400,000 by the early 1990s. Even more significant, transfers from governments to individuals and corporations also doubled. As Keynes predicted, this spending boosted the Canadian economy. It also contributed to one of the highest levels of public debt in the developed world.

There were great expectations that governments would help solve new problems of the post-war period – record increases in the number of job seekers, a higher incidence of single-parent families and a widening gap between growth areas such as Ontario and depressed areas such as Atlantic Canada. It was the engine of government, Canadians hoped, that would create the "just society"

Pierre Elliott Trudeau had promised. Billions of dollars were spent trying to even out opportunities and patch up some social problems associated with new hopes and new values.

Government debt began its climb in the mid-1970s. In hindsight, some critics blame all the spending on unconscionable politicians turning their backs on sound accounting principles in order to buy votes. But the federal government had racked up enormous debt before, notably during the Second World War, and had had no trouble paying it off. Moreover, most Canadians wanted to be bought. We weren't interested in anything that might deprive us of the good times that were the promise of this new era.

Federal Progressive Conservatives twice blundered when they strayed between the mother bear (the Canadian public) and the cubs (its deemed entitlements). In both cases the Tories had brave and reasonable intentions, and in both cases their noble gestures cost them an election. In 1974, PC Leader Robert Stanfield campaigned in favour of wage-and-price controls to cool down an overheated economy. He was ridiculed for making the suggestion by Trudeau, whose Liberals went on to win the election and impose wage-and-price controls. And in 1980, Prime Minister Joe Clark proposed levying a 15% tax on energy consumption; this came during a period of skyrocketing oil prices perceived to be caused by a critical shortage of world oil reserves. Again, Trudeau turned to ridicule. The Liberal Party's proposed solution was to keep oil prices artificially low by forcing Alberta to charge below-market prices for its crude (a move the Economic Council of Canada later said caused Canadian manufacturers to slip behind the United States in productivity). Once again, Canadian voters rewarded Trudeau with a majority government.

Government had an almost magical quality. When the rest of the world was bogged down in the energy crisis of the early 1980s, we could be proud of our own "made in Canada" approach. Unlike what happened in the U.S. and Britain, where the gap between the rich and poor widened during the 1980s, a combination of transfers to individuals and reforms in the tax law slowed this process in Canada. Time and again when distasteful events were swirling around in the rest of the world, Canadians cried, "No, not us," and government listened.

Election promises had always been integral to political success, but the sky had become the limit. Not only did the public expect more but a buoyant economy (and inflation that automatically pushed taxpayers into higher brackets) meant there was more tax money pouring in – and more to throw around. Elections became promise festivals, as parties offered everything from juiced-up retirement benefits and increased university funding to tax breaks for first-time home buyers and funding for day care. The federal government was everywhere, removing railway tracks from downtown Winnipeg, buying up land on Toronto's Harbourfront, helping P.E.I. consolidate its checkerboard of one-room schoolhouses, paying prairie farmers not to grow wheat. And so prevalent were government "bribes" to corporations that promised to create jobs that NDP Leader David Lewis started calling them "corporate welfare bums." In Saskatchewan, Tory Leader Grant Devine offered funds for any home owner who wanted to build or expand a rec room. He won the election, and thousands of Saskatchewan basements were turned into showpieces at taxpayers' expense.

As misguided as much of this spending may seem in retrospect, there is no question that it provided an important economic stimulant and helped deal with genuine national problems. John Kenneth Galbraith, referring to the growth in government in the U.S. during the past 40 years, made an interesting observation that bears repeating. "Welfare was not the creation of liberals or even unwed mothers acting with liberal support and encouragement," he wrote. "It was the result of one of the great migrations of modern times."[3]

In Canada, the "great migration" was more than the movement of people from rural areas and small towns to the cities. Our great migration involved the movement of millions of baby boomers, especially women, into the labour force. It was in good conscience that governments everywhere tried to ensure that demand created jobs. No government wanted the anguish of the depression to be revisited on Canada. And neither did Canadian voters.

GROWTH IN THE SERVICES SECTOR

Politicians spent a lot of time in the 1960s worrying about whether Canada would develop into an economy that could depend mainly on manufacturing rather than primary resources. We didn't want to be hewers of wood and drawers of water any more. We wanted an economy built on the production of finished goods, the kind of economy that created well-paying jobs, like the Europeans and Americans seemed to have.

There was only one problem with our brave aspirations. By the 1960s, these jobs were already on their way out. Automation was beginning to do exactly what the Luddites had feared: replace people with technology. Or rather, as Peter Drucker explained it in *Post-Capitalist Society,* the application of knowledge to work had made factories 3.5% to 4% more efficient every year for many decades until there was little work left to be done. In the 1950s,

Drucker pointed out, people who made things or moved things still constituted a majority in all the developed countries. By 1990, the percentage had dropped to 20% and was continuing to decline.[4] In Canada, for example, the percentage of workers employed in manufacturing dropped from 24% in 1961 to 15% in 1991.

Luckily, our maturing society created other needs, nearly all of them in the services sector. In 1961, 3.3 million Canadians worked in services. By 1971, the number had jumped to 4.9 million, and by 1991 to more than 9 million, accounting for more than two-thirds of all workers. That represented a threefold increase in service jobs during a period in which the Canadian population grew from 18 to 27 million. More women going out to work created more income for new "necessities" such as restaurant meals, labour-saving devices, automobile tune-ups, clothes for work, cleaning ladies, gardeners and home handymen. It also produced more income for new "luxuries" – new houses, more trips to the hairdresser, more expensive vacations. Again, that generated jobs – in real estate, personal services, tourism, in numerous areas of the service sector. These were "traditional" services. More economic activity also produced more jobs in the "dynamic" services sector – communications, finance, advertising – as well as in "non-market" services such as teaching, policing and administration.

The growth in services was an outgrowth of two developments. The first was the continuing transition from labour-intensity to capital-intensity in the expanding goods-producing industries: manufacturing, farming and resources. A century of ever-more-efficient technology had not only raised levels of productivity; it had, in each successive decade, sharply cut the need for labour itself, both in manufacturing and in the resource sector. In 1924, 74 hours of labour were required to produce 100 bushels of wheat. By 1960, it was 12 hours, and by 1986, it was 7.[5] Increased demand for manufactured products was easily surpassed by increased productivity. As a result, the demand did not translate into huge numbers of new blue-collar jobs. The job needs of the baby boomers had to be met elsewhere. The explosion in services came along at exactly the right time.

The new service jobs were far more appealing to ordinary Canadians than most of the jobs that had earlier been available – bellhops, waitresses and the like. Many traditional jobs were on farms or in the resources sector, outdoor jobs that often depended on good weather, good crops and fluctuations in the commodities markets.

The new jobs had a more upscale flavour. They were cleaner, more stable, even more creative. Most were in the white-collar sector: the professions, corporate management, teaching, the public service, retail, financial services, telecommunications, journalism and marketing. They offered the prospect of long-term employment that was safe, dignified, interesting and collegial. Many of these jobs – teaching, journalism and the public service – even came with a sense of mission. People could perceive themselves as helping to build a better Canada while earning first-rate salaries. In an era that still dreamed of Camelot, the combination seemed divine.

The result was a busy, bustling country, devoted to growth and more growth. Canadians, it seemed, had found the formula to guide us for the rest of our lives, and for our children's lives as well. What we forgot was that, while the forces that created this lifestyle were powerful, they were not eternal. We assumed that hard times were history. We were wrong.

THE END OF AN ERA

The unraveling of the Spend-and-Share era did not occur overnight. Indeed the warning signs were evident almost from the beginning.

The oil crisis of the early 1970s, which sparked much of the inflation that would dog this era, sent a strong signal that the postwar
economy was shifting gears. A decade later, a major recession threatened the economies of much of the developed world, sending a
clear message that the good times couldn't last. Yet it wasn't until
the end of the 1980s that the forces that had propelled this era
finally flamed out. Growth in the labour force, consumer spending,
government programs and jobs in the services sector continued
through the 1980s, creating a surreal sense of continuity. And then
the sky fell.

Canadians today find themselves in the midst of value changes as
profound as those of the 1960s. Unfortunately, this time the
momentum is against us. Then, we were coming off two decades of
postwar prosperity. Now, we are coming off two decades of very
limited economic progress. Average unemployment rates have
increased every decade, averaging 6.7% in the 1970s, 9.5% in the
1980s and about 11% through 1995. So has government debt. At the
same time, average real incomes (taking inflation into account)
have stopped growing and are now in decline. In the 1960s and '70s,
we saw ourselves as young, idealistic and optimistic. In the 1990s,
we are beginning to turn grey, worried about where we go next. Our
polls show that roughly one-third of Canadians fear that they or
someone close to them will lose their jobs. And there is considerable
anxiety that the social safety net we have constructed will have
considerably frayed when baby boomers hit old age.

The security that Keynesian economics offered is gone, replaced by
a realization that Canada is now so integrated into the global marketplace that much of our economic fate lies beyond our grasp. When
borders become meaningless, any attempt to stimulate demand
dissipates quickly. Besides, Canadian governments have no money.

By 1990, the engines that had propelled Canada for more than a generation had been virtually silenced. Overall labour force growth was in steep decline – down to 0.9% from 2% as recently as the 1980s. During the first half of the 1990s, the percentage of working women actually dropped – by 2%.

The golden age of government has ended as well. Today's government downsizing is part of a broader process that began, innocently enough, with talk about deregulation in the early 1980s. Since then, successive governments have ceded control to the free market, first by reducing or eliminating regulations limiting foreign competition, then by privatizing Crown corporations, and finally through program cuts and user fees that have affected everyone from hospital patients to national park visitors. At first, it seemed that we had a choice – free market alternatives were appealing because we believed they would give us lower prices and better service. Lately our governments have told us we have no choice. If we resist, foreign brokerage houses and credit raters warn that we may be forced to swallow the same kind of economic medicine meted out to Mexico in 1995.

Once, the good jobs in education, retailing, social work, banking and a host of other categories had made everyone who had one feel like a somebody. By the late 1980s, it was clear that many of these jobs had started to inspire nightmares of shattered expectations. New management theory emphasizing "delayered" hierarchies and flexibility rather than size have reduced the need for many executives. Middle managers who used to fire people found themselves scanning the help-wanted ads.

If the forces that created the Spend-and-Share era were on the wane, so, too, were the values that fueled those forces. Liberation may have been the impetus that propelled women into the workforce in the 1960s and '70s, but by the 1990s most of those working were doing it for reasons of economic survival. A 1994 national survey conducted by the Angus Reid Group in partnership with the Canada Committee for the International Year of the Family found that almost half of all working mothers agreed that "If I could afford to I would stay home with the children." The same survey found that two thirds of all adults believed "It is not possible to support a family on one income."[6] The badge of freedom had become a leg trap. During the '90s, family debt mounted as Canadians continued to spend as though incomes were still increasing faster than inflation. That, however, was often no longer the case. In fact, by 1993, income was at its lowest level in 18 years. True, the average salary of the country's 14.4 million workers rose slightly in 1994 to $23,746 from $23,544. But the 1.8% inflation rate meant a net loss of $300. In many parts of the country, house values plunged because of shrinking demand. The boomers had already purchased, and few younger Canadians could afford to. For most of Canada's 950,000 single-parent families (82% headed by women), the very concept of material progress was a bad joke. Almost half of all single mothers and about 25% of single fathers were not in the labour force in 1989. There was one food bank in Canada in 1981; 10 years later, there were nearly 300. Statistics Canada estimated that more than three million Canadians – including 934,000 children – lived below the low-income cut in 1989.

Confidence in government, so strong during the 1960s, has turned into anger and cynicism. By the early 1990s, it was increasingly clear that national governments were less capable of controlling economic destinies, particularly when those governments were saddled with excessive debt. Increasingly, it seemed, national governments were too small to cope with international pressures and too big to cope with more immediate local and regional problems. As Mathew Horsman and Andrew Marshall pointed out in their book, *After the Nation-State*, a "counter-revolution" was under way against the social democratic solutions nation-states had often proposed. The anger and resentment spilled over, affecting government bureaucracies. In the 1970s and 1980s, when the private sector still offered job security, there was only a mild gnawing irritation that federal and provincial bureaucrats could never (it seemed) be fired. But in the '90s, when so many Canadians were seeing their own wages stagnate and job insecurity increase, they voiced anger at the salaries and perks of public servants.

Margaret Atwood once defined "survival" as Canada's national motivation. Survival depends on people pulling together when times get tough. But the frustration of trying to pull together increases when people sense that others are cruising more comfortably in another boat. We have never shown much enthusiasm for "special status," either for individuals or for provinces, and the seemingly privileged position occupied by bureaucrats has not enhanced our affection for the state.

Nor is the resentment misplaced. Compared to the private sector, government workers have done well in recent decades. So have their friends the politicians, at least in terms of one very visible perk: pension benefits. Federal politicians, whose salaries are relatively low ($64,600 plus some tax-free benefits) compared with those of lawyers and other professionals, compensated by voting themselves gold-plated pensions. Until recently, these pensions extracted $5.61 from the taxpayer for every dollar contributed by an MP.

Canadians had begun to lose confidence in their own safety nets. In a 1993 Angus Reid Group poll, 65% thought medicare would provide "much more limited coverage" when they were elderly, and

21% thought it would no longer exist; 55% thought the Old Age Pension would provide "a good deal less in benefits" when they qualified for it, and one in four thought it would no longer exist; 50% thought the Canada Pension Plan would offer far less in benefits in their old age than it does now, and roughly one in three thought it would not exist.[7]

Corporations may have laid off workers faster than governments, but it was government that took much of the blame. In a 1992 survey of citizens in 16 countries, Canadians ranked themselves dead last in their satisfaction with national government.[8] This was more than revulsion against Brian Mulroney and Meech Lake. People were simply fed up with government. The implicit promises of the Spend-and-Share era – a healthy economy, good jobs and a secure future – had not been delivered. The individual Canadian's share of federal debt was $860 in 1965. By 1995, it was $18,535. Incomes were falling, taxes were rising, yet governments had far less to offer. Politicians who pledged to put governments on a diet instead of distributing goodies, such as Ralph Klein and Mike Harris, started winning elections.

But government wasn't the only casualty. Materialism, which for many Canadians had replaced religion as a guiding light, had begun to flicker – out of necessity more than anything else. In the 1970s and 1980s, rising wages and the growth of two-income families made it seem that Canadians were becoming increasingly prosperous. The truth was otherwise. Real income (taking inflation into account) increased by 43% during the 1950s, and 37% during the 1960s, giving us all the confidence needed to go on a spending binge. But in the 1970s, real income increased by only 8.5%, and by a mere 2% during the "me" generation of the 1980s.

One early casualty was the optimism that had done so much to spark the spend-and-save era in the first place. By the 1990s, Canadians had begun to speak bleakly about the future. The sense of continuous "progress" which had characterized public opinion during the "Spend-and-Share era" had quickly eroded. In 1989, 74% of Canadians believed that they were "better off" than their parents had been at the same stage in their life. By 1992, those holding this attitude had dropped to 56%, and at the end of 1995, only 47% of Canadians made this claim. Among those 18-34, the decline in optimism has been even more striking. In 1989, 65% of Canadians in this age group believed that they would eventually be "better off" financially than their parents. Six years later, only 29% of younger Canadians held this belief.[9]

Finally, the party was over. In fact, the band had gone home long ago, but we in our blindness had continued to dance. The intoxication of the 1960s had taken more than two decades to wear off. The hangover is now upon us, and we don't have much time to shake it off.

Four

THE SINK-OR-SWIM ERA

*"We live in a very turbulent time, not because
there is so much change, but because
it moves in so many different directions."*
Peter Drucker, MANAGING FOR THE
FUTURE, THE 1990s AND BEYOND

When I was 14, I almost drowned. My friend Larry Mudge and I
were navigating Omans Creek in Winnipeg on a summer's day. We
were cocksure sailors in my dad's rowboat, a little outboard motor
rigged up on the back. Omans Creek is normally dry, but heavy rains
had turned it into a boiling white-water river. Two teenagers set out
to tame it, and lost. A huge tree had fallen in the creek and lay partly
submerged. These things are called sweepers. You can see the water
sweeping over the top of the trunk; what you can't see is the surge
beneath it. "Now *this* is fun," I remember thinking as I gunned the
little outboard toward the tree, angling for clearance to ride the rush
of water over the top. *Wham!* Before we knew it, we were submerged,
sucked down by that hidden torrent beneath the tree. I remember
knowing one thing more clearly than I had ever known anything
before: *we were drowning.* To this day, I don't know what saved me,
but just as the motion picture of my brief life began to race through
my mind, Larry and I spurted into the air on the other side.

Ever since, I've been more wary about the undercurrents of life. One minute you're comfortably riding the crest, the next – who knows? Canadians spent the better part of three decades believing the river they had ridden on was safe. Now there seem to be sweepers everywhere.

A new era is taking shape in Canada. When I started this book a year ago, most Canadians understood that there was trouble in the air, but it was pretty much invisible. Even now, the general mood is ambiguous. It shouldn't be. What's happening has to be understood. Another unique set of technological, economic and demographic currents is gaining strength. Only this time the consequences will be far different and the transition far more difficult. The new age is still in its infancy, but the broad outlines of the future can already be deciphered: tumultuous change in the working lives of Canadians, a fundamental shift in the role and significance of the household unit, and a political climate unlike anything we have known. Amid the cry, "Every man for himself," the lifeboats are being lowered. Welcome to the Sink-or-Swim era.

All of us clearly need to understand the nature of this change. I would like to use this chapter to answer three questions:

How? Do we understand the new technology that is making some Canadian hearts despair and others hum like computers?

Where? "Canada" is the obvious answer, but the world's geography is changing. Canada is getting blurrier on the map.

What? What's happening to our demographics, particularly with regard to that nasty bit of business known as ageing?

THE TECHNOLOGY

"Each technology has an agenda of its own."
Neil Postman, *Amusing Ourselves to Death*

The single most important technology of the Spend-and-Share era was television. Television rewired our political antennae to respond viscerally instead of intellectually, helped usher in a fundamental change in gender roles and, perhaps most important, projected the images of identity and success needed to stimulate a culture that worshipped at the altar of consumerism.

The single most important technology of the Sink-or-Swim era is the computer, a device capable of projecting multiple personalities, from smart cards and the Internet to encyclopedic knowledge banks and, yes, even television itself. The computer carries far more revolutionary potential than television. It is taking Canadians across the frontier, into a new dimension, an ethereal territory with new laws, lots of opportunities and plenty of risks.

The world's first fully functional computer was built in 1943. It contained about 750,000 parts and almost 500 miles of wire and could perform about three additions per second. Successive improvements culminated in the launch of the IBM 360 in 1964. The basic 360 could perform about 100,000 additions per second, cost in the neighbourhood of $3 million and required a squadron of technicians to maintain it.

Over the next quarter century, computers slowly began to swallow up large sections of the Canadian workplace, then invaded our households. At work, computers became not just recording devices but corporate memories, not just communications mechanisms but control centers. Filing cabinets and typewriters began to disappear, swept away by more efficient electronic means of storing and transmitting information. As late as 1985, only 15% of Canadians were using computers at work. But by early 1996, that figure had skyrocketed to 55%. At home, the growth of computer ownership was much slower, but in recent years has soared from one in six Canadian households in 1989 to nearly one in two in 1996.[1]

The implications of the computer revolution are starting to emerge, some brimming with optimism, some more fearful. The most obvious effect is that the production and distribution of goods and services is undergoing a radical transformation. On the economic front, there are hundreds of billions of dollars up for grabs on the new frontier, and some of the world's most powerful corporations are moving quickly to cash in.

But while thousands now boast of their new capabilities with the mouse, keyboards and other devices connecting the human mind to a seemingly infinite supply of electronic impulses, nobody talks much about how we got here – or where we are going.

The computer revolution burst upon the late twentieth century much as the automobile burst upon our grandparents and great-grandparents at its dawn. Several technological streams converged almost simultaneously to create an entirely new machine that at first seemed odd but soon became commonplace, and changed our lives.

Computers gained speed because the tiny engines that turn electricity into commands – computer chips – became more sophisticated and more powerful. Speed is vital when it comes to processing words, but much more vital when the task is to process pictures, sound and video. Gordon Moore, the founder of Intel, the world's largest chip manufacturer, estimates that computing power has been doubling every 18 months over the past decade.[2] Intel's fifth-generation chip, the Pentium, contains 3.1 million transistors, can churn out more than 100 million bits per second and is barely the size of a postage stamp. As microchips get more powerful, they also become cheaper. As the *Economist* observed in 1993, "early in the next decade the central processing units of 16 Cray YMP supercomputers, now costing collectively some $320 million, will be manufacturable for under $100 on a single microchip."[3]

Faster and cheaper chips have not only made computers easier to use; they've permitted the miniaturization that makes today's laptops more powerful than the huge mainframes that dominated corporate data processing centers in the 1970s. They have also made it possible to use computers as multimedia devices, capable of harnessing an increasingly vast array of audio and video information. This transition was further facilitated by dramatic improvements in the size and cost of computer storage. In 1965, for example, it cost $30,000 to purchase a device to store one megabyte of memory. By 1990, the cost had dropped to $5. These, then, were the key revolutionary ingredients for the technocrats: dazzling speed, shrinking costs and enormous memory capacities hidden in tiny places.

For the average Canadian, another catalyst was crucial: user-friendly software. Apple was the first major computer company to appreciate the importance of catering to the technologically challenged, but its Macintosh applications were expensive and relatively slow. By the early 1990s, developments in chip technology (most notably by Intel) and software technology (most notably by Microsoft) meant that people with no specialized training could finally have it all: speed, storage and a variety of applications at a reasonable cost. The bow that tied this wonderful technology together and turned it into a world-wide communications phenomenon was better networking, both within offices and across huge distances. The move toward low-cost but powerful personal computers was at first accompanied by a significant drawback: it was a clumsy process to move information from one computer to another. In fact, information was often carried by hand, in the form of floppy disks.

Reliable network technology was not introduced to the mass market until the late 1980s. It has since served as the backbone for services such as e-mail, which has dramatically altered intra-office and inter-office communication. Now, e-mail mailboxes often get so stuffed that users can be heard wondering aloud whether they haven't become bogged down by efficiency. A strange concept, but one worth contemplating.

In recent years, systems incorporating modems, cables and fiberoptic strands, have been developed to transmit data quickly from one computer to another, even over long distances. Physical metaphors like "pipewidth" and "highways" convey the underlying concept of how changing technology increases the volume of "traffic" flowing between computers. To reduce congestion, coaxial cable and fiberoptic lines are capable of handling vast quantities of digital information. According to the New Paradigm Learning Corporation, conventional telephone lines have the capacity of a three-foot garden path; fibreoptics are like a one-mile-wide super-highway. This technology is eliminating the final obstacle to the rapid transmission of words, sounds and images over long distances at much-reduced costs. The *Economist* has concluded that "the demise of distance as the key to the cost of communicating may well prove the most significant economic force shaping the next half century."[4]

It's all quite breathtaking. A new information age, with unlimited access to just about anything that can be transferred in digital form – not just numbers and words but great works of art, music and guided tours of the seven wonders of the world – and the ability to communicate with literally millions of other humans around the world for little or no cost. The evangelists of this new age include a diverse cast of characters, among them Microsoft's Bill Gates, writer Nicholas Negroponte, futurists Alvin and Heidi Toffler and Newt Gingrich, speaker of the U.S. House of Representatives. They prophesize a coming utopia that is at once egalitarian, decentralizing and empowering. The digital revolution when applied to communications, according to consultant Don Tapscott, may be the biggest technological revolution ever: "A new medium of human communications is emerging, one that may prove to surpass all previous revolutions – the printing press, the telephone, the television, the computer – in its impact on our social and economic life."[5] Since the printing press alone played a pivotal role in the Reformation, the rise of democracy and the industrial revolution, it's not hard to get weak in the knees thinking about the implications of recent technological breakthroughs.

The application that has ignited these superlatives is, of course, the Internet. The Internet is more than computers; it's a social movement, the holy water of the new digital religion. It's free and easy to use, yet confers special powers to those who use it. As in many great religions, the mythology about the Net comes, in part, from its humble origins. As the *Economist* noted, "almost anything that made a difference on the Internet was produced by people whom the corporate world might consider nobodies." The legend of the Net has been reinforced by the startling pace of its adoption. The Internet has doubled in size every year since 1988. In October 1994, Internet analyst John Quarterman put the number of users around the world at 13.5 million. "No communications medium or consumer electronics technology has ever grown as quickly," he noted. "Not the fax machine, not even the PC. At this rate, within two years the citizens of cyberspace will outnumber all but the largest nations."[6]

World-wide, according to more recent estimates, there are some 50 million Internet users. By 2000, according to New Paradigm Learning, as many as one billion people will have Internet access. In Canada, Internet access, which stood at less than 2% in 1990, had swollen to 18% by mid-decade. By 2000, it may well approach 50% of the population.

The full implications of all this aren't entirely clear, but there is no doubt that the Internet is going to make some people enormously wealthy. Just as the Net is growing exponentially, so will the wealth it creates for those bankrolling its development. The reason is obsolescence. With more users on the Net, R&D spending on hardware, software and infrastructure increases rapidly (witness the huge appetite on Wall Street and Bay Street for new technology issues). The result is new software and hardware products that make what people currently own seem completely out of date. The 386 desktop system, perfectly adequate only last year, is suddenly a boat anchor. The cycle of product improvement and obsolescence isn't new to computers; it's existed since the start of the industrial revolution. What's new is that the cycles are getting shorter.

The other reason that a few people will make a lot of money is that most of the useful or entertaining Net content will likely be controlled by a small number of providers, just as TV programming is today. The commercial applications of the Net fall into three broad categories: entertainment services (movies, games, TV and music); news (broadcast and print); and information (libraries and books). Already huge corporations are jostling for position. Consider the Disney takeover of ABC/Cap Cities and Microsoft's planned joint venture with NBC. And large corporations, according to James Boyle, a law professor at American University, are doing more than buying content; they're also hiring lawyers and lobbyists to develop stricter intellectual property laws to ensure that they get paid by users. "We are in the middle of an information land grab and no one seems to have noticed," Boyle warned in the *New York Times*. "We need to figure out how the world changes when information becomes one of the most important forms of wealth and power, when everything from the pattern of purchases revealed by credit card receipts to the pattern of your DNA can become a byte of information, to be bought and sold in the marketplace."[7] In the next few years, Boyle added, even browsing the Internet could constitute copyright violation. Make no mistake: the Net is about big business as much as it is about the empowerment of ordinary citizens.

Nor will every company prosper because of the Net. Many, especially those in the communications sector, are faced with a direct competitive threat. E-mail is an obvious example. It's cheaper and faster to send letters and documents over the Net than by conventional means. What does that mean to Canada Post? You can bet Bell Canada and the other phone companies will adjust and make the new technology work on their behalf; after all, they've wired the world. But just when Canada Post is starting to deliver decent service, its whole *raison d'être* is suddenly open to question.

Paying bills and checking bank statements from a computer at home is faster and more convenient than waiting in line at a bank, or even driving to an ATM – good news for bank customers, depending on how adept banks are at finding ways to charge for this service. The Net offers unprecedented convenience when it comes to paying bills, looking for a job, buying used cars, perusing movie reviews or researching term papers. It can turn the home computer into a personal command center, similar to those in the workplace. But what does that mean to bank tellers, librarians, travel agents and people who have made their living putting newspapers together?

Beyond economics, the Net has the capacity to connect human beings in a variety of important ways. The potential for intellectual interaction or emotional bonding is clearly enormous. In minutes a Net surfer can have access to many of the world's largest libraries or strike up an exchange with a stranger halfway around the world. What a boon for shut-ins and people who live in remote places. But there are legitimate questions about the Net's value to the vast majority of Canadians.

Does the Net really give most users access to minds and sensibilities that they could never find close at hand? Will it give shy individuals the chance to initiate potentially rewarding relationships or become part of stimulating discussion groups in ways that they couldn't in the physical presence of other people? Will this electronic pump-priming translate into more successful interaction when people are actually in the room? Or will it always be, by definition, a cloistered, private, on-line experience? Will Net users broaden their outlooks by connecting to people with viewpoints they wouldn't find in their own communities? Or will it do the opposite: narrow their horizons by encouraging them to bond only with like-minded Net users?

Many analysts doubt that people who spend hours peering into computer screens, communicating with others who spend hours staring at computer screens, are going to take humanity to exciting places we haven't been before. As for meeting new people: "No doubt, the networks are certainly great places to meet men," observes Clifford Stoll, the sardonic author of *Silicon Snake Oil*. "There are several guys on-line for every woman. But, like the outlook for women in Alaska, the odds are good but the goods are odd."[8] Of course, if the Net doesn't offer what some would define as "the real world," is that so terrible? Nobody has ever had a problem with people who establish pen-pal relationships with people in distant lands, friends they may never meet. And nobody goes around scolding those people who like to spend weekends reading a good novel. Is there a touch of anti-Net snobbery in the air?

Perhaps. On the other hand, given the track record of the twentieth century, I think it's important to have a healthy suspicion about any technology that sports exaggerated claims. Television was supposed to be our salvation, and it certainly had that potential. But the medium seems to have narcotized rather than stimulated us. Robert Putnam, a professor of government at Harvard, has lamented the erosion of "civic virtue" in North American society that has led to a decline in public interest in democracy and the institutions that make democracy work. He places part of the blame on television, contending that people who were once active in the community are now stuck in their family and recreation rooms. TV, he says, "privatizes our public time." Is the Internet really a mind opener, or one more "privatizer"? Since the industrial revolution, most of us have equated technology with progress, and it is indisputable that technology has brought the world widespread benefits. But its dark underside seems to be causing increasing problems. The Net is unlikely to be an exception to the rule.

Furthermore, other than being a cheap and comprehensive communications device, the Internet's touted advantages seem somewhat overblown at this point. All these electrons were supposed to replace paper and save trees, for instance, but people still prefer to do a goodly amount of their reading away from the computer screen. In 1995, *Forbes* magazine chose Hewlett-Packard as its outstanding company of the year. Interesting: HP is the world's leading producer of computer *printers.*

The Net may yet become a valuable tool for ordinary people, just as its early promoters envisioned. After all, in the beginning only the rich owned telephones, and now just about everybody with an address has one. But at the moment, most of the Net's benefits are going to wealthier households. In the fall of 1994, an Angus Reid Group survey found that only 18% of Canadian homes earning less than $30,000 annually had a computer, and not a lot of them had modems. In households reporting income of more than $60,000, 63% had a home computer, 31% with a modem attached.

We tend to celebrate anything that promises to connect human beings, because we know too well the dangers of becoming estranged from beliefs, ideas and concerns. But what if the Net proves to be a masquerade? What if it diverts us from genuine interpersonal relationships? Clifford Stoll calls the cyberworld of the Internet "an unreal universe, a soluble tissue of nothingness. While the Internet beckons brightly, seductively flashing an icon of knowledge-as-power, this nonplace lures us to surrender our time on earth. A poor substitute it is, this virtual reality where frustration is legion and where – in the holy names of Education and Progress – important aspects of human interactions are relentlessly devalued."[9]

The Internet is the sexy technology of the 1990s. But technology as a force of change involves far more than the mixed blessings of cyberspace. Matched with new principles of work organization pioneered by such management gurus as Michael Hammer and James Champy (*Reengineering the Corporation*), computers are yielding huge increases in productivity. They are also redefining – and in many cases eliminating – the jobs of tens of millions of workers around the world.

Of course, there is a bright side. The new technology is creating demand for highly specialized knowledge workers who earn extra pay for their ability to manipulate the tools of the knowledge society. It is also enabling home-based businesses and telecommuters to reach new levels of independence and power.

But it's hard to escape the darker undercurrents. Thousands of workers – especially those in the services industry – are discovering redundancy. Many of those still working have become mere appendages to machines. Contrary to the mythology, the advent of the knowledge society doesn't mean that all jobs require more knowledge. In many cases, less judgment is required. Many employees are relegated to reading and taking instructions from computer screens. As Simon Head observed in a 1996 feature story in *The New York Review of Books*: "Just as Henry Ford once found a substitute for skilled craftsmen in rows of machines arranged along an assembly line, so the experts called reengineers have combined the skills of specialist clerks and middle managers into software packages that are attached to desktop computers."[10]

Unquestionably, the computer has enabled corporations and organizations to do more things, better, for less. That should spell success for institutions that own them, because ferocious wars are being waged in the international marketplace over who can deliver the best-quality products at the lowest possible prices, and who can bring shareholders the best return on their investments. Clearly, then, computers offer institutions great opportunities. The question is: What do they offer humans? Perhaps Newt Gingrich is right. Perhaps all our problems would be solved if everyone were given a laptop. But as American social commentator Barbara Ehrenreich puts it, "you can't do much with a laptop if you haven't had your lunch."[11]

GLOBALIZATION

In their book *Global Dreams*, Richard Barnet and John Cavanagh write that, "The world is getting smaller... but it is not coming together. Indeed, as economies are drawn closer, nations, cities, and neighbourhoods are being pulled apart. The processes of global economic integration are stimulating political and social disintegration. Family ties are severed, established authority is undermined, and the bonds of local community are strained."[12]

Globalization has been the dream of tyrants, poets and entrepreneurs since the beginning of history. Tyrants dreamed of global domination. Entrepreneurs dreamed of unlimited markets. Poets dreamed of harmony among nations. "This is the grass that grows wherever the land and the water is," wrote Walt Whitman. "This is the common air that bathes the globe." Globalization had that romantic wistfulness about it. No more hot wars, no more cold wars – just humanity, acting in common interest, rather than scheming to promote parochial ambitions from behind the fortress walls of nations. Even multinational corporations managed to sound poetic when they called for "world peace through world trade."

The yearning for a global human bond swept over millions of people in 1969 as they gazed in awe at Earth through the eyes of Neil Armstrong and Buzz Aldrin, the first astronauts to land on the Moon. No border demarcations, no different colours for different countries – just ethereal vapours drifting over a breathtaking orb so full of life and potential. Two years before they landed, Canadian philosopher Marshall McLuhan had predicted globalization, and even told us why: "with instant electric technology, the globe itself can never again be more than a village."[13]

McLuhan was right. In 1989 three powerful forces – one political, one technological and one economic – converged simultaneously; globalization was the fruit of the union. The fall of the Berlin Wall ended the 45-year-old East – West conflict, which had split the world into two armed camps. The rise of fast computers and wide-spread electronic networks connected via satellites meant that people who knew how to exploit these systems could know virtually everything happening in the world moments after it happened. It was, indeed, like living in a tiny village, but one village with a very large marketplace.

For people who dedicate their lives to manipulating wealth, heaven was within reach. Speculators and international corporations spent five years climbing St. Peter's ladder and were formally ushered through his pearly gates in 1994, when the Uruguay Round of the General Agreement on Tariffs and Trade produced the most comprehensive pact for the elimination of trade barriers since GATT negotiations began in 1947. The GATT breakthrough had been preceded by regional trade agreements that were even more comprehensive, among them the Canada-U.S. Free Trade Agreement of 1989 and the North American Free Trade Agreement in 1992.

Financiers had been waiting for a long time for this moment and were quick to take advantage. Francis Bacon had defined the formula in 1597: "knowledge is power." But now knowledge was far more powerful than it had ever been, because it could be translated into power so quickly – every second of every minute of every day. And knowledge abounds. It's been estimated that more information has been moved around the world in the first half of the 1990s than was moved during the rest of the century. John Maynard Keynes once compared securities investment to a contest in which participants are asked to pick the six prettiest faces from one hundred photographs. The investor who comes closest to guessing the preferences of the other contestants will win. In the case of the global marketplace, a tiny percentage of the world's six billion people are using modern communications technology to discern the preferences of others. During the last Quebec referendum campaign, for example, the slightest movements in opinion polls were tracked by traders in Tokyo and London, many of whom made small fortunes on currency speculation.

Dismantling borders, the economists said, would be good for everyone. The ability to produce things as cheaply as possible, combined with the freedom to compete everywhere, would provide the lowest prices possible for all consumers and, furthermore, would give people in poor countries a chance to catch up. No longer would their products be blocked from richer markets by the constraints of old-fashioned tariffs, quotas and other barriers.

On paper, it was a good idea. It was this very principle that led left-wing students into the streets of Paris in 1968 chanting "Down with borders!" Open borders and fewer trade restrictions have provided material benefits to significant numbers of people in

Singapore, Thailand, Indonesia and other emerging countries. But not without serious problems. So efficient has the world become that many people are no longer needed – even as consumers. By 1995, almost one-third of the world's 2.8 billion workers were either unemployed or clearly underemployed. Furthermore, as Richard Barnet and John Cavanagh point out, "of the 5.4 billion people on earth, almost 3.6 billion have neither cash nor credit to buy much of anything."[14]

"The world is breaking down into two tribes," mused Keith Bezanson, president of the International Development Research Centre. "There are the included, and the excluded. Unfortunately the number of excluded is rising quickly, and those who are included are becoming a very select group."[15] Bezanson also noted that, for the first time, a significant number of the excluded live in what we have always known as rich countries, such as Canada.

"Some day we will all live as one," sang John Lennon. I think he meant we would all live relatively well in global unity. So far, at least, the picture doesn't exactly fit the song.

GLOBALIZATION AND CANADA

The new international forces are exerting great pressure on Canada. Some of these pressures may strengthen the country, but others are threatening to tear us apart. There is no doubt that the Canadian economy is increasingly influenced by events beyond our borders – a reality that became painfully evident to most Canadians when the collapse of the Mexican peso in 1994 led to a temporary increase in interest rates in Canada. The specter of new global competition has Canadian corporate leaders fretting in fields as diverse as transportation and banking. Today, when Canadian finance ministers issue budget forecasts, journalists are more likely to seek reaction in New York (where our debt is largely held) than in Vancouver.

The virtues of globalization, then, depend on where you sit. Most business leaders – especially those in the resources sector – sing hymns of praise to the global deity who has delivered access to foreign markets (particularly lucrative when the Canadian dollar is low). For union leaders, whose memberships have already been hit hard by automation, globalization (and its inherent threat of low-wage competition from abroad) represents a menace that is eroding the hard-won gains of Canadian workers. For the arts community, globalization means that the cultural walls that protected them for decades have been breached. For the president of a Canadian airline company, globalization offers the thrill and challenge of competing in more markets. For a flight attendant, it means the probability of salary cuts, required so that the airline can pursue business in those markets.

During the Spend-and-Share era, national political, economic and cultural imperatives were more important than international relations. The department of external affairs then saw its job as exerting Canadian influence in the political discourse among nations. Since our voice was not of breathtaking importance on the world stage, few Canadians paid much attention. Now, the department is officially known as Foreign Affairs and International Trade, and the mandarins who inhabit it are far more interested in talking trade than in discussing the nuances of the latest UN resolution.

Conservative philosopher George Grant was one of the first to recognize that Canada's independent spirit was waning quickly. In *Lament for a Nation,* he declared Canada a lost cause, blaming the loss on the failure of both Conservative and Liberal politicians to develop a cultural vision different than that of the United States.

Diefenbaker, he observed, had at least tried to resist the Americans on issues such as whether Canada should be forced to mount nuclear warheads on its joint defence missiles. But Diefenbaker failed, according to Grant, because he had not understood the crucial importance of Quebec to Canadian identity. Other Conservatives had abandoned the age-old Tory concern for preserving tradition in exchange for greater opportunities to earn the almighty dollar.

The Liberals, Grant charged, "failed to recognize that the real danger to nationalism lay in the incipient continentalism of English-speaking society, rather than in any Quebec separatism." Looking out on the twin juggernauts of commerce and ever-improving technology, at a time when they possessed only a tiny fraction of the strength they now have, Grant threw up his hands: "What happens to nationalist strivings when the societies in question are given over, at the very level of faith, to the realization of the technological dream? At the core of that faith is service to the process of universalization and homogenisation... But how can a faith in universalism go with a desire for a continuance of Canada?"[16]

Pierre Trudeau considered himself a philosopher, so he presumably read Grant. Certainly his government made gestures at fighting a rear-guard action against continentalism, even if it did enact the Canadian Charter of Rights and Freedoms. The Charter was built around an American-style emphasis on the sanctity of individual rights, rather than the overall well-being of the community, which Canadian law had always championed. But the Trudeau Liberals were sensitive to charges that the governments of Mackenzie King, Louis St. Laurent and Lester Pearson had been too continentalist. In 1972, External Affairs Minister Mitchell Sharp (himself branded a continentalist) issued a white paper called "The Third Option," which maintained that Canada would pursue a stronger alliance with Europe in order to avoid U.S. domination. Nothing much happened, but at least the sentiment was on record.

The Foreign Investment Review Agency was established and it demanded that foreign corporations investing in Canada show that their acquisitions were "in the best interests" of Canada. Few would-be investors were rejected, but at least lip service was paid toward the value of a Canadian identity. The National Energy Policy and rules covering everything from U.S. magazines operating in Canada to broadcast regulations emanated from a broader view that Canada could insulate itself from global influences, particularly the U.S.

One cannot pretend that there was massive public support for protecting Canadian identity at any cost, but there was certainly enough to keep politicians interested in the subject. Then came Brian Mulroney. By the end of the Spend-and-Share Era, we had a prime minister whose favourite cultural memory was singing Irish songs for Col. Robert R. McCormick, the American owner of the Tribune Co., which owned the paper mill in Mulroney's home town, Baie Comeau. It was not a good sign.

By the 1990s, Ottawa was so hamstrung by debt that protecting a distinct Canadian society with distinct cultural values was no longer a priority. The very popular governments of Ralph Klein and Mike Harris behave as though the Bible had been written by Newt Gingrich, and the federal Liberals are too worried about the deficit to mount much of a protest. George Grant has been dead since 1988, but he still speaks from the grave: "Our hope lay in the belief that on the northern half of this continent we could build a community that had a stronger sense of the common good and the public order than was possible under the individualism of the American capitalist dream... This lament mourns the end of Canada as a sovereign state."[17]

Five elements of the current shift toward globalization have particular relevance for Canada.

LOWER TRADE BARRIERS

The development of regional and international trading agreements covering traffic in goods and services has been a feature of the Canadian landscape for most of the post-war era. For example, the 1965 Autopact represented the most comprehensive bilateral economic agreement Canada had ever signed. Earlier, leaders such as Mackenzie King had avoided making economic deals with the Americans, fearing that Canadian voters might view them as anti-British and continentalist. Nevertheless, trade flows north and south had increased dramatically since the 1960s. Between 1965 and 1990, when the total volume of world trade doubled, trade between Canada and the U.S.A. more than tripled.

As impressive as these gains were, they do not come close to matching the increases recorded since 1990. The FTA, NAFTA and GATT have had a much more profound impact on Canada, simply because of their scope. Never have our borders been open on so many fronts. And never have we surrendered so much of our sovereignty, in terms of control over our economy, to achieve these goals.

During the first half of the 1990s, a time characterized by sluggish consumer markets and high unemployment, the movement of goods and services between Canada and other nations grew faster than at any time in our history. Canada exported $252.9

billion worth of goods and services in 1995, a huge jump from $157.8 billion in 1989. Exports as a percentage of GDP now represent a whopping 41%, compared with 27% at the height of the Spend-and-Share era. Of course, trade is a two-way street; imports are also at record levels.

The opening of borders holds the potential of better and cheaper products for consumers and improved access to foreign markets for producers. That's the good news. The bad news – at least in the short term for Canadian workers – is that open borders also imply more competition, which means that Canadian producers must get their costs in line. Competition has become the number-one justification for many of the anomalies we see creeping into the Canadian economy. Noting that some of Canada's largest companies, such as General Motors, were cutting back staff in spite of rising profits, *Globe and Mail* business columnist Peter Cook offered an all too familiar rationale: "Nowadays, to raise wages in Detroit or Windsor," he observed, "is to risk challenge from Wolfsburg or Pusan. Competitiveness requires that a company strive to be the lowest-price, highest-quality manufacturer, or service provider, in the global market. And, like it or not, there ain't much we can do about that."[18]

GLOBAL MONEY LENDERS

Under the watchful eye of the International Monetary Fund and other international institutions, Canada's growing dependency on foreign money lenders has skyrocketed, especially since the late 1980s. The reason boils down to simple mathematics: government debt requirements have outstripped the lending capacity of the domestic economy. In 1969-70, Canada's net public debt was 21% of GDP, 5% of which was held by foreigners. By 1993, the national debt had climbed to 67% of GDP, 21% of which was held abroad – the highest percentage of foreign-held debt in any G7 country. In the mid-1990s, Canadian governments were borrowing more than $20 billion a year to finance operations. The growth of Canada's debt in recent years has been nothing short of stunning. The fact that so much of it is held offshore is alarming. Italy has a much higher annual deficit and cumulative debt than Canada, but nearly all of it is held internally. Our dependence on foreign lenders increases the pressure on Canadian interest rates and makes Canadian economic and social policy at least partly dependent upon the whims of nonresidents. According to economist Thomas Courchene, "This is tantamount to a unilateral transfer of fiscal and financial sovereignty to the 'kids in red suspenders.' Not surprisingly, the 'kids' – bond and treasury traders – are exercising that sovereignty, and the 1995 federal budget is merely the first installment."[19] While many have bemoaned the loss of sovereignty associated with free trade, it may be the international bankers and bondholders who have done the most to rearrange the social landscape in Canada.

To be sure, Canada is not alone. In the early 1990s, Mexico became too dependent on foreign investment, especially in short-term bonds that could be quickly liquidated and taken out of the country. Chile has put strict limits on foreign portfolio investment, and South Korea restricts the ability of foreigners to invest in its stock market. Both countries are considered part of the economic miracle of the decade. As American economist Tom Petruno observed recently about Mexico, "never in history has the country been populated by so many capitalists, and never before have they had the ability to transfer entire fortunes across borders in the blink of an eye, thanks to technology."

THE GLOBALIZATION OF CULTURE

Despite George Grant's lament that Canadian governments did not do enough after the Second World War to sustain a distinctive Canadian culture, several efforts were made, particularly under the governments of Pierre Elliott Trudeau that dominated Canadian politics between 1968 and 1984.

The establishment of the Canadian Radio-Television and Telecommunications Commission in 1968 represented an aggressive move to control the Canadian airwaves. Early in its mandate, the CRTC introduced regulations aimed at ensuring that Canadian radio stations played large amounts of Canadian content, a move that encouraged development of Canadian recording artists who otherwise might have been buried by American domination of the industry. Canadian content regulations were so strictly monitored that all the songs from Bryan Adams' album *"Waking Up The Neighbours,"* with the exception of the chart topping *"Everything I Do (I Do It For You)"*, didn't qualify as Canadian content (and therefore for the Juno awards) because his co-author and producer was British. Briefly, during the 1970s, TV satellite dishes were outlawed on Canadian soil, an attempt to force viewers not hooked up to cable to watch Canadian television. That rule was not popular, particularly in the North.

But it has become increasingly difficult to hold back the tide of American culture. Some rules are still in place, but there now seem to be more exceptions than rules. Rules that once restricted the ability of foreign companies to purchase Canadian publishing companies have largely been abandoned in the wake of the policy changes in the early 1990s. One of the most spectacular purchases of cultural assets occurred in 1994, when American communications giant Viacom received approval to buy the Canadian businesses of Paramount Communications and Blockbuster Entertainment. The deal means that Viacom controls the Famous Players movie chain, the licensing and distribution of syndicated TV shows and movies to 40 Canadian television stations, including pay TV's First Choice and Super Channel, and two book publishers.

Examples of resistance to the tide of American culture still crop up occasionally. Cultural industries were exempted from the FTA and NAFTA at Canada's insistence, but U.S. trade representatives keep fuming that the exemption's days are numbered. After more than a year of publication, the *Sports Illustrated* "Canadian" edition was given the same treatment by the Chrétien government as *Time* had been by Trudeau. Again, the Americans made threatening noises. Culture is a major industry in the U.S., and those who export it have great difficulty understanding why anyone would want to treat its products differently from the way American society treats most other things – as a business.

In the end, that unrelenting pressure may wear us away. For all intents and purposes, the Canadian Broadcasting Corporation replaced the Canadian Pacific Railway in the second half of the twentieth century as the institution that symbolically tied Canadians together. But the CBC is in serious jeopardy. In the television market, its share of Canadian viewers in early 1996 stood at 12%, down from 13.2% during 1994-95. Its November 1995 decision to drop American programming will probably cost it more viewers. Izzy Asper's CanWest Global, a network that specializes in American movies, American sitcoms and American cop shows, spends a fraction of what the CBC spends, but runs neck and neck in the competition for viewers. In one 1990 Angus Reid Group survey, Canadians were almost twice as likely to give top grades to the quality of programming seen on the American Public Broadcasting System (PBS) than to the programming on the CBC.

The most bizarre political decision of this decade may be the Chrétien government's sale of licensing rights for properties associated with the RCMP to the Disney Corporation, America's most powerful cultural institution. The Disney decision was avoidable. But, for better or worse, new technology ranging from "Death Star" satellite broadcasting to the Internet makes it virtually impossible to regulate what Canadians watch and interact with. The wall has been breached, and the world is spilling in.

THE SUPREMACY OF CAPITALISM

Before the fall of the Berlin Wall there was a global competition between Adam Smith and Karl Marx. In the former's model, the pursuit of individual self-interest guaranteed the well-being of society; in the latter's, societal planning protected the interests of the individual. Canadians have never shown much interest in extremism, neither Marx on the left nor Smith on the right. But the tussle between the moderate left and the moderate right provided much of the drama in Canada's political passion play throughout the Spend-and-Share era.

The creative tension between the Progressive Conservatives and the New Democratic Party allowed the opportunistic Liberals to dominate the era, plucking proposals from the other parties whenever the need arose. As a result, the best ideas from across the political spectrum always had a chance of being implemented. The results may have been curious – a mix of Crown corporations, assistance to small business, foreign investment review boards and corporate handouts – but they reflected Canada's diverse needs and beliefs.

The fall of the Wall threw this neat balancing act out of kilter. For the left, it represented a decisive blow. For capitalists, especially corporate heavyweights, the 1990s have been a long-running festival that shows no signs of ending soon. The essence of leftism is government planning and control, ostensibly on behalf of all elements of society, particularly the vulnerable. The essence of the ideology that now dominates the globe is the inviolacy of personal freedom, individual self-interest and the needs of the marketplace. The big winners are the 300-odd corporations that account for a large proportion of the world's business, latter-day versions of colonial empires. They defend their positions not with machine guns or cruise missiles but with trademarks, copyrights and huge marketing budgets that dwarf the resources of many governments.

Capitalism's triumphs have dealt a serious blow to the precepts of Canada's mixed economy. The vulnerable are now in disrepute; in fact, they're blamed for many of the problems the dispirited middle class encounters. Corporate bosses have always argued that if governments would just leave them alone to operate independently and efficiently, the benefits would trickle down to ordinary people. John Kenneth Galbraith defined trickle-down economics in the following way: *"The doctrine that if the horse is fed amply with oats, some will pass through to the road for the sparrows."*

WORLD PUBLIC OPINION

In the spring of 1995, the British government announced that it intended to allow Shell Oil to sink the Brent Spar oil platform in the North Sea. Greenpeace, the ecological warrior movement founded in Vancouver and now based in Amsterdam, claimed that the rig contained vast quantities of contaminants. Feisty little Greenpeace was up against one of the most powerful governments in the world, and one of the most powerful corporations – Royal Dutch Shell Group, with global sales of $168 billion, 106,000 employees world-wide, and offices in more than 100 countries. It took a while, but Shell eventually capitulated, bowing to a growing boycott of its products in Europe and North America. Score: World Public Opinion 1, the tag team of Britain and Shell 0. This was not the first time that world public opinion had pressured a government to back down. The Canadian sealing industry collapsed in the late 1970s after Brigitte Bardot and the animal rights movement depicted the slaughter of wide-eyed seal pups in terms reminiscent of the Holocaust. In the end, the Canadian government was forced to place rigorous limits on the seal hunt. Score: World Public Opinion 1, Canadian government and the sealers (somewhat less prosperous than Shell) 0.

When Brian Tobin set out to win the 1995 Turbot War, he didn't go to sea; he went to New York – to convince the international media that his cause was just. The Canadian forest industry is far less concerned about public opinion in Canada than it is about public opinion in its major markets, the United States, Europe and Japan. If Jacques Parizeau had won the 1995 Quebec referendum, his first task would have been to convince the world that the vote constituted a mandate for a separate Quebec state. In fact, the Parti Québécois was so convinced it would win that before the polls had closed it started sending out notes consolidating its position to foreign embassies in Ottawa. Parizeau's biggest fear was that attempted separation would result in an armed stand-off with Cree in the Ungava region of northern Quebec. International polls suggest that world public opinion would side with the Aboriginals. The bottom line is that it isn't just economic decision-making or Canadian culture that is being heavily influenced by external forces. Political decision-making is taking the same kind of hit.

On August 27, 1995, two stories appeared in *The Toronto Star*. One quoted Herb Grubel, a Reform MP and professor of economics at Simon Fraser University, agreeing with several American economists that North America should have a common currency that might be known as the "Eagle." "All it would take is for the [U.S. Federal Reserve Bank] to add one or two districts for Canada and Mexico," said Grubel. "In five years, there will be one central bank for North America and one for the European Union." The second story reported that a proposal had been prepared in the U.S. – finalized with the assistance of the National Performance Review, Vice-President Al Gore's task force on reinventing government – to abandon immigration and customs inspections at airports and border crossings connecting Canada and the United States.[20]

Neither idea is really that far-fetched. The Europeans have already abandoned border controls between most countries in the EC and a common currency is coming soon. One currency and no border.... That wouldn't leave much to lament.

AN AGEING SOCIETY

> "Demographics explain about two-thirds of everything."
> David Foot and Daniel Stoffman, *Boom, Bust and Echo*

The traditional demographic chart of age groups in Canada looks like a pyramid: the bottom is the wide part, where the kids hang out. As we move up the triangle, the population becomes progressively smaller and older. This image describes Canadian society for as long as people have kept records – a lot more kids under 10 than seniors over 70. The triangle has been a symbol of safety and opportunity for Canadians. The children get a lot of attention; the smaller group at the top have plenty of younger people to look after them when they get old.

Not for long. Canada is marching inexorably toward a new society in which the number of Canadians in the older age groups (say 70 to 75) will be more or less the same as those in the younger age group (say 5 to 10). We are moving, in short, from a triangle to a rectangle. The squaring of the triangle has been in progress for decades, but the transformation began to accelerate rapidly in the mid-1990s. That acceleration will continue until 2036, when the first of the baby boomers turn 90. How many baby boomers can expect to see 90? More than most of us think.

This phenomenon is of more than passing interest, because the real effect of this remarkable demographic change will be felt much sooner. It is no secret that, for Canadians under 30, the preponderance of older people holding on to to a declining number of jobs is causing problems. Decent work, often any kind of work, is hard to find. More than four million baby boomers are now between 40 and 50. Their pre-retirement years are quickly approaching. If they hang around the workplace for as long as they can, it will only exacerbate the difficulties of younger Canadians. The boomers are the people who will finally add another corner to the triangle, with all the consequences that implies. The rectangle waits for them, like the monolith in *2001: A Space Odyssey*, unavoidable, moving toward them slowly, haunting their dreams.

Growing older has never been a barrel of laughs, but during

the Spend-and-Share era it did have its perks. Many seniors and even not-so-seniors managed to make quite a bit of money when the consumer boom boosted housing prices. Older Canadians also did well when the labour force started bursting at the seams in the 1960s and 1970s; companies and governments were growing, and those who had been employed the longest usually got promoted first. And taxpayers were generous; transfers to seniors increased more quickly than transfers to anyone else. High-quality health care was not only easy to get, it was free. Golden Pond really was gold.

In the Sink-or-Swim era getting older is getting dicier. At the beginning of this century about 5% of Canadians were over 65 years of age. By 1996, the number had increased to 12%. So it took a century for that age group to double. The next doubling will take place in less than half that time – about 40 years from now. Let's take a look at how three components of Canada's age equation are changing.

INCREASED LONGEVITY

Longevity has been improving in Canada for most of this century. In 1961, a 65-year-old Canadian could expect to live another 13.6 years if male, 16.2 years if female. Today, the average 65-year-old man will live another 16 years, a woman can expect another 21 years. Longer life expectancy is clearly one reason that the rectangle is forming.

We are living longer because of better medical care and healthier lifestyles. These two trends are likely to continue to improve. Medical science has advanced dramatically in its ability to treat and, in some cases, even cure the big killers of earlier generations. With a combination of new drugs and surgical intervention, heart disease is now more manageable. Transplants are now routine at most major Canadian hospitals, and new procedures such as angioplasty show promise. Cancer survival rates have improved dramatically over the past 30 years. The incidence of smoking is down significantly, despite the cigarette companies' assault on the youth market. Canadians are becoming more careful about what they eat. Alcohol consumption, on a per-capita basis, has been in decline for the past decade. People are wearing their seatbelts, and drinking and driving is no longer the merry prank it used to be. Even the incidence of tooth decay is dropping; in some cities, dentists are only moderately wealthy.

We used to calculate that someone over 65 might have a decade to live, at best. Now, according to a physician friend of mine, we have the "go-go's" (65 to 75) who are healthy enough to live life to the fullest, the "go-slow's" (75 to 85) who can still lead relatively active lives, as long as they get to bed by 7:30 p.m., and the "no-go's" (over 85) who are often disabled and require nursing or medical care.

Let us focus on the years leading up to 2010. Most of the younger group, many of them born during the Second World War, shouldn't encounter significant problems. The birth rate was low during the war, so these people won't apply undue pressure to the system in their old age. This has been a lucky age group all the way along. They found lots of jobs when the entered the labour force, just ahead of the baby boomers (and therefore ahead of them in the pecking order when promotions came up). They had access to cheap housing when they started families. And their twilight years should be pretty comfortable.

The older groups, however, will start clogging the system. If recent trends continue, many of these people will live well into their eighties. Caring for them will be one of the most important policy issues of the next decade. These are very special people. They lived through the depression, helped win the war and built a great society that started to unravel only after they retired. Not only are they special in their own right, they are special to a huge chunk of Canada's population: they are the parents of the baby boomers. The boomers will have to wrestle with the extra pressure these people are going to put on Canada's social safety net. Then, after a short breather, boomers themselves will begin to feel the incredible pressure of their own passage into old age.

THE AGEING OF THE BABY BOOM

The first wave of boomers will hit retirement age in early 2011. For the next 15 to 20 years, the ranks of retirees will swell. The rectangle will be fully upon us. Imagine a world in which one of every four people is over 65. The whole country will be like Victoria is today.

For the first five or six years after the boomers reach 65, they probably won't push the system toward collapse. Indeed, they'll be lumped in with the slightly older group born during the war, which isn't very big and will temporarily mitigate the boomers' impact. But by 2016, watch out. As good a time as we have had pushing our weight around for all these years, our problems keep growing as we get longer in the tooth. Most of us boomers are over 40 now; a few have even hit the half-century mark.

And we are going to hit the health-care system like a battering ram. The consequences will be enormous, particularly when you consider how little most of us have done to prepare ourselves for old age. Saddled with huge debt levels from the consumer binge of the 1980s, caught in the downdraft of falling wages, confronting less job security than at any time in our group's memory, many boomers are already starting to work themselves into a foul mood. All of this at a time when many of us find ourselves sandwiched between the financial needs of children struggling in a depressed job market and the emotional needs of parents struggling with old age.

The once bold and optimistic boomers are growing wary. Less consumption, more savings. More work (if you're still employed), less free time. A new look at what life – and death – really means, beyond all the shop-till-you-drop values of the old days. These are the areas in which the ageing of the fabled baby boom will be felt earliest, long before the queues begin to form at the golf courses and hospital waiting rooms.

DECLINING FERTILITY

The triangle is turning into a rectangle not only because there are more seniors at the top; there are also fewer juniors at the bottom. The reason: what demographers refer to as the "baby bust," the sharp drop in fertility rates that occurred when it was time for the boom generation to have children. Logically they should have produced more than their parents did, because there were more of them. They didn't. Blame the value changes of the 1960s.

Falling fertility rates have produced proportionately fewer young people in Canada than at any other time in our history. Canada's francophone communities used to be known for big families. For most of the last decade, they've held the world record for low fertility rates. Lucien Bouchard hit a raw nerve during the 1995 Quebec referendum when he chided francophone women to have more children. Separatists are painfully aware that the demographic trends in Quebec aren't favourable to their cause. Low fertility rates among francophone women, higher rates among immigrants (who normally vote no) and ageing population all threaten, in the long term, to shrink the separatist vanguard.

The decline in fertility rates has been observed everywhere in Canada since the late 1960's. In fact, if it wasn't for healthy doses of immigration over the past quarter century, we might be hurtling not toward a rectangle but at an inverted triangle. Depending on what happens with the family formation and fertility patterns of younger Canadians, we may still be. Between 1961 and 1991, the percentage of childless married women aged 35–39 grew from 9% to 13%; for women aged 25–29 the percentage increased almost threefold from 14% to 38%.

The strength of the Canadian social security net depends on the ratio of taxpayers (mostly people with jobs) to retirees. You need taxpayers, and many of them, to support a generous system of Old Age Security, Guaranteed Income Supplements, Canada/Quebec Pension Plans and universal health care. Lump these systems together, and the vast majority of benefits are paid out to people over 65. Except for Old Age Security, most of these systems were designed in the late 1950s and early 1960s, in the middle of the baby boom. The architects assumed that there would continue to be a ratio of about seven people paying into the system for every one beneficiary. The baby bust threw a statistical spanner into the works. We now have roughly five (potential) workers for every retired Canadian. And by 2036, we will have only half of that ratio – 2.5 workers (if there are jobs) per beneficiary. This means rapidly rising contribution rates – and taxes – to support the social security benefits being promised today.

In 1995, there were 4.3 million Canadians aged 20 to 29. In 1974, there were almost as many people in this age range, but the population was considerably smaller back then. These young Canadians may face the heaviest burden of the century – and we boomers are partly the cause. These are the people whose careers must bend the most to the uncertainties of the new era. They are often the first to be shown the door when companies and governments restructure. Twenty years hence, they and their children (if they can afford to have any) will be handed a monumental bill by the boomers, who in all their wrinkled splendour will not only want the same old age benefits of the generations that preceded them, but will want this new generation to pump an even larger percentage of their earnings into the Canada Pension Plan than they did; otherwise, the CPP will go under. These Canadians, now in their twenties, fall in right behind Generation X – a term coined by Vancouver writer Douglas Coupland to refer to Canadians born at the tail end of the baby boom in the early 1960s and now in their thirties. Though some demographers call this generation the baby bust, given the difficulties that they are facing finding jobs and the responsibilities that will fall on their shoulders when the boomers start to retire, wouldn't it make more sense to call them Generation Y... as in *why* us?

This combination of increasing longevity, the ageing of the boomers and the decline in fertility is about to create a historic "first": about 10 years from now, there will be more Canadians over 60 than under 15. This crossing of the demographic equator is not shown on any charts, but it's out there. And while the water will still swirl clockwise in the sink, many other things will start to turn upside down.

We can already see that the war between the generations will be fought on the battlegrounds of education and health care. For centuries, societies put far more emphasis on the care and feeding of the young than the old, because there were so many more of them. Already, the cries about the possibility of user fees for people staying in hospitals can be heard across the land. Meanwhile, younger Canadians are complaining about 30% increases in tuition fees, cutbacks in student grants and loans and the closing of community colleges. Something has to give.

What a potent mix of forces! Computer technology has changed the very nature of work and commerce. An international marketplace is playing by brand-new rules, most of them drafted by corporations, not elected governments. And that same population bulge that hit Canada at the start of the Spend-and-Share era is still hogging the stage, this time scattering problems rather than optimism and energy. Each of these forces, on its own, would have a major impact on Canadian society. Together, they constitute a typhoon. What makes the storm more threatening is the loss of many of the windbreaks. Consumer demand, traditionally an engine of growth, has been shut down. The squeeze on the service industries is continuing. Pressures on governments have left them limp and increasingly toothless. Canadian values, where they concern our jobs, our home life and our country are changing. The next three chapters will examine those changes in detail. At the dawn of the Sink-or-Swim era, knowledge may mean not only power but survival.

Five

THE TRANSFORMATION OF WORK

"... the only ones really competing these days,
it often seems, are the workers themselves
– against each other."

David F. Noble, PROGRESS WITHOUT PEOPLE:
NEW TECHNOLOGY, UNEMPLOYMENT,
AND THE MESSAGE OF RESISTANCE

Think about horses. A century ago, there were horses everywhere. Livery horses. Dray horses. Coach horses. Pony express horses. Mill horses. Carriage horses. Plough horses. All hard-working horses. The hardest working of all was the smallest, the pit pony, who lived his whole life underground, hauling coal in the mines. Every now and then, you still see the occasional horse, police horses, show horses, race horses, pleasure horses. But essentially, the horse is passé, replaced by the steam locomotive, the tractor and the automobile. Once horses had outlived their usefulness to humans, they started to disappear.

But what if most of them were still around? What if every city in Canada was filled with gaunt, angry horses, ribs exposed, teeth bared, stampeding up and down the streets, smashing through store windows. And what if those kind of protests were happening in every city in the world? And what if the demonstrators weren't horses but humans, and they were armed, and hell-bent on revenge?

At first these images seem overly dramatic. When you begin pondering the effects of computerization and globalization on the Canadian economy and you end up with horses running wild through your head, you worry. I was grateful, therefore, to open the *Financial Post* on October 14, 1995, and find a kindred spirit. Rod McQueen, a financial columnist highly respected on Bay Street, was writing a series called "The Nature of Work." In it, he quoted Tom d'Aquino, president of the Business Council on National Issues (which represents 150 large corporations), talking about the current transition in our economy. The current economic restructuring, d'Aquino said, "is like the period when we went from the farm to the city in the industrial revolution."[1]

D'Aquino was, of course, referring to the late nineteenth century, when masses of workers graduated from low-paying employment in the fields to newly created jobs in urban factories. D'Aquino is essentially optimistic that things will sort themselves out in the workplace. But McQueen followed d'Aquino's observation with his own rhetorical question: What if there is another parallel? What if this time we humans are the horses? What if computers replace *Homo sapiens*?

Exactly. Later, I discovered that economist Wassily Leontief, winner of the Nobel Prize, felt the same way: "The world of humans as the most important factor in production is bound to diminish in the same way that the role of horses in agricultural production was first diminished, then eliminated by the introduction of tractors."

There's an eerie similarity between the irrelevance of horses to twentieth-century economies and the growing irrelevance of large numbers of human beings to the labour forces of the twenty-first. As we approach the next century, new technological, economic and

demographic forces are converging on a sociological ground zero
that is defined by one word: jobs. Every month for the past decade
or so, the Angus Reid Group has asked Canadians which issues
should receive the greatest attention from Canada's leaders.
Throughout the 1990s, even after the mandarins in the department
of finance declared the recession "over," the issue of jobs has dominated the public agenda. In the late 1980s, concern about jobs averaged less than 10%; since 1990, the level of concern has stood at
about 30%. Numbers are usually pretty unemotional, but these
reflect widespread fear. The concern attached to them is real, and
deeply personal. It reflects more than what people are reading in
newspapers or watching on TV newscasts. It reflects anxiety among
large numbers of Canadians that they or someone else in their
household will lose their job or otherwise become unemployed over
the next year.

The Canadian economy has performed very poorly in job
creation during the 1990s. To understand the magnitude of these
changes, look at the number of people who have been affected – so
far. In 1989, slightly more than one million Canadians were unemployed; another 800,000 would enter the labour force over the next
six years as job seekers. That's a total of almost two million Canadians looking for work in the new economy. What kind of jobs did
this economy produce to meet this demand? Not nearly enough.
Full-time paid employment, the kind of employment that confers a
sense of security and allows people to plan ahead, *declined* by about
130,000 jobs. Thus, while almost two million Canadians were
looking for full-time jobs, employers came up with 130,000 fewer
positions. What grew, of course, was the number of unemployed
Canadians (increasing to more than 1.4 million by 1995) and the

number working in what the experts refer to as "non-standard" employment – part time jobs, temporary work and self-employment. University of Alberta sociologist Harvey Krahn estimates that between 1989 and 1994, non-standard employment grew from 28% to 33% of the workforce.[2] Welcome to the new economy.

The job situation would be even worse had not record numbers of young Canadians decided to stay in school and not bother trying to find a job. In 1995, there were 400,000 fewer Canadians aged 15 to 24 in the labour force (i.e., either looking for work or holding a job) than there were 1989. Only a fraction of this difference can be explained by the declining quotient of young people (the number of Canadians in this age group dropped only by about 5,000). The more likely explanation is that many young people have sensed the poor job climate and decided to stay in school. In so doing, they have masked an even more severe job crisis than the one that we readily see.

The current crunch is not unique to Canada; former U.S. Labor Secretary Ray Marshall has categorized it as "the worst employment crisis since the 1930s." Marshall stated flatly that "almost one-third of the Earth's 2.8 billion workers are either jobless or under-employed, and many of those who are employed work for very low wages with little prospect for advancement." [3] Noting that the U.S. and other industrialized economies have been in trouble for some time, Marshall observed that the main forces for change were technology and increased international competition. In other words, two of the three new forces – computerization and globalization – that were considered in chapter 4.

More and more social and economic analysts are concerned about the future of work. A few years ago, when computerization and globalization really started to affect the workplace, some people started to wonder out loud whether the contradictions Marx and Engels had speculated about more than a century ago weren't finally upon us. Marx was convinced that the capitalist system would eventually collapse under the weight of its unwavering drive to increase both efficiency and consumption. The production process, he predicted, would eventually become so efficient that there wouldn't be enough workers left earning wages to consume what was being produced.

Robert White, former president of the U.S. National Academy of Engineering, doesn't go that far, but in a 1991 speech he did express qualms unusual to his profession. As an engineer, White is naturally a great admirer of technology. In fact, he was careful to point out that "technological advance has been the most powerful job creation mechanism that society has devised." But he also asked: "Will the rate of creation of new industries be adequate to provide the jobs that are lost as a result of productivity increases?" His answer: "Nobody really knows ... We are witnessing the collision of philosophies and beliefs about economic growth, social equity and technology." Others have taken White's ideas further. In *The Jobless Future*, Stanley Aronowitz and William DiFazio state: "All of the contradictory tendencies involved in the restructuring of global capital and computer-mediated work seem to lead to the same conclusion for workers of all collars – that is, unemployment, under-employment, decreasingly skilled work, and relatively lower wages."[4]

Sounding a similar warning, economists Paul Krugman of MIT and Robert Lawrence of Harvard have argued that between 1979 and 1992, productivity in the American manufacturing sector increased by 35%, while the workforce shrank by 15%. For most of the 1980s, it was fashionable to blame the loss of manufacturing jobs in the United States on foreign competition and cheap labour markets abroad. However, Krugman and Lawrence suggest that "the concern widely voiced throughout the 1950s and '60s, that industrial workers would lose their jobs because of automation, is closer to the truth than the current preoccupation with the presumed loss of manufacturing jobs because of foreign competition."[5]

This theme has been enlarged upon by Jeremy Rifkin, president of the Foundation of Economic Trends, in Washington. In *The End of Work*, Rifkin warns that forces already in place will create a "near-workerless world." "The wholesale substitution of machines for workers is going to force every nation to rethink the role of human beings in the social process," he writes, adding: "Redefining opportunities and responsibilities ... in a society absent of mass formal employment is likely to be the single most pressing social issue of the coming century."[6] Featured in a CBC *Primetime* documentary in the fall of 1995, Rifkin painted a chilling portrait. The combination of global competition and new computer technology, he claimed, was eliminating good jobs at an alarming rate, creating conditions under which increasing numbers of people would soon be working in the "servant" class.

The controversy surrounding Rifkin's views has been so intense that the *Economist* – international bible of the business establishment – devoted seven pages to a denunciation of his book. Here in Canada, the CBC documentarians presented Stanley Hartt, a former deputy minister of finance and chief of staff to Brian Mulroney, as Rifkin's foil. The impeccably dressed Hartt, oozing corporate grace, elegance and calm, seemed astounded that Rifkin could get it all wrong. He cited the motor car: "At the time it was invented," he said, "if you would ask people, 'Will it employ masses of people?' they would have said, 'No. It'll never replace the horse and buggy.'" Technological development, according to Hartt, may involve short-term pain, but in the long term it frees up labour to produce things "we don't even know about yet."

Of course, Hartt has a point about technology. As Jean-Jacques Solomon observed in *The Uncertain Quest,* whether you see technology as a means of human enslavement and destruction or as a liberating Promethean force, you cannot walk away from it without walking away from the world's problems – from opportunities to reduce suffering, lengthen lives, attain higher levels of education, communicate more easily, gain access to greater social protection and leisure time and liberate much of humanity from the drudgery of manual toil.

During the past 200 years there have been two "industrial" revolutions, one in so-called primary industries such as agriculture, forestry and mining, and the other in manufacturing. Combined, they have contributed to a tenfold increase in output with only a twofold increase in employment. In 1911, more than 60% of Canadians worked in "goods-producing" jobs. As the century draws to a close, this employment has fallen to less than 25%, yet we all have lots more goods. This is the miracle of twentieth-century productivity.

Optimizing productivity is, for most economists, the key that unlocks the door to prosperity. They point, quite correctly, to a historical record that demonstrates how technology and increased global trade have stimulated economic expansion and yielded higher incomes and lower costs for huge segments of humanity. In 1913, 100 Model Ts rolled off Ford's Windsor assembly line each day, the products of boring, repetitive, low-wage work. Today, 1,200 Ford Taurus cars come off the line daily at Windsor. The workers involved make good money and the product is light-years better than the one you had to crank to get started.

One would truly have to be a prophet of doom to grouse about technology. Certainly, anyone who harbours doubts about where the mindless application of technology is taking us these days is made to feel like one. During his CBC interview, Stanley Hartt invoked the Luddites, the English textile workers who went around smashing mechanized looms in the early 1800s because they believed this machinery would destroy their livelihoods. For almost two centuries they've been held up as oddballs.

Never mind, as Kirkpatrick Sale points out in *Rebels Against the Future*, the Luddites saw clearly what was coming, and that great hardship overtook them once it came. Within several generations, the new technologies of the industrial revolution transformed many self-sufficient local communities into new economic units which devastated the multiple crafts of formerly independent workers and turned them into machine-minders. To an economist, the Luddites were still oddballs. It is hard to find an economist who doesn't believe that a more efficient world almost always makes for a better world. The very essence of being economical is getting the most out of the least.

What makes so many economists and business leaders excited about the changes sweeping the planet is this implicit promise of ever-increasing levels of productivity. Global competition forces companies to become more productive, and new technology provides them with the means to do so. As a result, many economic sectors are acquiring an increasingly profitable glow as new markets link up with lower production costs. Take exporters. There is no doubt that globalization and new technology (along with a low Canadian dollar) have been godsends to Canadian exporters. In 1993, Canada's exports increased by 10%. In 1994, they were up another 14%. In 1995, it was 12%. Without the export boom of the 1990s, the Canadian economy would have slumped into a permanent recession. During the 1980s, exports accounted for about 28% of Canada's GDP. By 1995 they had climbed to 41% and were continuing to climb.

The resource industries (especially oil and gas, mining and forestry) have all boomed during the first half of the 1990s, largely because of healthy exports. Profits in these industries have skyrocketed and stock market prices have soared with them. The combined revenue of Canada's top ten mining companies increased 10% from 1990 to 1994. Revenues of the top 10 forestry companies increased by 8% during the first half of the 1990s. The oil and gas industry has also seen hefty gains in both revenues and profitability.

The agricultural sector has also been celebrating. The competitive advantage of Canadian farmers, coupled with strong demand from Asian countries, has produced growing revenues. Gone is the image of the poor wheat farmer. When the Chrétien government rescinded the Crow Rate rail subsidy in 1995, there was hardly a murmur of dissent. Farmers have bought into the new free-swinging economy to the point that a vocal segment of the industry is demanding the freedom to bypass the Canadian Wheat Board and sell grain directly to foreign markets. The modern farmer barely has time to get mud off his boots, he's so busy hooking into the Chicago Board of Trade on the Internet. Total agricultural revenue in Canada jumped 6.5% in 1994, and experts estimated another 6.6% rise in 1995. Most of this increase has flowed from higher world demand and better international prices.

Then there's manufacturing. When you think of it, there's every reason the manufacturing sector should be a winner. Taxpayers have pumped billions of dollars over the past two decades into helping Canadian manufacturers become more competitive. That's what we were told the GST was all about – spreading taxes to cover services as well as goods, so that manufacturers wouldn't have to shoulder the burden on their own. Evidence from the early 1990s suggests that this new "value-added" approach is paying off, particularly for exports of manufactured goods. Aerospace, automotive and computer electronics lead the list of manufacturing stars that have contributed to Canada's recent export boom. No wonder Stanley Hartt felt so good as he challenged Jeremy Rifkin. Conventional wisdom stares you right in the face: advanced technology and globalization are clearly the keys to progress. Only a Luddite would argue that there's something wrong with this picture.

Nobody wants to be an alarmist, especially when all the experts keep saying that things are just great, and that Canadians are riding a wonderful wave of change like the champions we are. But why are so many people feeling they're under water? Are they right to be scared? Or should they just hold their breath and wait until the waves subside? The past will repeat itself and, before you know it, we'll be surrounded by security and prosperity, as we have been ever since the Great Depression. I'm sorry to disagree, but I think ordinary Canadians will be holding their breath for a good long time. In the real world, average incomes are down, job creation has turned into job depletion, workplace benefits are disappearing and the social safety net is badly fraying. Even if the economic wizards are right about the long term, the short term is upon us with a vengeance, producing one of the most severe periods of dislocation since the 1930s.

The manufacturing, resource and agricultural industries are not the job generators that they used to be. Fewer than 3% of Canadians now work on farms, and even with the boom, farm employment is lower than it was at the end of the 1980s. The manufacturing sector has shed almost 175,000 jobs since free trade came on stream in 1989. Revenues surged in the resource sector over the first half of the '90s, but employment levels declined.

And even if these industries were still job producers, they couldn't possibly compensate for the damage done in the service sector, which employs more than 70% of Canada's workforce. These are the jobs – often high-paying – that created all those opportunities and the economic demand in the 1960s, '70s and '80s. These are the jobs that are disappearing as quickly as you can say "downsizing."

Finally, the truth is emerging. It is beginning to dawn on people that a growing GDP, fostering a frenetic stock market and ever-rising TSE index, isn't quite the same thing as an economic "recovery" – at least not for most Canadians. The alleged recovery following the alleged recession has definitely conferred benefits, most notably on investors and captains of industry. But that isn't what we used to mean by the term *recovery.* The end of a recession used to feel good for most people. Now it only sounds good.

I have not heard a single convincing argument about how the vast numbers of jobs evaporating before our eyes are going to be replaced. We need to stare reality in the face and acknowledge that there may never again be enough jobs to approximate anything like full employment, especially if we are talking about full-time jobs, the kind of work that most of us have learned to center our lives around. Humans must either adjust to the new reality – and make it work for most of the world's growing population – or large numbers of formerly middle-class people, in Canada and elsewhere, will learn a definition of suffering they never thought would apply to them. The majority of Canadians, like the majority of citizens in other "rich" countries, have often been exempted in the past. This time around, dispensations will be few and far between.

To understand what is happening to the job market, we must begin by looking at how the very nature of work is changing in response to the twin pressures of computerization and globalization. There are really two kinds of work. Since binary numerology is in fashion these days, let's call them Work 0 and Work 1. Work 0 is work that can be broken down into its essential steps. These steps can be duplicated by non-human devices – animals in the old days, mechanical technology after the first industrial revolution, and more likely robots, computers or other types of electronic machinery today. Sometimes, the steps cannot be completely duplicated by non-humans, but their inventors figure out how to use unpaid workers to help out. If discount supermarkets can persuade customers to assist the electronic checkout devices in return for a few pennies in savings, they don't need as many cashiers.

Peter Drucker, the American management guru, says that it was Frederick Winslow Taylor (1856-1915) who first applied knowledge to the study and engineering of work. In *Post-Capitalist Society*, Drucker explains how Taylor could not go to Harvard because he had poor eyesight, so he took a job in an iron foundry. After closely observing his co-workers, he reached a revolutionary conclusion: there was no such thing as "skilled" work, only a series of repetitive motions, "each of which had to be done in its own right way, its own best time, and with its own right tools."[7]

What became known as Taylorism created a revolution in the way work was organized. It laid the foundations for the development of mass assembly manufacturing, one of the most important technological developments of this century. Careful study of the techniques of skilled workers allowed management experts to determine the exact physical actions required to build a product. The hundreds or even thousands of actions (lifting, turning, molding, etc.) could then be organized in sequence along an assembly line, with each worker given a small number of precisely defined tasks to perform. Once individual tasks had been explicitly defined, it was only a matter of time before highly specialized tools were developed to improve the efficiency of workers. Eventually, many of the most specialized tasks could be performed entirely by tools known as robots. This is the miracle of industrial productivity improvement in the twentieth century.

Although many jobs in the service sector have not been immune to automation, most of us have assumed that the more sophisticated service jobs – nursing, real estate, teaching, law, translating, managing, accounting, doctoring, brokering, etc. – would always be exempt. They seemed to qualify as Work 1 – work that cannot be easily duplicated. But we should have known better. With computers now beating top-ranked chess champions with regularity, there are few functions that designers won't be able to make them perform.

And when computers are matched with new management techniques, the potential for massive gains in productivity in services jobs is enormous. The Frederick Taylor of our day is Michael

Hammer, who claims that most work can be "re-engineered" to produce huge productivity gains. "Re-engineering," he boasts, "takes 40% of the labour out of most processes. For middle managers, it is even worse; 80% of them either have their jobs eliminated or cannot adjust to a team-based organization that requires them to be more of a coach than a task master."[8] As they were with Taylor almost a century ago, workers today are suspicious of Hammer's approach. But Bay Street is delighted.

This delight is not without irony. Normally, the investment community relishes high unemployment numbers, which are often a consequence of delayering and new technology. A high monthly unemployment figure invariably boosts the TSE index, because it means a cheap, plentiful supply of labour is available with little inflationary pressure to wreak havoc on the value of investments. You may also have noticed that when a corporation announces it has discarded another battalion of workers – often devastating these people's lives – the market invariably rewards the corporation by boosting the price of its shares.

But now for the irony. On October 12, 1995, a headline in the *Globe and Mail* read "Instinet Sends Chill Up Bay Street." A company named Instinet had developed stock-trading terminals that allowed clients to "enter their trading order on a computer screen, thus enabling money managers to trade directly with each other, rather than through brokers." What had Bay Street so worried, said the *Globe*, "is the fact that Instinet allows clients to bypass the broker and cut into their livelihood." What does this mean? It means the real world has come to the money market. These are service jobs – relatively sophisticated ones – and many of them will be gone soon. The brokers are being hoist on their own petard.

All the Porsches and BMWs on the streets tell you that many people are still making good money at their work stations. Nevertheless, it is getting increasingly difficult for a job to qualify under the good job heading, Work 1. Work 1 is done primarily by people Rifkin calls "symbolic analysts or knowledge workers." In the United States, he estimates, these account for only about 3.8 million people out of a population of nearly 300 million. But they are the managers of the new high-tech economy. They move information around – information that can be used to better fit production to consumption in any given place. It can also be used to speculate on stocks, bonds, derivatives, commodities, currencies and the like. Speculation is where the money is. Twenty years ago, most international currency movement was to pay for goods and services rather than speculation. No longer. Knowledge workers help create products, services and information to help people bet on what's hot and what isn't. "The knowledge workers are a diverse group united by their use of state-of-the-art information technology to identify, process, and solve problems," Rifkin writes. "They are the creators, manipulators, and purveyors of the stream of information that makes up the postindustrial, post-service global economy. Their ranks include research scientists, design engineers, civil engineers, software analysts, biotechnology researchers, public relations specialists, lawyers, investment bankers, management consultants, financial and tax consultants, architects, strategic planners, marketing specialists, film producers and editors, arts directors, publishers, writers, editors and journalists."[9]

For anyone intending to use this list as a guide, beware the pitfalls that lie within many of these categories. Some of these people are clearly doing extremely well. On the other hand, there are plenty of unemployed architects, engineers and journalists. Not nearly as many, however, as you'll find within the hundreds of occupations that now fall under the heading of Work 0.

The most symbolic of these, for my money, is not the common labourer, replaced by a vast variety of construction equipment, or the receptionist, replaced by voice mail, or the middle manager, bypassed and delayered. Beyond all these, consider the fate of the musician, often a person of great talent, replaced by the synthesizer. Synthesizers can reduce any sound to digital impulses. All the talent a musician develops over a lifetime can be captured in a string of ones and zeroes, then stored. Entire symphony orchestras can be reduplicated by one little machine operated by one person. Notes played by great musicians are often "sampled" – that is, extracted and stored – and recombined in performances that the original artist never had anything to do with. In *The End of Work,* Rifkin relates the haunting story of one musician whose skills were pilfered from him before he knew what was happening. "Buell Neidlinger, a string bass player, describes a recording session where he was asked to play 'every note of the chromatic scale.' After the session, Neidlinger noticed that a sampling machine had been hidden in the corner of the room behind the coffee machine. 'He had stolen my sound,' Neidlinger later recounted. Henceforth, the studio could use the notes to compose and produce any piece it desired."[10]

The message here is that no matter how gifted you may think you are, no matter how clever you may be at thinking, talking or performing, somebody is busy designing a circuit board that will outstrip your talents. When that task is completed, there will be a virtual you, and your talents will be made available cheaply, on demand, 24 hours a day. The longer this process continues, the more all those vital occupations on the Work 1 list will stumble off to join Work 0.

I'm reminded by friends who study economic history that "progress" usually involves some casualties: gifted artisans who can no longer find work or entire occupational categories that are no longer needed. The invention of the steam engine, they lecture me, left little demand for blacksmiths, but considerably enhanced the quality of travel and, in the end, produced many more occupations than were lost.

Maybe some day our grandchildren will look back at our time on Earth with the same detachment we feel toward the personal agonies experienced during the industrial revolution. But they will probably also know that *our* revolution involved two key differences: First, the *speed* of technological change is much faster. The first steam engine was produced in 1769 yet did not begin to increase agricultural productivity until a century later. Second, the *scope* of change is much broader. Although some jobs changed dramatically during the first hundred years of the industrial revolution, the majority did not. Most people continued working on farms and living in rural areas well into the twentieth century. Our revolution is affecting more people, more quickly than any technologically induced transformation in history. This time, the technology is particularly well suited to yielding huge gains in the productivity of service sector work – where 75% of us are now located – and the expanding pressures of global competition demand rapid gains in productivity. Maybe these changes will produce a better life for all of us. But when, and at what cost?

A highly respected estimate comes from Paul David, of the Center for Economic Policy Research at Stanford University. He forecasts that by 2010 to 2015, levels of general prosperity and upward mobility in the United States will equal or surpass those experienced during the 1950s and 1960s. Until then, David warns, Americans will pass through a painful period of diminishing national prosperity, falling levels of public services and a weakening social safety net.[11] If these estimates are applied to Canada, it means we're facing as many as 20 years of tough sledding.

Yes, that sounds bleak. On the other hand, human beings still hold a measure of collective and individual control over their destinies, and the situation will become desperate only if we fail to recognize the enormous challenges we face. Without a clear understanding of how this new economy is changing our lives, it will be impossible to launch the massive effort required to help Canadians adjust. I've already examined how, at least when it comes to jobs, the promise of the export sector during the 1990s has been largely illusory. However, it is in the services sector, whose incredible expansion kept the Spend-and-Share era going for 25 years, that the most telling blows are now being struck.

Six

THE SHAKEDOWN IN SERVICES

> *"Nothin' shakin' on Shakedown Street.*
> *Used to be the heart of town."*
>
> The Grateful Dead

The services sector – filled with all those clean, high-paying and even idealistic jobs that represented Canada's growth during the Spend-and-Share era – has sputtered in the 1990s. Teachers, nurses, managers, bureaucrats, social workers, real-estate brokers, insurance brokers, salesclerks, lawyers, dentists, architects, journalists, bank tellers, railway workers, these and dozens of other trades and professions are feeling the squeeze in the Sink-or-Swim era. The services sector is going through a major shakedown. Some categories of employment, like computer services and market research, have benefited from the growing demand for information, but many others have not.

During the Spend-and-Share era, services sector jobs grew at a rate of 3.4% a year.[1] True, not all of these jobs were glamorous. But many of them were secure positions in government, corporations and the retail sector. Since 1989, growth in service jobs has been at a virtual standstill – up a puny 1.2% a year, slightly lower than the growth in the working-age population. In mid-1989, the percentage of working-age Canadians with jobs peaked at 62.4%. Slightly more than 7 out of 10 of them were in the services sector.

Later that year, the balloon burst. By 1995 the number of working-age Canadians with jobs had dropped to 58.7%, and the shrinking services sector was becoming the labour market's number-one problem. When the transition from full-time to part-time jobs was taken into account, this sector – which nine million Canadians still count on for employment – was in the midst of a major upheaval. Between 1989 and 1995, full-time positions in the services sector grew by less than half a percent per year, part-time positions grew over 2%, and the number of self-employed workers grew by more than 4%. With this shift, a new rule of the Sink-or-Swim era has begun to surface: don't count on the economy to produce new jobs – you've got to produce them yourselves.

To understand how jobs in the services sector will change, it is necessary to examine the changes currently under way in the category's occupational groupings. But be warned: the results of this analysis are not for the weak of heart.

In its 1990 statement *Good Jobs, Bad Jobs*, the Economic Council of Canada divided the service economy into three sectors: dynamic, traditional and non-market services.

Dynamic services include:
- Utilities, communications and transportation (all types of transport, pipelines, storage, broadcasting, telephones, postal and courier, utilities, etc.)
- Wholesale trade
- Finance, insurance and real-estate (banks, trust companies, credit

unions, mortgage and insurance companies, investment dealers, real-estate operators, etc.)
- Business services (employment agencies, advertising, architectural, scientific, engineering and computing, legal services, management consulting)

Traditional services include:
- Retail trade (stores, auto repair shops, gas stations, etc.)
- Personal services (restaurants, hotels, bars, the entertainment business, hair salons, laundries, car rentals, photographers, travel agencies, funeral services, security guards, etc.)

Non-market services include:
- Education (schools, colleges, universities, libraries, museums, etc.)
- Health and social services (hospitals, nursing homes, doctors and dentists, day care, crisis centers, psychologists and social workers)
- Public administration (governments and their agencies)

DYNAMIC SERVICES
About one in four Canadian workers is employed in this broad category. This sector believes deeply in wealth, and there is good money to be made here. Since 1989, employment growth in dynamic services has fallen to about a third of the pre-1989 rate. Many of these jobs are particularly sensitive to the principal ideology of the Sink-or-Swim era – increased competitiveness. Deregulation and privatization are freeing management from the constraints of government control and public accountability. And new technology is creating significant improvements in productivity. The result is generally good news for customers but a new environment for workers.

Utilities, Communications and Transportation

This category is like a large moving van, stuffed with everything from mattresses to natural gas, to bytes of information. Canada is a big place, so moving cargo and energy and data is critical to our economy. During the Spend-and-Share era, growing consumer demand opened up a lot of these "delivery" jobs. Many were well paid, including unionized positions for some of Canada's largest Crown corporations (CN, the CBC, Air Canada, Ontario Hydro, etc.). This is still a growth sector, but almost all of it's happening among either part-time workers or self-employed entrepreneurs. Between 1967 and 1989 employment grew at an annual rate of 1.5%. Over the past six years total employment growth still looks respectable at 2%, but during that period 10,000 full-time jobs have vanished. All of the new jobs are either part-time or contract positions. And the real cutting has just begun. Announced job reductions in 1995 are expected to make this a no-growth job sector for the rest of the decade. Large companies are being broken up. Small independents, heavily into the latest technology, are making inroads. Anyone remaining on the payroll is likely to be asked to do more – for less.

Utilities

In 1992, at the very nadir of the recession, 156,000 Canadians were employed by power, gas and water utilities. Most worked for big companies like Ontario Hydro and Hydro Québec. By 1995, with the so-called recovery well under way, employment levels at utilities had dropped to 142,000. The longer-term prognosis is bleak. One well-placed industry insider told me that in the electrical generating industry alone, total cuts could amount to 40% of the 1989 labour force. Say goodbye to 31,500 jobs. Ontario Hydro alone will eliminate 15,000 to 20,000 jobs.

Two factors are at play in the downsizing: intense competition from alternative energy sources, and hostile regulators who have correctly sensed public resistance to price increases. As a result, utilities have been forced to look inward for efficiencies. Layers of management have been shed and operations streamlined through more sophisticated computer billing systems, automated customer inquiry systems and new remote monitoring and sensing technologies. Pilot studies now under way may soon set the stage for the total automation of electricity delivery through remote monitoring of all users, including residences. Such systems will do more than throw thousands of meter readers out of work; they will allow electrical companies to introduce special pricing to encourage appliance use outside "peak load" periods. That's the bright side: more efficient energy consumption and lower prices. People who do laundry at 2 a.m. will get a real bonus. People who read meters for a living or build hydroelectric dams won't.

Computer-based sensing is already revolutionizing the natural gas industry. Canadian Western Natural Gas of Calgary, and Northwestern Utilities of Edmonton were among the first companies in North America to install automated meter reading. In Calgary and Edmonton alone, they had been spending $6 million a year. This innovation is expected to yield significant savings. Meter readers were often forced to return two or three times to read indoor meters, because people weren't home. Not any more.

Communications

In theory, jobs should be plentiful here. Dozens of new communications services have been formed. The telecommunications and broadcasting industries are spreading their wings. If you can't get the information you want out of your computer, telephone, fax machine, television or radio, there's a good chance it doesn't exist.

The reality so far as jobs are concerned is less impressive. In 1989, employment in the communications industry stood at 328,000 workers. By 1995, after the greatest explosion of new services in the history of the industry, the number of workers was virtually unchanged. What had changed was the employment mix; full-time positions were down 10,000, while part-time and self-employed workers were up by 11,000. Again, the prognosis for the remainder of the decade is not encouraging. New efficiencies and increased competition are snuffing out jobs – especially full-time work. In 1995, Bell Canada announced it was laying off 10,000 workers. Other telcos have followed suit. In the wake of its 1990 privatization, Alberta's AGT has shed about 4,000 positions. Saskatchewan's telephone company has reduced its payroll by 1,000. BC Tel has cut 1,500 jobs. Consumers have benefited from these restructurings through huge reductions in long-distance rates.

Computerized technology will reduce the need for staff in areas such as billing and customer service. In the U.S., it's estimated that by the end of the decade 10,000 telephone operators will be performing the tasks that 60,000 were responsible for in 1994. New voice-recognition systems are already starting to monitor your information requests; while these systems have their glitches, the technology is rapidly improving and users are growing more accustomed to interacting with computer-generated voices.

Here, then, is the paradox: the same information systems that are generating all the excitement are breeding despair in the job market. If communications isn't creating jobs, which sector will? If communications can't create jobs now, when will it? Ironically, many of the workers helping to build the new information infrastructure are among the first to be laid off. It's not unlike being ordered to dig your own grave.

A 1996 advertisement in the *Globe and Mail* by Rogers Cantel and Bell Canada warned that the information highway "raises the ante in competition. If we don't act, Canada and Canadian companies will be left behind." In this case, "act" means becoming more efficient, which translates into replacing people with microchips.

Next to Ma Bell, Canadians' most familiar electronic companion over the past half century has been the CBC. But the "Corp" is quickly becoming "the Corpse." The free market is in the ascendancy, and entrepreneurs have never liked having to put up with a government-subsidized competitor. In 1987-88, the CBC employed 10,571 Canadians. A decade later, fully 25% are expected to have been "delayered."

Once, undeniably, the CBC was a bloated institution. In Ottawa, producers sent out five-person film crews to cover Parliament Hill assignments that CTV and Global handled with two people. In doing so, they gave the politicians ammunition for the firing squads that would follow. After several rounds of belt-tightening, however, the CBC is starting to look emaciated. Most of its employees are overworked and underpaid. One more place not to look for a job.

Private broadcasters are also cutting a wide swath through their organization charts. Lower advertising revenue (the result in part of sluggish consumer spending), intense competition, deregulation and new technology are all responsible. CTV, for example, employed 447 people in 1991. Four years later, it had slimmed down to 384. At Toronto's City-TV, the same person often serves as reporter, camera operator and editor. Telemedia Communications and Pelmorex Broadcasting, which together own the two radio stations in Sault Ste. Marie, Ontario, reduced their total staff from 45 to 21 by agreeing to share sales, administration and technical operations, automated programming and the use of satellite network services. Rogers' AM outlet in Winnipeg switched to a network program source (delivered via satellite) and trimmed more than half its staff.

The Internet poses a serious threat to both radio and television. Angus Reid surveys reveal fewer viewing hours among Internet surfers and an increasing use of Net-based audio. Progressive Networks, a Seattle company, is already into "netcasting." Its "RealAudio" program adds live sound to products such as Netscape and Mosaic. RealAudio turns computer pages into talking picture books. Warner Brothers' hit movie *Batman Forever* has added Real-Audio to its Web site, allowing Gotham City Radio to broadcast over the Net – and the CRTC is powerless to stop it.

Over the next decade the expansion of the Internet threatens to exacerbate the trend toward audience fragmentation already evident in Canada. This will further erode traditional ad revenue in radio and television, leading inevitably to further downsizing. The technology is already in place to allow broadcasters to make do with fewer staff. Recently, I had a glimpse of one possible scenario during an interview with CNN in their New York studio. My interview took place in a studio with no camera operators or technicans. Everything was remote controlled – from Atlanta.

Transportation

Since 1989, Canadians employed in what Statistics Canada calls the "transportation and storage" field increased from 539,000 to 559,000. But all of this growth was the result of part-time jobs and increasing numbers of self-employed workers. I suppose this could be called good news. But it's apt to be short-lived.

Employment at Canada's railways dropped from 82,000 in 1987 to fewer than 50,000 in 1995. The trend is straight downhill, because increased trade between Canada and the U.S. is forcing Canadian railways to streamline operations to compete. U.S. rail carriers have operating ratios as low as 66% (meaning operating costs are 66 cents for every dollar of revenue). In 1994, CN and CP reported operating ratios in the 90-92% range. Both companies have begun restructuring in order to chop costs and boost profitability. When CP announced it was relocating its head office from Montreal to Calgary, it also slashed 700 head-office jobs. That's in addition to the 6,000 positions eliminated since 1993. CN announced in early 1995 that it would permanently erase 11,000 jobs. Later that year, it said that further reductions would cut the total workforce by about 1,000 positions a year "over the next few years." In its preliminary prospectus, prepared for investors in advance of its 1995 public offering, CN said that it expected its remaining workers to become more productive, otherwise outside contractors would perform their duties.

In the transportation sector, business is shifting away from railways to trucking. The chief beneficiaries are smaller trucking companies. Owner-operated trucking is growing and large truckers are hanging on by the skin of their teeth. The proportion of total trucking revenues derived from north-south trade has increased 20% since the early 1990s.[2] Canadian trucking companies face stiff competition on these routes. Wages and benefits are lower in the U.S., and Canadian operators must push themselves harder to compete. Here, too, new technology is having an impact. Telemetry, for example, has already made trucking companies far more efficient, tracking loads by computer. But the computer operator may soon be surplus. Federal Express and other firms have launched services on the Internet that allow customers to monitor the movement of their own products. And Coca-Cola has begun putting microprocessors in Coke machines; central dispatchers will thus know exactly what's in the machine before the Coke truck arrives. This advance could significantly improve the productivity of distributors, who will know exactly how much of each soft drink and potato chip to load on the truck. The result – you guessed it – less staff.

The Canadian airline industry doubled in size between 1955 and 1968, tripled by 1978 and quadrupled by 1991. Employees shared in the success. The increase in salaries was almost fifteenfold by 1978 and fortyfold by 1991.[3] Since then, things have gone into a bit of a stall. The villains: new technology, increasing competition and declining demand in the highly profitable business-travel segment. Computerization has revolutionized the industry, especially in areas such as flight scheduling, reservations and ticketing. Computerized instant ticketing eliminates the need to purchase a ticket from a travel agent or to check in prior to boarding. WestJet, a new regional carrier in western Canada, estimates that savings achieved through automatic ticketing will allow it to cut prices by 30%. With the proliferation of home computers and access to the Internet, savings will likely accelerate, but with consumers rather than employees at the controls.

It is true that the recently enacted Canada-U.S. Open Skies agreement may be creating opportunities for the Canadian airline industry. For example, between late 1995 and the spring of 1996, Canadian Airlines created 700 new jobs in Vancouver. But it is also bringing more intense competition. There has already been a rapid increase in cross-border traffic – up about 20% from January 1995 levels. Like the railways, the Canadian airline industry must bring operating costs in line with U.S. competitors. That means only one thing: more cutbacks or wage rollbacks. Since 1991, Canadian Airlines has reduced its full-time staff by 15%, while the number of permanent employees at Air Canada decreased by over 9% between 1990 and 1996. Employees at Canadian Airlines have lost ground to inflation over the last five years, and the worst could still be ahead. In addition to U.S. competition, Canadian must deal with two new regional airlines that are discounting fares in its key market, western Canada.

Finally, the airline industry in Canada must cope with the prospect of declining levels of business travel. More video-conferencing already means fewer business trips. Video-conferencing is joining the computer and the fax machine in the category of key tools in the modern office. It reduces costs and increases productivity. Sales of video-conferencing systems are "exploding" according to Greg Funk, manager of Compression Labs of Markham, Ontario; its own revenues were up nearly 40% between August 1994-1995. Desktop video-conferencing systems should double in number to about 3,000 by the end of 1996, predicts Jack Keating, of NBI/Michael Sone Associates of Toronto. Hardware prices are falling; long-distance phone charges will soon be in the same cost neighbourhood as local calls, and new desktop video-conferencing systems are getting easier to use. And there's no jet lag.

Wholesale Trade

Wholesale trade once generated thousands of new jobs. During the Spend-and-Share era, this category grew at more than 2% per year, reaching about 600,000 jobs by 1989; 8 in 10 of these were full-time positions. Since then, the wholesale sector has lost about 10,000 full-time jobs. The few jobs created have been either part-time or self-employment. Why has employment growth come to a virtual stop? First, because consumption has fallen, so there is less to ship. Moreover, large retailers like Wal-Mart are increasingly going direct, bypassing the wholesale level. This doesn't necessarily imply the death of the wholesale sector, because other forces are also at work. Globalization may eventually create more jobs in this field. More and more manufacturers are centralizing production facilities, because the decline in tariffs means that branch plants no longer need to be located in foreign markets.

The Canadian wholesaler is affected when production plants move from Canada to the U.S. or another country. That invariably means a loss of manufacturing jobs. But it can also mean an increase in wholesaling jobs if a "middleman" can help distribute American or other foreign products in Canada. Already, something of a ware-house economy has grown up in Canada, a new string of giant ware-houses and distribution centers for products shipped from abroad.

That's a genuine plus for job creation. But new economics and new technology are having a reverse effect. Retailers, under the pressure of intense competition, are increasingly squeezing wholesalers. Think of everyday consumer items such as shoes, food, household appliances and drugs. How badly do retailers need a wholesaler when orders can be placed by computer directly to the manufacturer? In New York City, International Close-out Exchange Systems' on-line database matches buyers and sellers of excess close-outs – goods, toys, clothes and electronics sold for pennies on the dollar. The company bypasses the wholesale level, linking vendors directly with retailers. The big U.S. chains invariably deal directly with the manufacturer, and the retail sector is increasingly being influenced

– if not yet dominated – by U.S. "big box" retailing monstrosities. Companies like Computer City or Toys 'Я Us that have huge selections and very low prices. They're monsters, often pay low wages and are driving smaller Canadian competitors out of business. But consumers are pinching pennies, and in difficult economic times it is hard to blame anyone for looking for bargains.

Finance

Throughout the 1970s and '80s financial services – banks, credit unions, trust companies, brokerage houses and insurance services – proliferated. When Canadians weren't spending money, they were borrowing, saving or investing it, and the financial institutions were only too willing to think of creative ways to be accommodating. Pre-boomers did more saving and investing and boomers did more borrowing, but both groups kept the financial people smiling those can't-lose smiles.

Between 1967 and 1989, jobs in this category expanded at a healthy annual rate of 4.1%. Since then, job growth in financial services has averaged less than 1% per year. Full-time employment has dropped by 11,000 positions; the little jobs growth achieved is all part-time or contract work. And the real changes are only beginning; the full force of globalization, new technology and restructuring have not yet been felt.

It took 20 years for the ATM to become a permanent feature in Canadian banking and financial quarters. Today, they're everywhere. Debit cards gained faster acceptance, particularly among women, who tend to be wary of carrying cash. But much more is coming: telephone banking, 1-800 brokering, more electronic transactions and, of course, the Internet, to be used for every financial

transaction short of giving spare change to panhandlers. Money is
as easy to handle as words on the Internet. Although fewer than 1%
of Canadians are currently using the Net for banking services, it
won't be long until the convenience of keyboard banking catches
on. More than half of all banking transactions are now performed
electronically. By the end of the decade, it will be 75%. The implications are profound. Banks have always seemed so solid and enduring, but many of their bricks-and-mortar branches will become Pizza
Huts and Starbucks in the not-too-distant future. Who needs
branches when most bank business is conducted by modem? And if
you don't need branches, you won't need tellers.

Once again, globalization is teaming up with technology to eliminate jobs. Foreign banks are still relatively minor players in the
Canadian banking system, but they have been given more regulatory room to play. When competition heats up, managers will find
new ways to make cheap and efficient electronics replace people.
On the other hand, as boomers age, there will be increasing
demands for financial services, which may have some moderating
effect on the people squeeze in the industry.

Banks, Trusts and Credit Unions

For Canadians, banks are both darlings and devils. Our laws have
provided a handful of huge banks with a comfortable environment
in which to build vast national branch networks. On the positive
side, this has created one of the safest, most convenient banking
systems in the world and a lot of employment. On the other hand,
Canadian banks have extracted breathtaking profits from the pockets
of Canadians. In 1995, for example, the seven largest banks earned a
combined return of more than $5 billion – an average return on

equity of about 14%. That compares rather favourably with the 6% paid on Canada Savings Bonds, especially if you argue, as you reasonably might, that the banks constitute a secure investment.

Nevertheless, the future is not exactly rosy in those gleaming Toronto banking towers. There's always that tiny element of doubt, rather like a Saudi prince wondering if the oil will run out. U.S. and other foreign banks are lining up at the border, eyeing what has been a captive market. With lower operating costs, higher productivity and massive capital reserves, some of these global traders may well give the banks in Canada a run for their money. The *Financial Post* has observed that "recent megadeals among six U.S. regional banks could have a fatal impact on the competitiveness of Canadian banks, their global standing and their lock on the home market."[4] Wal-Mart-type bankers may surface. If U.S. banks offer better service at cheaper rates, nobody doubts that Canadians will respond. Even long line-ups at bridges didn't stop cross-border shopping in the early 1990s, and soon, it won't be necessary to cross the bridge to get to the nearest American bank.

Canadian banks aren't patsies, however, so there is a credit side to this ledger. The Canadians are already doing some invading of their own. Toronto-Dominion, for example, "has essentially sidestepped corporate Canada as a major source of business growth," Ann Shortell wrote in *Money Has No Country.* "Half of its corporate loans [in 1990] were in the United States and the balance would soon tilt in Manhattan's favour; ... its strategy dovetailed with the plans of every one of the largest six Canadian banks."[5] Bank of Montreal owns Harris Bank (Chicago) and a major piece of BanComer (Mexico).

Which brings us back to banks as employers. Obtaining precise numbers can be tricky, but nobody questions that the employment boom of the 1980s is headed south. Deloitte & Touche's financial services group estimates that in the U.S., 450,000 banking jobs will disappear over the next decade. In Canada, 5,000 positions have disappeared since 1989 – despite the banks' entry into a broad range of nontraditional banking services, including credit cards, insurance and brokerage products. Credit union employment is also down from its high-water mark in 1991 (59,000) and is expected to continue its decline throughout the decade.

Employment at trust companies is riding the same toboggan. Many trusts have been swallowed up by the banks. Others have simply faded away. Between 1990 and 1995, the number of trust company employees dropped from 34,000 to 25,000, and we still haven't reached the bottom of the hill. Increased competition, deregulation and management restructuring have all been part of the people squeeze. However, nothing can compare to the importance of computer technology in rendering financial services workers obsolete. The future is located at the newly renovated CIBC flagship branch in Toronto, which features 38 banking machines and 16 tellers. You can access the ATMs on the main floor; to see a teller you have to descend one floor. CIBC says customers want speed, convenience and efficiency, preferences that give machines an edge over people.

Perhaps even Toronto isn't the real wave of the future. Bank representatives from around the world are making pilgrimages to Leeds, England, for a glimpse of an extremely successful branchless banking operation. First Direct, the world's leading telephone-only bank, is the fastest-growing bank in Britain, signing up 2% of the nation's banking customers in only five years. On an average day in

Leeds – a location chosen mainly for its low cost – 150 phone recep-
tionists (fewer at off-peak hours) handle 24,000 calls a day. On the
walls are scoreboards flashing the number of customers on hold and
how long they've been waiting. Needless to say, given its negligible
overheads, First Direct is able to offer extremely competitive rates.

Whether it's through phones or machines, banks clearly want
their customers wired. To push people toward their ATMs, First
National Bank of Chicago is charging customers $3 for involving a
human teller in transactions a machine could handle. Citibank has
taken a more carrot-like approach; it's eliminating all fees associated
with electronic transactions. It has been estimated that half of all
bank teller jobs in the U.S. will be eliminated by the end of the
decade. Most remaining jobs will be converted to part-time status. It
costs a bank $1.07 every time a customer conducts a transaction
with a teller, according to the American Bankers Association. The
same transaction at an ATM costs 27 cents. A telephone transaction
that does not involve human contact costs 35 cents. Shifting more
employees into part-time positions lets branches operate longer
with fewer and cheaper employees. Most part-timers do not receive
the benefits that full-time employees do. They can also be
summoned on an as-needed basis.

In fairness, most redundant tellers at Canadian banks are not
being fired; they are being retrained and relocated, as the banks
scramble to sell every other financial service imaginable. Even so,
banks are unlikely to be the sources of new employment that they
have been in the past. Marie Gohier, manager of corporate recruit-
ment for Royal Bank of Canada in Montreal, says that in 1989, 60
to 65% of new positions were filled by hiring from outside. Today,
that's down to 30 to 35%.[6] That hardly makes it any easier for all

those over-qualified applicants to find jobs in the banking system. MBAs are being forced to apply for entry-level jobs, just to get a foot in the door.

The computer revolution in the banking industry has been nothing short of stunning. According to several senior officials I have interviewed, employment levels will decline 30 to 50% over the next decade. Technology is remaking the entire monetary system.

Microsoft president Bill Gates recognized that reality when he went after Intuit, the personal-finances software maker. The deal fell through, but not before giving the banking community a scare. They could see Microsoft wiring its 70 million Windows customers into the electronic-commerce networks Gates intends to put together – with or without help from the banks. Gates has also hooked up with Visa on a system designed to secure credit-card transactions completed over the Net.

Insurance and Real Estate

The insurance industry is undergoing a world-wide transformation. Lloyd's of London is facing its biggest cash crisis in 308 years, partly as a result of huge settlements for environmental claims. In Canada, the demise of Sovereign Life in Calgary and Confederation Life in Toronto caught a lot of analysts by surprise. While the industry claims these are isolated incidents, there is no doubt that insurance companies (and therefore their employees) are facing a radically new environment. There were more than 100 Canadian insurance companies, employing 144,000 workers, in 1988. By 1995, employment had grown by a mere two-tenths of 1%, to 147,000. During the same period, the profits of this industry advanced by 35%.

Again, new technology and increased competition are the driving
forces. Forty per cent of insurance company income is now earned
outside Canada.

In the property and casualty market – a $16-billion industry in
1994 – middlemen are becoming vulnerable. In Britain, Direct Line
Insurance entered the market in 1985, basing its business entirely
on direct sales that eliminated brokers. Direct Line now controls
approximately 25% of the British market. Consumers buy casualty,
property and auto insurance products by calling a toll-free number,
which puts them into contact with an insurance underwriter.
Networked computers allow the underwriter to examine the caller's
claims history and other factors before quoting a price. The administrative cost is about 20% of the premium dollar, compared with
more than 30% under the traditional brokerage system. Consumers
win; independent brokers lose.

In Canada, the first major foray into telephone-based insurance
sales was made not by an insurance company but a bank. In early
1995, the CIBC's new insurance arm began selling policies through
a 1-800 number in Ontario. In its first three months, this service was
swamped with an average of 14,000 calls a week. (Mind you, part of
this volume was attributed to independent brokers who called repeatedly, attempting to tie up the lines. Who would have thought of
insurance brokers as modern-day Luddites?) By the year's end, CIBC
had declared the service a success, announcing it would go national.
Other financial institutions, both Canadian and American, were
expected to offer similar services. Internet-based services are already
available, although they are not expected to achieve a significant
market share until the end of the decade. According to some
observers, more than half of all property and casualty insurance sold

in Canada will be sold directly within the next ten years. "The distribution revolution ... may very well prove to be the most profound change this industry has experienced in its 200-year history," says Ted Belton, director of research for RBC Underwriting Management Services, the insurance arm of the Royal Bank of Canada.[7]

That a bank was the first to launch large-scale telephone-based insurance provides a clue to the second problem facing the insurance industry – new competition. With the deregulation of financial services, banks and major American-based financial institutions pose a serious threat. Confederation Life's suicide plunge has left many Canadians wary. In 1995, the Standard and Poor's rating agency downgraded three major Canadian life insurers because it felt that future market conditions would make it more difficult for them to compete. These signals unsettle consumers; insurance shouldn't be about taking risks. Buying insurance means playing it safe. Canadian insurers should be worried. If Canadians get spooked, they are likely to turn to the only thing that seems both larger and more enduring than the Canadian Shield – the banking system. Even though the federal Liberals have restricted the ability of banks to sell insurance products, none of the major banks has retreated from this lucrative business.

Once again, these pressures can only impinge on jobs, wages and working conditions. Several consortia of insurance brokers have sprung up to help brokers market their services collectively and make new technologies affordable. Even if these efforts are successful, independent brokering – the quintessential small business – will likely demand longer hours for less revenue. (There are currently about 30,000 independent brokers in Canada.)

In 1989, the Canadian Real Estate Association, the licensing body for real-estate agents in Canada, boasted 93,000 members. By 1995, membership had dropped to 75,000. The decline was clearly a function of the stagnant market for residential and commercial property. Among the 75,000 licensed agents, almost a third earn less than $20,000 per year. The problems confronting these agents involve more than a cyclical downturn in demand and a temporary oversupply of product. The function of property and buildings is being fundamentally redefined. A combination of corporate downsizing, greater use of technology and the rise of home offices is contributing to a long-term decline in demand for commercial office space. For example, in 1994, some 35,000 U.S. based AT&T employees were telecommuting at least one day a week; another 12,000 were in virtual offices, using cell phones and laptops. Combined, these groups represent nearly 20% of AT&T's workforce. The company is said to have saved $80 million last year by closing offices. AT&T is also responding to U.S. federal pollution-control requirements that push companies to cut down on employee commuting.

The residential market, too, is suffering from oversupply and a chronic weakness in demand. The latter is the result of shifting demographics, precarious household finances and changing values concerning the form and function of housing. And like other middlemen, real-estate agents are facing elimination, courtesy of new technology. The Internet is already a first-rate real-estate catalogue, allowing buyers to surf through listings, view properties and exchange e-mail messages with vendors. The MLS real estate service has a website allowing potential purchasers access to information on over 100,000 properties listed by real-estate agents in Canada. Newcomers are starting to provide other services that offer sizable discounts to vendors, traditionally saddled with 5-6% real-estate fees. The Toronto Real Estate Board, which had 26,000 members in 1989, had 21,000 in 1995, and president Carl Fox expected the number to go "down to 15,000 or 17,000 before it stops."[8] It goes without saying that the technology will just keep getting better. Prospective home buyers will soon view properties by downloading video clips onto their home PCs. While agents will still play a role, it will be a reduced one. Even now, says Dave Higgins, president of the Canadian Real Estate Association, 80 to 85% of real-estate revenues go to 15 to 20% of agents.[9] Over the next decade, these super-sellers will likely be the ones who exploit the new technology to their best advantage.

In sum, it will be harder and harder to earn a living in real estate in the coming years. Would-be brokers are beginning to figure that out. The Real Estate Council observed in 1995: "Demand for the salesperson's pre-licensing course has dropped with the decline in market activity ... The total number of licensees decreased 5% over the past year. It would now appear that for the first time in ten years, the licensee population has stabilized." The number of licensees may have stabilized, but you can bet the number of Canadians making a living in real estate will keep on dropping.

Investment dealers

Before the market crash in October 1987, brokerage and investment dealers employed approximately 27,000 Canadians. Since then, profits have surged and revenues per employee have more than doubled, but the number of people working in the industry has declined. By the end of 1993, employment was down to 22,523. Computer-based trading gives investment dealers tools that substantially increase their productivity, part of the reason why revenue per employee has increased so quickly. Discount brokers offer cost-efficient keyboard and computer trading. Several – including the discount brokerage services operated by Royal Bank of Canada (Action Direct) and Toronto-Dominion Bank (Green Line) – will take orders to buy or sell securities 24 hours a day, seven days a week. One advantage: people busy during the day can enter orders the night before. The obvious danger is the martini-inspired trade.

The incursion of Canadian banks into the investment industry – through brokerage takeovers, the launching of mutual funds and discount brokering – hasn't killed Bay Street's entrepreneurial spirit. Small, specialized boutique investment houses have established their presence over the past several years. The industry is looking at new ways of doing things, and new things to do. The emergence of discount brokers has forced more traditional brokers to focus on niche markets. More small firms operate as "introducers," gregarious people with a knowledge of the marketplace who can keep clients dabbling while larger brokers handle the mechanics (or electronics) of putting deals through. Small shops with a veneer of expertise are doing quite well.

Investment and brokerage dealers, like others in the middle, are being squeezed by all the market competition. Their employees are being squeezed by the new efficiencies within the industry. The outlook for new jobs is gloomy; the outlook for profits is pretty darned good. That's not an unusual combination these days.

Business Services

This third component of dynamic services is quite diverse: It includes architects, engineers, lawyers, accountants, management consultants and computer programmers, all jobs traditionally thought of as Work 1 – hard to imitate with bits, bytes, circuits and machines. And these are coveted jobs, knowledge jobs, that were gobbled up by educated young Canadians during the Spend-and-Share era. Remuneration and working conditions are usually good, and there is often a measure of autonomy and creativity involved. The average annual growth rate in this category between 1967 and 1989 was 7.3%, the highest of any group.

In fact, even in the 1990s, business services have rung up a comparatively good record for creating employment – almost 4% a year. That's better than every other sector, but still well off the heady pace of the good old days. While there has been a boom in some categories – most obviously computer services – this expansion has been muted by weak performances in areas such as architecture, engineering and law.

Computer Services

It will be no surprise that this sector is performing like Secretariat running against a field of plough horses. From 1989 to 1995, employment growth in computer services averaged 15% per year, the fastest rate for any employment category in Canada. By the end of 1995, fully 123,000 Canadians, about 1% of the labour force, were working in computer services of one kind or another. With the massive deployment of computer resources through both private and public sectors, levels can be expected to continue to boom for the foreseeable future. One 1992 federal government study found a shortage of at least 9,000 software workers (people who write computer programs). Only three years later, the estimated shortage had climbed to 20,000.

Clearly this is one of the few truly bright spots on the employment horizon. Educational institutions are racing to fill the growing demand, and filling their pockets in the process. In British Columbia, the Vancouver Film School is charging students $15,000 for an intensive 10-month multimedia course; there is no shortage of applicants. VFS students typically have a university degree and are willing to pay these steep tuition costs in order to gain a foothold in the new economy.

But as good as it all looks, there may be quicksand just around the corner. The same 1992 federal study found that many software creators were out of work because rapidly advancing technologies had rendered their highly developed skills essentially worthless. Twenty-five-year-olds too busy to keep up with new systems find themselves replaced by 20-year-olds whose minds are in mint condition, armed with the latest ideas. Train, train and retrain, and pray you don't fall off the merry-go-round as it gathers speed. Computer giant IBM once boasted in its employee handbook, "In nearly 40 years, no person employed on a regular basis has lost as much as one hour of working time because of layoff." That was 1981, when it employed more than 400,000 people world-wide. Today, it employs about 225,000.

The demand for expertise in this field may be illusory, for two reasons. The first involves the globalization of software design. Multinational companies contract software development on a global basis. Programmers in Pakistan come at a far lower cost than young North Americans. More sophisticated software is increasingly being assembled overseas. Who knows what effect this will have on young Canadians rushing to fill the job void in computer software? Furthermore, software is getting progressively easier to use. Internet-based services such as the World Wide Web require almost no training – even I can do it. Intuitive and flexible programs such as Intuit's Quicken can be used by amateurs to perform tasks that would have formerly required specialized programming abilities. ·

While many experts predict huge employment growth in this area, some are more dubious. They contend that as computers become more standardized and easier to use, they will require less technical support. Still, it's a better bet than studying to repair type-writers.

Architects and Engineers

The number of Canadians employed as architects or engineers has stagnated since 1989 at about 160,000. Full-time employment has dropped by 5,000, offset by growth in the numbers of architects and engineers who are self-employed. Some are at the cutting edge of developments (they're on the Work 1 list); others are scrounging for work. There are plenty of new graduates in these traditionally attractive fields, but opportunities are limited, particularly by the decline in construction activity. Again, new technology is making the work easier and workers more replaceable. Design engineers often command hefty fees these days. But they are helping to design systems that make design easier through the use of – what else? – computers. Computer-aided design (CAD) has been around since the early 1980s, but only in recent years has it started to make a difference. All of a sudden, fewer architects and fewer engineers can do a lot more work.

Consider the following example. California-based Pacific Gas and Electric uses CAD to design wiring for huge concrete-and-steel developments. Technical drawings that used to take 500 hours of highly trained professionals' time can now be done in 50 hours. The side effects are predictable: a cornucopia of unemployed and under-employed architects and engineers. The situation will get worse when those construction firms that still like to do things the old way – two-dimensional black-and-white plans – are inevitably drawn on stream. Calgary architect Barry Pendergast says that many builders are only beginning to accept that the revolution is at hand. Clients increasingly want to be involved in design and that's one of the areas where the computer is invaluable. Construction firms that don't catch on in a hurry will disappear.

Lawyers

How the mighty have fallen. Is any other field so glutted, with the possible exception of East Coast fishermen? For a quarter of a century, the number of lawyers just kept growing. In 1995, the bubble burst, the number of active lawyers dropping by 3,500, in one year. More than 3,000 lawyers graduate every year, but the Canadian market is pretty well saturated. Some young lawyers pay law firms for the opportunity to article. An estimated 20% of lawyers with less than five years experience were unemployed in 1995.

This used to be such a cozy profession, but suddenly there are too many lawyers and too little money. Politicians like Mike Harris aren't making things any easier. His Ontario government has eliminated 20 classes of services from the legal aid system, beefed up eligibility requirements and reduced fees. Legal aid work wasn't making criminal lawyers rich, but they needed it to keep them busy when more lucrative clients weren't buying. In recent years, it's accounted for up to 75% of criminal lawyers' incomes.

Law offices now rely on computers as much as any other sector.

CD-ROMs linked with on-line services keep firms abreast of changes in the legal system, particularly tax law and its accompanying regulations. In the past, some law firms traditionally kept two or more people on staff collating and storing updated material. Now, hypertext and other advanced search engines allow small firms to compete with larger ones, whose huge research libraries no longer offer such a distinct advantage. New technology is also changing the look and function of the law office. Increasing numbers of lawyers do their own secretarial work using PCs. Modems and faxes allow more lawyers to work from home. During the 1994 G7 summit in Halifax, for example, one of that city's largest law firms donated its office space to the federal government. For many of the senior partners, the experience was an eye-opener: they found they could work at home as efficiently, or more efficiently, as they could from downtown.

At least one legal specialty stands to do very well, however: lawyers who understand the new world of high-tech international business transactions and intellectual property. Industries with very deep pockets are willing to spend generously to defend or enhance their marketplace opportunities. That means huge fees for a limited number of people who have had the time, energy and money to train both in law and in other high-tech fields. But for many other lawyers, as well as their paralegal and support staff, the scramble for tight revenues is the order of the day.

Accountants

The accounting profession is doing marginally better than law. Since 1990, growth has averaged about 2.5% a year. Two-thirds of this increase is the result of growth in part-time and self-employed accountants.

Your average Canadian accountant is starting to have problems, because computer software such as Quicken makes doing accounts and income tax relatively simple for anyone with a keyboard. On the other hand, accountants who can quickly assimilate methods that dovetail with the needs of the over-heated knowledge industries – understanding how to work with intangible assets such as patents and other intellectual property – can prosper. According to Robert McLean, executive director of the International Federation of Institutes for Advanced Study, the accountants who will lead their field will be those who can "measure, over the long run, return on investment in people skills, information bases and technological capabilities within organizations."[10]

TRADITIONAL SERVICES

About a quarter of all Canadian employment falls under this category. During the Spend-and-Share era, jobs in traditional services grew at an annual rate of 3.3%; since 1990 that has dropped to 1.3%.

Retail Trade

This sector was particulary hot during the Spend-and-Share era. Average annual employment growth was 2.8%, a response to ever-increasing consumer demand. By 1989, 1.7 million Canadians were working in a retail establishment. Since then, the sector has produced no new jobs. In fact, it has lost ground: 30,000 full-time jobs were wiped out since 1989. Of course, this was offset by a trend evident across the economy: more part-time and self-employed workers.

Retail sales haven't exactly withered and died. They've been increasing by 2% a year. But retailers are meeting cost pressures by finding ways of making staff a less-important part of the sales equation. The Internet, of course, lurks on the horizon – a more efficient way of buying, and selling, and a most efficient way of eliminating jobs. Add increased foreign competition and you have fewer and less- lucrative employment opportunities.

The casualties are everywhere. Woodwards and Brettons have faded into history. Dylex and Cadillac-Fairview are hanging on by their fingertips. The Bay, Eaton's and Sears – the growing retailers of earlier decades – have fallen on tough times. We have passed a turning point: since 1990, department store revenues have been decreasing while those for other retailers (mainly "big box" stores and specialty retailers) have been increasing.

Part of the retail story is predicated on somnolent growth in consumer demand, which is important enough to consider separately in the next chapter. After climbing by 4.3% per year for almost 25 years, consumer demand has slowed dramatically to an annual average of about 1%.

Then there's the "big box" competition from the U.S., using all its buying muscle on a continental basis. Retailers such as Wal-Mart Canada, Future Shop and Price Club/Costco are "category killers," capable of monopolizing whole niche markets and driving other retailers out of business. Almost all of these chains run non-union shops and pay close to the minimum wage, with minimum benefits. And they are deadly competitors; by 1995, sales in traditional major department stores, such as Eaton's, Sears and the Hudson's Bay Company had dropped for three straight years. Even Zeller's, the darling of the Canadian retail trade for most of the 1980s, is hurting. Earlier in 1996, it announced plans to move its head office from Montreal to Toronto in order to gain "operating efficiencies."

The announcement followed a 72% drop in fourth-quarter profit.

In tandem with lower demand and more competition, there's our old friend technology. Inventory control is now largely handled by computers, so human beings are no longer needed to take stock. Just-in-time delivery – goods that arrive in warehouses only days before being shipped to stores – means fewer workers. Price scanners make cashiers more efficient, so fewer of them are needed. And it's going to get worse. With new portable scanners, developed by U.S.-based Symbol Technologies in cooperation with a Dutch supermarket chain, customers will become their own check-out clerks. A hand-held device about the size of a cell phone, the scanner reads bar codes, totals the bill and even allows consumers to pay with credit cards. Argyll, the owner of Safeway and Presto supermarket chains in Britain, plans to eliminate 1,000 employees under a "re-engineering" plan that centers around self-scanning. Estimated savings: about $40 million a year.

Employees in customer service departments may also be headed for the door. Take the Hudson's Bay Company. The Bay's four interactive systems handle 15,000 to 20,000 telephone calls a week. Three connect with customers, dealing with inquiries about balances, bill payments and credit limits. Another handles in-store calls. Only half of these calls still require a live operator. And the Bay is preparing to move to voice recognition next, which will handle the 50,000 calls a year that deal with changes of address.

New technology in the retail sector isn't always a job killer. Take the example of Shoppers Drug Mart which has invested heavily in computer systems and software to provide its pharmacists with information on drug interactions, allergies and possible medication abuse. Unlike the U.S., where drug stores are forced to cope with the loss of market share to mail order giants like Medco, the Canadian regulatory environment which controls pharmacare prescriptions has so far limited the growth of this distribution channel in Canada.

In unregulated sectors, however, new technology, especially the Internet, poses a real threat to retail jobs. American catalogue giants such as Land's End, L.L. Bean and J.C. Penny have been quick to adjust to the advantages of the Internet which has the promise of offering consumers a combination of convenience, low prices and quality merchandise. In addition to providing access to products, Internet-based services allow users instant access to real time videos on subjects such as how to take measurements for a shirt or how to assemble a piece of furniture. Still in its infancy, Internet shopping will grow quickly as virtual malls spread through cyberspace. The key will be development of secure systems for conducting financial transactions over the Net.

To that end, a new kind of electronic money is being launched by financial interests around the world. This is E-cash, currency that moves along multiple electronic channels largely outside established networks. These channels enable consumers and businesses to send money to each other more cheaply, conveniently and quickly than through the banking system. Emerging brands include Mondex, DigiCash and Cybercash.

Citicorp is developing what it calls the Electronic Monetary System, an entire infrastructure for using electronic money issued by it and other banks. Just as surely as pieces of eight were replaced by paper currency, we will soon think very differently about money. Like E-cash, digital money will permit on-line shopping, where you will zap money to a merchant over the Internet. All of this may be ho-hum in a few years, but Tracey DeLeeuw is on top of it already. DeLeeuw, a 28-year-old single mother with a high-school degree and computer smarts, put 350 technology-related products up for sale on the Internet. Within six hours she had 240 orders and 1,000 requests for information.[11] DeLeeuw's company, Winnipeg-based ManGlobe Virtual, is a Net-based electronic shopping mall as well as a financial processing, distribution, customs and currency exchange center. Because she wasn't set up to accept credit cards and had not anticipated customs costs, she ran into some early problems. But the problems were a blessing in disguise, because they forced her to come up with solutions. If Canada Post took care of distribution and customs brokerage, and if the Royal Bank managed financial transactions and currency exchange, and if the phone company looked after telecommunications and Internet access, then, she thought, "This might work!" DeLeeuw, a former salesclerk, coordinated it all and is on her way to being one of those self-made women (or men) who the optimists say will rise from the ashes of all those destroyed retail jobs. Whenever they do, it will certainly be exciting. But how many Tracy DeLeeuws will be able to make a decent living in the future of Canadian retailing?

Personal Services

Except perhaps at its seamier edges, this is is not a sector in which many people get rich quick. But during the 1960s, '70s and '80s it was a sector where a high-school degree – or less – could earn you decent money. Personal services included jobs at hotels, restaurants, beauty salons and amusement and recreation centers. It included car washers, security guards, bartenders and babysitters. The jobs still exist, but they are increasingly part-time.

In this category, the number of people who can make enough money to get by usually depends on the shape of the economy; many services involve expenditures that are to some degree discretionary. For example, barbers know that in tough times people get fewer haircuts. Canadians are still spending money on personal services but have started to cut back. Between 1967 and 1989, employment growth here averaged just under 4% per year. Since then, full-time positions have grown by less than 1.5%, while part-time employment has expanded by almost 5%. (The two fastest-growing job categories in the American economy are security guards and maids, a combination that certainly has a Newt Gingrich ring to it.)

If you are looking for a job that serves mass market consumers, prospects are less than encouraging. Once again, the electrons are on the prowl for ways to nudge us to the sidelines. Some fast-food drive-through restaurants are replacing order takers with touch-sensitive menu screens. And your morning wake-up at the hotel is more likely than not to be digitized. Using computers, a fast food outlet can now change menu boards in two minutes; it used to take five hours. At the hair salon, digital hairdos are all the rage. Clients can have their image scanned into a computer, where it is digitally manipulated with various hairdos; clients see what they'll look like before the scissors go into action. So far, at least, human beings are still doing the actual clipping.

Despite these developments, personal services is where many people end up after being evicted from the mainstream economy. Secretaries become hairdressers, meter readers become security guards. On British Columbia's Sunshine Coast, you can get your hair cut by a man who lost his job at the gas utility. In Toronto, I am frequently driven by cabdrivers who once had better jobs. Companies call it downsizing. For their discarded employees, downgrading is a more appropriate word.

There will always be jobs in personal services, but many of them have a common denominator: they don't pay well. Security guards, car rental jockeys, laundry workers, bartenders, taxi drivers, couriers, theatre ushers, manicurists, hairdressers, valet parking attendants – these kinds of jobs come open from time to time, and young Canadians grab them as fast as they do. They won't get rich, and they probably won't be contributing to a pension plan. But they do pay the phone bill. Don't be surprised if the young man or woman collecting your FedEx parcel has a university degree. For many young people, that's all that's out there these days.

NON-MARKET SERVICES

Non-market services, as the name suggests, are essentially community services, services performed outside the marketplace, usually paid for by taxpayers. These jobs were almost the signature of the Spend-and-Share era, when governments were deemed to be part of the solution, rather than part of the problem. The electorate wanted better schools, more social services, improved health care, new recreational facilities – the works. Hundreds of thousands of jobs opened up for teachers, social workers, public servants, health-care personnel, recreation workers or just about anyone who wanted to help build a better society and make pretty good money at the same time.

This sector grew by 3.5% a year from 1967 to 1989, when more than one in five Canadians worked in non-market services, either as public servants or in taxpayer-supported fields such as health care or education. Since 1989, employment growth has plummeted (to an average annual rate of about 1.2%), then stopped altogether; since 1994 it has actually started to drop. This decline came before the Harris government in Ontario announced plans to drive a bulldozer through the public sector. It also occurred before the first round of federal cuts, scheduled to trim 45,000 civil servants.

Not only are real employment levels dropping, but opportunities for advancement are drying up and wage levels are either flattening out or in decline. There are three main sub-sectors in non-market services: education, health and social services, and public administration. Each is having problems.

Education

Each spring in the late 1960s and early '70s, school board recruiters fanned out across the country seeking new teachers at universities and teachers' colleges, often bidding against one another for the services of "B" and even "C" students. At the University of Manitoba, the shortage of teachers in the late 1960s was so acute that the government waived tuition fees for education students. They even allowed new teachers into the classroom at the elementary level with only one year of post-secondary training. (That's how my wife, Margaret, started her teaching career at the tender age of 18. So young did she look that she was asked for a date by a young man in the sixth grade; she declined.) These days, "A" and "A+" graduates apply for teaching jobs whenever there's an opening, then wait, and wait, and wait. During the 1970s, the number of teachers increased by about 8%, and by about 4% during the 1980s. But in the '90s growth in Canadian education slowed and in 1995 there were nearly 20,000 fewer jobs in the sector than in 1994. The prognosis is gloomy for all the usual reasons: surplus workers, delayered management, privatization, shifting demographics and increased productivity through new technology.

There are now an estimated 18,000 surplus primary and secondary teachers in Canada. Qualified teachers are accepting jobs as teachers' assistants. Some are so desperate that they are doing volunteer work in schools in order to gain experience. At the post-secondary level, the Association of Universities and Colleges of Canada reports that in 1995 there were 15 applicants for each new position. About 2,000 teachers graduated from universities and teachers' colleges in 1995. The odds that many of them will be standing in front of a classroom anytime soon are not good.

Nor is this a short-term phenomenon. Several factors are likely to constrain educational employment for a very long time. The cash crunch faced by all levels of government is leading to a massive overhaul of the education system. This will involve more round-the-clock use of facilities, longer school years, larger classes, more user charges and reduced salaries and benefits for teachers. In Ontario, Grade 13 has finally been retired. Administrators are being pared accordingly. Alberta has merged 141 school boards into fewer than 60. Similar changes are taking place in Ontario, where a purge is under way aimed at downsizing, reorganizing and rationalizing major administrative functions.

At community colleges, funding cutbacks are narrowing course options and increasing tuition fees. Federal grants, which once provided as much as 25% of community college funding, have been cut to near zero. Winnipeg's Red River Community College has eliminated 70 teaching positions since 1990, and you don't need a crystal ball to see that more are coming. Federal support to universities has been in steady decline for years. Increases in tuition fees and reductions in programs and staff have followed in their wake. Many tenured professors in their late sixties are refusing to retire, blocking opportunities for younger people.

Of course, part of the reason that teaching jobs aren't coming on stream is that young people aren't coming on stream. The percentage of Canadians under 18 has been declining for the past 15 years. During the boom era, that might have meant smaller classes and more money for libraries and other amenities. But not in the Sink-or-Swim era. Total funding levels for education are dropping, by about 2% in 1995. Deeper cuts are in the works.

No profession requires greater "people skills" than teaching, but that doesn't mean improved technology isn't costing jobs. It is easier for teachers to handle split classes when they have machines as helpers. At the primary level, a host of new computer and CD-ROM teaching tools are coming to market that may revolutionize the teaching of basic skills. The Amazing Writing Machine from Broderbund, for example, features a built-in thesaurus and spell checker, and helps children illustrate their own stories, poems and letters. Games like Spell It from Davidson reinforce spelling skills through games. And Math Blaster Mystery teaches math through the use of clever prompts. These computerized devices help children learn at their own pace. So central have computers become to learning that there is growing concern that the large gap in computer ownership between high and low-income households could boost the educational advantage that rich kids have traditionally enjoyed.

At the junior and senior secondary level, CD-ROM encyclopedias are used for research. They come with note takers, so students can take notes and download text, pictures, music, video clips and animation. In Cross-Country Canada, a CD-ROM interactive teaching program, children take the wheel of a truck and drive across Canada, learning about the country on the way. Dinaparktycoon, created by the Minnesota Education Computer Consortium, simulates a business that markets dinosaurs. How much do you need to feed them? How many people do you need to take care of them? What happens when you forget to fence them in? If you handle your dinosaurs right, you make money. If you don't, you go broke.

At the post-secondary level, the Internet makes it possible for more students to share professors with the best credentials. Indeed, professors without an electronic following may soon have trouble keeping their jobs. The concept of tenure – guaranteed employment to maintain freedom of speech among university teachers – is fraying at the edges. Trevor Hodge, a professor of classics at Carleton University in Ottawa, calls tenure a myth. "The real issue," insisted Hodge in the *Globe and Mail*, "is not tenure or non-tenure for new staff. It is that, as the budget is cut and senior, and expensive, professionals retire, they are increasingly replaced by sessional lecturers. These are part-time employees hired on a one-year contract for one course, often at a salary so ludicrously low that it would be pure exploitation except that the university can afford nothing better."[12] In the halls of academe, like everywhere else, more electronics means fewer employees. If sound studios can steal musicians' notes, can cartoon-character "professors" spouting stolen ideas through your home computer be far behind?

HEALTH AND SOCIAL SERVICES

More than 10% of Canadians earn their living in the health and social service sector. During the Spend-and-Share era, employment in this category grew at a rate of 4.3% a year, the fastest rate of growth for any except business services. But since 1994, employment growth has averaged 2%. This decline is merely a harbinger of the job losses that will cut into this sector during the rest of the decade. Federal reductions to provincial health and social service budgets – almost $7 billion – will not be fully implemented until 1997.

Intense fiscal pressure is leading to gut-wrenching cuts in hospital and medical services. There is a national surplus of nurses, dentists and primary-care physicians. About 20,000 hospital beds have been closed since 1990. Entire hospitals are being shut down across Canada. Medical school enrollment has been cut by 6% nationally, and in some training facilities the intake of interns has been trimmed by as much as 30%.

There is evidence of a dramatic shift in the nature of work in the health-care sector. Hospital cutbacks have forced allied health professionals, such as nurses and LPNs, into positions that do not use their full range of skills. Underemployment is a growing problem. The Canadian Nurses Association estimates that thousands of nurses are unable to find jobs that use their full talents. Many work at private nursing homes, with poor pay, casual hours and few benefits. According to one insider, as many as 10,000 have not been able to find a job at all.

"Why are nurses so expendable?" the *Edmonton Journal* wondered in a 1995 editorial. The answer, of course, was that the provincial government had just finished cutting $734 million from its health-care budget. In the first year of those cuts, the United Nurses of Alberta lost 10% of its membership. More nurses and hospital workers will lose their jobs all across Canada as Ottawa cuts health-care payments to the provinces and the provinces do likewise in their own jurisdictions.

Hospitals have begun replacing nurses, dietitians, social workers and physiotherapists with nursing assistants and others with less training. For example, there is a movement to replace registered nurses with licensed practical nurses. It's happening everywhere and could cost thousands of RNs their jobs. Computers and other sophisticated technology permit people with less training to monitor electronic instruments that signal danger – the kind of danger signals registered nurses have always kept in their heads. Nurses who manage to keep their jobs have had to adjust to the new economic realities. In 1995, Quebec's 45,000 unionized nurses approved a contract that would give them a 0.5% wage hike in 1996 and 1% in 1997 and 1998. Meanwhile, few, if any, new nurses were being taken on.

If nursing assistants are cheap alternatives to nurses, nurses are cheap alternatives to doctors. In 1994, Ontario's NDP government began training groups of nurses to perform tasks previously reserved for doctors. Medical personnel will be in greater demand when the baby boomers hit their seventies, but that's a two-decade wait.

Patients are being encouraged to keep their stay in hospital as brief as possible. New mothers are now sent home as quickly as 36 hours after delivery. Medical treatment for a host of conditions, including kidney stones and narrowing of the arteries, are handled on an out-patient basis. In an effort to reduce the number of chronically ill patients likely to require years of treatment, some hospitals are spurning elderly patients.

From hospital administrators, you will hear a litany of complaints about reduced funding and increased patient demand. Dietary and food service operations at many of Canada's leading hospitals are being contracted out to private companies such as Nestlé Canada or the U.S.-owned Marriot Food Services Group, both of which use "cook and chill" technology to mass-produce meals at central locations and deliver them to hospitals "just-in-time" for the dinner hour.

New laboratory technology allows specimens to be evaluated with fewer technicians at a far lower cost. Surgery, once performed from nine to five, is now performed around the clock at many hospitals. Improved drugs are reducing the need for so many care-givers and surgeons in the treatment of patients. These drugs, produced in virtually workerless environments, often prove more effective and less costly than surgery. Fifteen per cent of Canada's health-care expenditures now is allocated to drugs – more than is paid out to physicians.

Canada is reputed to have the best health-care system in the world, but that doesn't seem to make it a great place to find work. In 1995, most of the graduating class from the occupational and physiotherapy program at the University of Manitoba accepted jobs south of the border. Major U.S. employers regularly conduct success-ful raiding operations in Canada looking for nurses and physicians. A study published by the Canadian Medical Association estimates that between 1990-1994, 2,500 physicians relocated to the U.S.[13]

When people lose jobs, as they are throughout Canada, they tend to have more economic and social problems. But that doesn't mean there will be people there to help them. In July 1995, *Toronto Star* social policy reporter Laurie Monsebratten painted a vivid picture of job prospects in the social services field after the Quebec govern-ment introduced experiments in work-for-welfare. Her first four sentences tell the story: "When Alain Lacasse went to college to study the sociology of ageing almost 10 years ago, he believed he was preparing himself for the jobs of the future. Today the 34-year-old Montrealer is on welfare and spends 20 hours a week as a recreation assistant for the elderly at a provincial nursing home. For his efforts he receives $100 a month – about $1.25 an hour – on top of his $550 welfare cheque. What's worse, the union says he is doing the work of a woman who was recently laid off and was making more than $12 an hour. 'Not only are my job prospects slim, but I have stolen another worker's position,' he says."[14] In the spend-and-share era, nobody would have believed that story. In the Sink-or-Swim era, it no longer comes as much of a surprise.

PUBLIC ADMINISTRATION

Canadians have always had a far greater belief in the ability of governments to improve society than Americans have; it's one of the few ways people have been able to tell these two nations apart. But Canadians became disenchanted with governments in the late 1980s and early '90s, and pressures mounted to deflate bureaucracies. Employment in all levels of government declined by 36,000 in 1995, a drop of 1.6%. Public sector wages and salaries also declined. Both will likely continue to drop, in response to further fiscal restraint at all levels of government.

In 1995, the federal human resources development department (HRD) was wedged between two huge problems: high unemployment and growing government debt. When a department committed to creating jobs announces that 3,500 jobs are being eliminated at federal job centers, you know that debt takes precedence over the unemployment. The department believed it could save the government $2.8 billion over three years by streamlining department operations. Part of the plan involves closing 150 Canada Employment Centres, replacing them with – what else? – job-killing technology, in the form of 400 kiosks dispensing job information electronically.

A nice irony: the very federal department specifically designated to create jobs is deploying technology to cut its own costs. Lesson: the job problem is going to get a lot worse before it gets better. Ever-increasing efficiency has won the day, at every level of the private and public sector. There is no looking back.

The HRD, in fact, is a leader in technological innovations that replace people with equipment. This department uses voice processing to respond to the public's information requests over the telephone, allowing reduced numbers of employees to concentrate on Work 1 kinds of decision-making. The department receives more than 30 million calls a year about unemployment benefits. Periphonics Corp. has installed a service that can handle inquiries on 840 telephone lines. For example, with an application called Insurance Services, available 7 a.m. to 11 p.m., callers learn how to qualify for benefits, where the nearest Canada Employment Centre is and how and when to file claims. On another application, recorded messages are available 24 hours a day with job information and employment programs. Tests showed that nearly all calls were made outside normal business hours, and that 65% of callers voluntarily chose the recorded message rather than switching to an operator. Efficient? Unquestionably! Responsive? Absolutely! Saving tax dollars? No doubt. Creating jobs? No, actually – killing them.

The public service, in short, is no longer a happy hunting ground for young Canadians in search of jobs. In her 1995 report to Parliament, Clerk of the Privy Council Jocelyn Bourgeon noted that the federal public service has one of the oldest workforces in the country. Without new blood, Bourgeon said, the federal bureaucracy faces a leadership vacuum within 10 years, when 70% of its executives will be able to retire.

Brad Cline, 33, graduated from Carleton University in 1986 with a master's degree in public administration, but left the government for the private sector in 1993. "I don't want to sound like a Generation X whiner," he told the *Ottawa Citizen* in 1995, "but people my age are just stuck. Any job I could do in government is either going to be abolished or some 45-year-old is in it." [15]

The shakedown in services is happening across the entire spectrum. The reasons are well known to the millions of workers who have already been affected: intense competition (often from new foreign players), tight margins, shrinking revenue, high debt levels and the arrival of new technology that enables many jobs to be performed more efficiently and others cut. But what of the consequences? What happens when so many people are simultaneously affected by powerful new forces that threaten the security of their jobs?

I'm not convinced that the new economy has any magical power to correct the dislocation being experienced by millions. Of course, there are individual stories of stunning successes in the new economy – young entrepreneurs who have become millionaires, disabled people able to perform new tasks, companies that have triumphed in a digital global economy. But these anecdotes hide the harsher reality of the past six years: good, secure jobs are getting harder to find. This is not a short-term downturn, but part of a broader transformation that can't be ignored.

No economist, and no entrepreneur, should be allowed to maintain that the job situation will sort itself out before long – especially if we are talking about the "safe" full-time jobs of the past. When? How? Are exciting new jobs going to open up in biotechnology? Yes. Are there going to be many of them? No. Are there several exciting new fields similar to biotechnology? Indeed. Are they going to supply nearly the number of jobs being displaced by technology? Not that I can see.

I have asked all kinds of optimistic experts to explain how the magical transformation to a new, high-employment economy is going to happen. Sooner or later, they start muttering that it "has always" happened before, that technology "has never let us down yet." It is time to pull our heads out of the sand and adjust to a painful truth: the new economy is going to estrange more people from good jobs. What the new economy *is* producing is job insecurity, longer working hours, a surplus of labour, more part-time workers, a social safety net full of holes and the potential for growing income disparities between rich and poor.

I have a friend who is a senior administrator at a community college. Most mornings, he arrives at work at six and isn't home until eight at night. He's working harder than ever – with no extra pay – for two reasons. Several of his colleagues have been fired in recent years as part of the college's downsizing program and he has to do their jobs. Also, like many people, he believes that if he works even harder, he can escape the next bullet. In a survey we carried out late in 1995, about two-thirds of all Canadian workers reported that they were working longer hours compared with a few years ago; only about a quarter said they were getting paid for this extra effort.

Especially in services, too many people are chasing too few jobs. The unemployment figures hide the full extent of the labour surplus Canada currently faces. As many as 7% of Canadians have simply left the labour force because they have abandoned hope of finding a job. That means people who have succumbed to despair are responsible for making terrible unemployment rates look merely bad. And every time a few thousand jobs are created, the unemployment rate doesn't drop the way it used to; that's because an equal number of these invisible unemployed decide that conditions may be improving and start looking for a job. The largest group waiting to enter the job market is made up of young Canadians, many of whom have retreated in the 1990s to the safety of post-secondary education.

It's a harsh economy when people are forced to take on two or three jobs, often without benefits, to make ends meet. The movement to part-time, flexible work is swamping the job market. We're talking about the creation of a new "servant class," whose main role will be to attend to the personal needs of the wealthiest 20% of the population. This is the 20% that advises ordinary people to make themselves "flexible" in the workplace. As labour historian Jamie Swift points out in *Wheel of Fortune*, when some people speak of the advantages of flexibility, they are really talking about the advantages of compliance.

Unequal access to hours of work is a major cause of the increasing inequality of earnings in Canada. The use of a "core" of full-time workers, many of them working longer hours, supplemented with increasing numbers of part-time, part-year or contract workers, provides companies with greater flexibility. It allows them to focus training and advancement on a diminishing number of core workers. In effect, it creates two classes of workers. One of the most widely debated issues of the 1990s is the possibility of the decline of the middle class. Traditionally, Canada has taxed progressively and spread its wealth around relatively fairly. It has never come close to being the socialist society that the more privileged classes bemoan, but it hasn't done badly for a capitalist economy struggling to compete on the same continent with the most capitalist nation in history.

This is beginning to change. Richer Canadians are getting richer. Poorer Canadians are getting poorer. Good jobs still pay a lot. Bad jobs still pay a pittance. The problem is that jobs in the middle are evaporating. "Modern economic forces," reported Alanna Mitchell in a 1996 *Globe and Mail* series, "are shaping the labour force around two poles: the haves and the have nots. But it's not just wages. This polarization is manifesting itself on many fronts: people who work too many hours compared with those who work too few; people who have long and valuable tenure in their jobs compared with those who are deemed disposable."[16] A sense of fairness also seems to be evaporating. Our surveys show that wealthy Canadians – those who are benefiting from the new economy – are the most likely to applaud when social programs are cut back, when talk turns to even more deficit cutting and when tax cuts are advanced as the means of solving the problems facing the less fortunate.[17] The only thing holding back the kind of widening gap between rich and poor experienced in the U.S. is Canada's systems of taxation and income transfers. The transfers have already been cut, but the full force of reductions won't be felt until 1997. As for taxation, the Reaganesque rhetoric is already in evidence in Alberta and Ontario: cut programs and put more money in people's pockets and jobs will reappear.

Several analysts, including the *Toronto Star*'s respected economics editor, David Crane, see a solution in retraining. That sounds nice, and to some degree it makes sense. But it assumes that there will be plenty of work in the New Utopia if only we can match our skills to the changing needs of the marketplace. There's a kernel of truth here – some job vacancies do go wanting because Canadians have not been trained to fill them. But not many. Crane's theory is helpful at one level but ultimately dangerous at another, because it does not deal with the essential problem: it doesn't matter how willing, or how trained, workers are if improved technology and a global marketplace are creating a society in which there will not – cannot – be enough decent jobs to go around.

In fact, the effect of globalization and new technology in many sectors is to reduce, not increase, the skill requirements of workers. Many now spend much of their day watching machines work. Telephone operators sit for hours, rarely talking with callers, as computers do their jobs for them. The cash register now tells the salesclerk how much change to give the customer. That makes for fewer mistakes, but it doesn't make for sharper cashiers. David Livingston, a sociology professor at the Ontario Institute for Studies in Education, cites one U.K. study that suggests most workers use more complex skills driving to work than they do once they arrive.

The training myth is largely based on the fact that university-educated Canadians have a better chance of finding jobs than do people with less education. On the other hand, large numbers of people – particularly younger Canadians – are working in fields completely unrelated to the area in which they studied. Their specific training is largely wasted; they are hired simply because it's assumed that they will be brighter and more adaptable than those people who didn't graduate. But it doesn't prove that raising training levels will create job opportunities. Statistics Canada data show that almost one-quarter of all workers are over-qualified. Yes, it is better to be trained at something than to not be trained to do anything. But training per se is not going to automatically solve the problem of disappearing jobs.

I know all of this sounds gloomy. I'm not gloomy by nature, and frankly my own experience in the new economy has been satisfying.

But I think it's time we faced the truth that Canada is in the middle of a very difficult time. The hopes and dreams of millions of Canadians are being swept away. The Spend-and-Share era is disappearing in the rear-view mirror and the forces of the new economy are creating congestion on the promised road to the better tomorrow. It's time we understood that the problem is much bigger than making the right choices, getting better training, working hard and being flexible. We are in danger of extending the ideology of privatization – already a core precept of the Sink-or-Swim era – to its final and most bizarre conclusion: that adapting to the new economy is fundamentally a private affair with winners and losers each masters of their own fate.

What is the future of work in a post-services society? True, new technology is freeing us from repetitive jobs, jobs that by definition machines can do. That leaves us with two problems. The first is obvious: How are most people going to make a decent living? Second, what about the principle that has been so central to the Protestant ethic dominating our society – that work gives us dignity?

Capitalism has a way of providing privilege and status to individuals who work and undermining the privilege and status of those who do not. And you can't confer any kind of status or dignity on people by forcing them to do jobs that mean little or nothing or that rob other people of legitimate jobs, as in workfare. What's the alternative to social assistance in a society in which good jobs – or any kind of jobs that might some day lead to good jobs – are increasingly scarce? The most important question in our future may not be how to find jobs, but what to do with labour that is simply not needed in the conventional wage economy. There is a simple moral question here. The new economy is conferring many benefits. How do we share them?

The current job crisis is likely to get a lot worse before it gets better – if it gets better. The full impact of new technology and globalization has yet to be felt in many job categories. Government budget-cutting and downsizing has yet to hit with full force, particularly in the provinces. Economists keep looking to the horizon, seeking ways to stimulate the consumer demand that once kept our economy expanding. But consumers are retreating into their shells. Why wouldn't they? Opportunities are disappearing, and nothing augurs well for any kind of shared prosperity in the future.

I started this discussion by talking about horses. Let's end with a horse – a horse named Boxer. One of George Orwell's most famous books is a parable called *Animal Farm*. In it, Orwell lampoons communism by comparing humanity to a barnyard in which the animals take over the farm from the humans. Before long, the shrewd and tyrannical pigs are running things in their own interests. But it isn't until a faithful old work horse named Boxer is finally hauled off to the glue factory that the other animals finally understand just how horribly the pigs have betrayed them. The moral, of course, is that socialism – supposedly devoted to the best interests of workers – is a cruel hoax. Which is exactly what it turned out to be in nearly every society that tried it.

Socialism's failure was capitalism's gain. Nearly every economy in the world has now bought full-tilt capitalism. Some formerly socialist countries, such as Russia, are having trouble adapting to capitalism In the Sink-or-Swim era. Some traditionally capitalist countries, such as Canada, are also having trouble adjusting. Unless ordinary people in all economies gain access to jobs, or other mechanisms are designed to allow them to share in the fruits of the marketplace, Orwell's pigs may start taking on new faces.

Seven

THE TRANSFORMATION
OF THE CANADIAN HOUSEHOLD

"To every action there is
always opposed an equal reaction."

Isaac Newton

In the fall of 1995, I had dinner with several Canadian CEOs whose companies manufacture or sell consumer products. All were eager to boast of the bold steps they had taken to improve the efficiency of their companies. In each case, they told upbeat stories about the benefits of new technology, muted somewhat by more somber asides about loyal employees who had been let go – the price of maintaining profits in an increasingly competitive marketplace. Eventually we started talking nuts and bolts. "How's business?" I asked. At first, a few replied that things weren't *that* bad, but before long, most admitted that sales were lousy. "We're having a lot of trouble getting people to spend money," said one CEO, a man with a long-standing reputation for success in the marketplace. "Even people with decent jobs are worried about whether they're going to keep them, so they're not spending." So there it was: the perverse irony of the Canadian economy today. The people in charge are brandishing the sharpest knives they can find, each one whetted to a razor-sharp edge, cutting the fat out of their operations. All in the name of profits, of course. The problem with knives is that they sometimes have two edges. If you're careless, it's easy to end up cutting your own throat.

I'll begin with the obvious: the knives being wielded are being pointed outward at the competition even more fiercely than they are being pointed inward at perceived inefficiencies. A street fight is under way in the international marketplace, the likes of which the world has never witnessed, not even during the swashbuckling years of the robber barons of the nineteenth century. Those old buccaneer capitalists – the Rockefellers and Morgans and their friends – were nasty, but they lacked the transportation or communications technology to wage war in every nook and cranny of the universe. Their successors lack none of these weapons. Those lines mapmakers draw on globes no longer represent latitude and longitude; they represent store shelves, stretching from your local shopping center around the world and back again. It is on those endless shelves that the war for consumers is being fought.

Business wars have always been cutthroat, but this is a no-holds-barred struggle for survival. The international commercial war escalated when the nuclear-charged cold war faded in the late 1980s. And, strange as it may seem, this fight to the death in the marketplace is the business world's idea of a peace dividend. Business people argue that no matter how intense this conflict gets, it is healthy, because if Adam Smith was right, it will benefit humanity rather than littering the landscape with discarded workers.

Even those zealots who concede that not *all* of humanity is likely to reap the rewards of unrestrained economic competition argue that *most* people will benefit, or that *many* people will benefit, or that the people who *count* will benefit (an argument usually made in private). The private argument makes some sense; the public ones are dubious. Moral arguments don't carry much weight in the 1990s. Warnings about excessive preoccupation with building a competitive rather than a humane society tend to be dismissed as outdated knee-jerk liberalism. Forgetting morality, however, there are pragmatic arguments as to why the international commercial street fight could well end up damaging combatants as well as innocent bystanders. I base one of these arguments on Newton's first law of motion: to every action there is always opposed an equal reaction. Actions in the workplace will inevitably cause reactions in the home. As surely as Canadians' personal well-being is being threatened by cost-cutting in the marketplace, the adjustments they make in their personal lives will rebound to threaten the well being of marketplace operators. Canadian business leaders may have no choice but to slash costs if they are going to compete in an open market. But nobody should pretend there won't be both an economic and social price to pay. Nor are businesses themselves likely to walk away unscathed.

When we talk about personal lives being threatened, we are talking about the fate of nearly 30 million Canadians and approximately six billion more people around the world. Depending on who they are and where they live, some will benefit from the commercial wars (lower prices, the constant search for new production centers) and some will not (the relentless pressure to replace humans with technology). In the domestic context, let's consider what are likely to be the three most important changes to the working lives of Canadians: cutbacks in jobs and benefits, the supremacy of new technology and the abandonment of loyalty to employees. These actions are dominating the workplaces of the Sink-or-Swim era. What will be the reactions in the home?

Cutbacks at work – loss of jobs, lower wages and benefits – inevitably create cutbacks at home. People with less money to spend do something fairly predictable: they spend less. Decreased household spending, of course, means decreased demand for consumer products. And decreased demand for consumer products, as any Economics 101 textbook will tell you, leads to more cutbacks at work, wherever these products are produced. This can become a vicious circle, which is what happened during the Great Depression. Unless a company is focusing entirely on foreign markets, there is a message here: don't expect improved domestic demand if ordinary people are afraid to part with their money. Even exporters aren't exempt – they will eventually have to accept that a low exchange rate on the Canadian dollar and economic expansion in countries such as China and South Korea won't carry them forever. If other countries are also replacing workers with technology (which they are, even in relatively low-wage countries such as Mexico), demand will decrease in those markets as well. So the first reaction to cuts in the workplace is that many consumers will simply not be able to buy as much product, or will be wary of buying as much product, because they have lost their jobs, are afraid of losing their jobs or have been shunted into low-wage jobs.

The second reaction, I predict, will be attitudinal. If employers are going to be ruthlessly efficient, why shouldn't consumers? If leanness and meanness create a more efficient workplace, why can't ordinary people create a more efficient home the same way? If employers are willing to go to any extreme to cut corners, why shouldn't consumers? Many of us were willing to pay a premium for image in the 1980s when brand names were the fashion. But why be a sucker if you know that with a little patience, you'll be able to buy a product of decent quality on sale? Why be loyal to a particular brand, Canadian or not, if another one is cheaper? If producers are going to inordinate lengths to squeeze workers, why not go to inordinate lengths to squeeze back?

There is a third factor. If employees who used to mean so much to the economy are suddenly expendable, why not declare things we've been purchasing for years expendable in the home? How much of what we buy do we really need? During the Spend-and-Share era, it was fashionable to indulge ourselves, buying what we wanted, whenever we wanted it. What if living more intelligently, more frugally, not only becomes more important but actually becomes fashionable? Frugality is certainly fashionable in the business world (with the exception of upper-end executive salaries). Why not at home? And if Canadians pared down their own consumption patterns, wouldn't that cause more Canadian-based companies to close? Or to be absorbed by huge corporate interests that are gaining a tighter stranglehold on the international marketplace?

If you read past the stock market analysts on the business pages, you will see that Newton is already swinging into action. Retailers in many fields are already beginning to fret. Cash registers aren't humming the way they used to, especially during traditionally high-volume periods like Christmas, when sales of high-profit merchandise compensated for slower seasons. In December 1995, a young woman interviewed on a news show put other shoppers' reticence in a nutshell: she said she now feels "foolish" if she pays more than the sale price – for anything. In short, the Draconian measures that companies the world over are taking will backfire, shrinking national economies as well as people's means of earning a living. Competition may be exciting, but not when there becomes less and less to compete for.

Economics, of course, isn't everything. In this chapter, I'd like to consider both the economic and non-economic consequences that the profound changes associated with the Sink-or-Swim era are likely to have on our personal lives, and the effect we will have on the marketplace. This new era is having a major influence on nearly every aspect of our personal lives. It will alter our internal space – our dreams, our values, our identities. And it will alter our external space – where, with whom and how we live.

Not since the mid-1960s has the Canadian household displayed such a wide range of new (and sometimes conflicting) trends. After serving as the primary engine of economic growth for two generations, household purse strings have begun to tighten. But other things are happening as well, many of them spinoffs from the new economic situation. The Canadian household is showing signs of a new stability. After years of focus on personal independence, today stronger family ties and a greater respect for interdependence seem to be returning. The divorce rate is down. More young people – and old people – are living at home. The home is becoming the hub that it hasn't been for decades. Not only are more people living at home, more people are working there. That reverses a trend that began a century ago when people started to leave the farms for more urban settings. Many Canadians displaced from the traditional workforce and others who left voluntarily have set up offices at home. In fact, the Small Office, Home Office (SOHO) phenomenon is mushrooming. In 1995, there were 1.65 million SOHOs in Canada, and by the year 2000, an estimated 40% of North American households will include at least one person running a business from home.

This is at once an economic phenomenon and a human phenomenon. Not only is the home becoming more of an economic hub, it is once again becoming an emotional hub. Your office may well be there, but so may your spouse (employed or unemployed), your mother and one or two of your grown children. It is ironic that housing, the major asset of the majority of Canadian families, is worth considerably less than it was five years ago in many markets, yet the home seems to be becoming worth more to all kinds of Canadians, young and old.

For all the stresses involved in living together, the household has a pretty functional set of shock absorbers; it is probably the most resilient institution we have. People muddle their way through tough times better when they can hold someone's hand now and then, talk things through, have the odd laugh, do what people do when they are not performing for the outside world. Canadians are going through a massive adaptation as they come to terms with the new realities. We hunker down. We pull together as best we can. "The root of the state," said Chinese poet Mencius, "is in the family."

I don't want to push the new emotional import of the family too far. I'm not saying that we are becoming like the Waltons, with all their cozy farmhouse values. Given that most Canadian families are now decidedly urban, and that intergenerational attitudes have changed, "family values" aren't ever going to be romanticized in that way. But when people are threatened, they behave differently than they do when things are going smoothly. And many Canadians are indeed threatened.

Let's take a closer look at what is happening in Canadian house-holds of the 1990s. The changes affecting them fall into two broad categories: new patterns of consumption, and new values that go beyond consumption.

CHANGING PATTERNS OF CONSUMPTION

In 1990, the longest period of sustained consumer demand in Cana-dian history shuddered to a halt. For almost 30 years, real growth in household consumer spending had increased, on average, by over 4% per year. Only once (1982) did the growth rate drop below 2%. The next year it rebounded and it flourished throughout the rest of the decade. Fully 60% of GDP growth between 1965 and 1989 was based on increased consumer spending.

During the first five years of the 1990s, however, growth in spending has inched forward at 1% a year. In only one year (1994) did it rise above 2%. When per capita spending is taken into account, consumption of personal goods and services actually declined between 1989 and 1995.

When consumer spending first began to topple in 1990, analysts blamed the country's national scapegoat, Brian Mulroney. And why not? Mulroney's government had introduced the reviled GST in 1990, which immediately made a host of household goods and services more expensive. Canadians shuffled south to make GST-free purchases, creating temporary mini-booms in such cities as Buffalo and Bellingham. By 1992, the shock of the GST had started to wear off. The declining value of the Canadian dollar made U.S. purchases increasingly expensive. But even with most Canadians staying home, consumer spending growth didn't return. This time post-recession blues were blamed, which meant that there was nothing to worry about, really. Recessions were part of the normal business cycle and hadn't been anything to get exercised about since the 1930s. One bank economist (echoing dozens of others) said that Canada was undergoing nothing more than "the kind of adjustment that normally follows a recession." Indeed, by 1994 it seemed that the worst was behind us. Consumer spending growth finally rose above 2% that year. But it proved to be a blip. By 1996 it had become obvious that there was nothing traditional or short-term about the "adjustment" taking place in the economy.

Now, retailers and manufacturers are increasingly concerned that emaciated consumer spending will be a chronic symptom of the post-1989 economy. They have every reason to worry. The current state of household finances in Canada is not encouraging. In fact, it's alarming. The unemployment rate, hovering between 9% and 11%, is clearly understated, given the hordes who have given up finding work and aren't counted as jobless any more. Even for those working, average take-home pay has declined. Debt levels have risen. Assets – particularly homes – have lost value in nearly every part of the country. The jobs available are more and more likely to be low-paying, meaning there is less chance to earn what was once deemed a good living. Not to mention the widespread fear that the safety net constructed for the sick, disadvantaged and elderly may soon be unrecognizable.

ANXIETY ABOUT TODAY: THE FISCAL SQUEEZE ON CANADIAN HOUSEHOLDS

Since 1990, individual take-home pay has fallen by approximately 5%. The decline can be blamed on a combination of wage cuts, fewer hours worked and increased taxes. At the same time, debt levels have increased from 79% to 92% of personal disposable income. Housing prices, which kept increasing during the Spend-and-Share era, giving homeowners the feeling that they were getting wealthier, have dropped significantly in most cities, particularly in eastern Canada.

The decline in take-home income follows a dozen years of little or no income growth. In spite of this, consumer spending continued to grow during this period. Why? First, there was a sizable increase in dual-income households (particularly in what comedians then referred to as DINKS – double income, no kids); hence, disposable *household* income actually increased during these years. Second, there was inflation which encouraged consumption because of expectations of rising prices and incomes.

The debt loads borne by Canadian families today make it difficult for all but the most affluent to consider major new purchases. In the past, Canadians have quickly paid down their debt during tough economic times. For example, household debt dropped from 75% to 62% of disposable income during the recession of the early 1980s. The failure of consumers to rein in debt levels this time around demonstrates how seriously household balance sheets are out of whack. Who's making the big bucks lately? Surprise! The people we owe money to – the banks and the credit card companies.

Through most of the 1970s and 1980s, continuous inflation left the impression that assets would just keep increasing in value, making the debt level seem progressively less onerous. For example, the average selling price for houses increased by 25% during the 1980s. Inflation made our pay packets seem generous; the number of dollars the typical wage earner brought home actually went up by more than 70% over the decade. But what many of us didn't notice was that those dollars were getting thinner and thinner. Since most Canadians had grown used to feeling better off, and since they naturally *wanted* to feel better off, many decided to ignore the warning signals. The result was an orgy of spending.

Today, a far different dynamic is evident. Inflation is minuscule, pay cuts are as prevalent as pay raises, and household savings have been laid to waste. Many Canadians find it touch-and-go just keeping up with monthly bills. For many more, the situation has deteriorated into the once unthinkable world of personal bankruptcy. In the first seven months of 1995, there were 36,118 consumer bankruptcies across Canada, up 16% from the same period in 1994 and 1% higher than the record recession-ridden year of 1991. Visa and MasterCard balances surged to $17.4 billion in 1995, an increase of 13%, even while Canadian pay increases averaged only 1%. And Gib McMullen, executive director of the Credit Counselling Service of Ottawa, predicts, "The record bankruptcies of 1995 are going to be nothing compared with 1996."[1]

ANXIETY ABOUT THE FUTURE: JOBS, RETIREMENT AND THE FATE OF THE SAFETY NET

During the 1990s a lot of Canadians have become alarmed about their financial security. My sister's family in Oakville is a case in point. Anne is a nurse who has been working for about eight years at a Hamilton-area hospital. Like many nurses, she has become increasingly concerned about her future in the wake of budget cuts announced by the provincial government. She and her husband have decided to delay plans to purchase a new car and are carefully re-evaluating how they spend their money. She hopes she won't be laid off, but there is always a chance that her hospital could be closed. This is not the time to spend. Scores of other nurses are probably feeling the same concern. Odds are that only three or four will lose their jobs. But who can be sure? So everyone cuts back, just in case. Thus does job anxiety sap the lifeblood out of the consumer economy.

Uncertainty has a way of magnifying problems out of all proportion, thereby creating additional problems. In the spring of 1996, about 30% of Canadian's told us they felt that they, or someone in their family, would probably be laid off or become unemployed in the next 12 months. That adds up to about 3.3 million households. Of course, 3.3 million Canadians are not going to lose their jobs next year. But what if all these people really believe that they could be the unlucky ones? That's a lot of new car purchases delayed, shoes resoled and a significant increase in the number of Kraft Dinners served. Sooner or later, the GM plant in Oshawa, the Sears shoe department in Burlington and the Loblaws meat counter in Hamilton are going to feel the effect, if they haven't already. Perception becomes reality. Prophecies – even false ones – often fulfill themselves. Job anxiety is poking at the lives of Canada's disillusioned middle class. What used to constitute fear for the young, the uneducated and seasonal workers has crept into more refined neighbourhoods. The anxiety can be expected to worsen as the full effect of dislocations associated with the transition to the new economy hits home.

All of this would make anyone, of any age, nervous. But older people, except for those already retired on fully indexed pensions, tend to be more jittery than young people, and the big bump of baby boomers is ageing quickly. Cockiness is turning into caution.

Canadians over 40 are now starting to worry about their savings.

Belatedly, I am one of them. Despite all those polls I interpreted in the 1980s, despite all the warning signs, I didn't save a nickel before I was 40. Now the rudest of the f-words, fifty, is staring me starkly in the face. Suddenly, I'm turning the cushions over on the couch looking for change to invest in retirement funds and wondering if the golden years will be made out of aluminum.

According to one recent survey, my queasiness is shared by a lot of other boomers who feel that they too have skimped on their futures. Like most, I don't have a pension plan. Like many of my friends, I didn't invest in RRSPs until interest rates became uninteresting, leaving us at the whim of mutual funds when a stock market "correction" is long overdue. Just one more worry, as tens of thousands of boomers who started saving late gamble that the TSE is their ladder to serenity.

Data on Canadian savings patterns are somewhat contradictory. Though the official "savings rate" has been in decline throughout this decade, investments in RRSP's are at record levels. Boomers are now putting more emphasis on saving than spending. Many of the expenses associated with forming families are behind them – homes have been bought (if not always paid for), the appliances are still working and the kids have part-time jobs and are buying their own clothes. So it's time to put some money aside. Good for the banks, but bad for retailers and salesclerks, especially considering that "clerk" is the country's number-one job designation.

For a huge number of Canadians, the future is becoming an obsession. Less certainty of employment. Lower wages for those lucky enough to have a job. Less protection, after welfare and unemployment insurance reform, for those without jobs. And increasing levels of debt for everyone. Consumer confidence, according our measures, is at best anemic. All of this reflects what the economic writers like to call "cautious consumers." This is a euphemism for people mesmerized by fear. Let's not be delicate. Let's not call it caution, or reluctance or uncertainty. Let's call it *trauma*.

THE NEW CANADIAN CONSUMER IS VOLATILE

People who used to buy one brand out of habit – often a habit ingrained by television advertising – have become far less monogamous. Today, the odds are no better than 50-50 that a person who picks up a product at the grocery store one week will buy the same brand a few weeks later. [2] Merchandisers, who know that it costs approximately five times as much to win a new customer as it does to keep an old one, are frantically trying to figure out how to pitch products in a way that will keep people in the fold.

In fact, customer retention has become the hot marketing issue of the decade. Clients of mine that used to spend advertising and research dollars trying to attract new consumers now funnel that money into keeping the customers they have. It's a tough job. The old slogans just don't seem to work any more. It's as though Canadians have sensed a declining commitment to them as employees and are fighting back, displaying declining loyalty when they take their hard-earned money to the stores. Air travelers used to have clear preferences for either Air Canada or Canadian. Now, they choose whoever offers the best deal. Department stores and retailers watched in horror as tens of thousands of once loyal customers marched off to Wal-Mart when it entered Canada in 1994. U.S.-based price clubs have made a huge dent in the grocery market. Even the banks are worried. Despite record profits, every bank CEO knows that they can no longer take customer loyalty for granted. Our surveys show that at any given moment, as many as 20% of all bank customers are thinking of switching banks.

THE NEW CANADIAN CONSUMER IS VALUE CONSCIOUS

Consumers with less money to spend get careful. The "I deserve this" attitude of the 1980s may still be popular with the Rolex set, but for most Canadians the splurge days are history. Bargain bins, dollar stores, second-hand sports equipment and clothing, and home renovations are now among the hot items. Says George Kosich, president of The Bay, "We no longer have the ego-intensive, free-spending consumer of the 1980s; we now have the well-informed, value-intensive, functionally inclined, price-sensitive customer of the '90s. The value-seeking customer is no longer at the lower levels of income, but at all levels of income."[3] People want the biggest bang for their buck. Some of the selling points that are most important to them fit under the following headings.

If It Saves Time, I Want It.   One of the great ironies of the Sink-or-Swim era is that we live in the most efficient society in history, but nobody seems to have any time. About 60% of Canadians we polled in early 1996 said that over the past five years their leisure time has shrunk. Not suprisingly, people crave time. Time savers ranging from McDonald's to Speedy Muffler have been growing in the marketplace since women started going out to work, and they are becoming even more precious as nervous employees log longer hours. Ottawa used to be known as a government town with a slack work ethic. No more. Much of the city's economy now depends on the computer software industry, which is known for obsessiveness in the workplace. Furthermore, employees who still work for the federal government are now often as overworked as they used to be underworked, and there is desperation in the air as public servants scurry to demonstrate why cutbacks should target somebody else, not them. One successful Ottawa dentist I know complains that he is suddenly having trouble getting patients to come in for treatment – not because they're not covered by government dental plans (they are) but because they worry about missing time at the office.

Function Over Fashion. Several months ago I scheduled a meeting at our Toronto office with some marketing people from IBM. Into the room walked two pleasant chaps, both dressed in jeans. "Sorry," I said, thinking they might be people we had hired to help with telephone surveys. "This room is reserved for a meeting we're having with IBM." "That's us," they replied. And it was. In the free-form '60s, IBM fired people if they didn't wear suits, white shirts and ties. Now, at IBM and elsewhere, function has begun to rule over fashion. Let's face it – if you're going to spend 10 to 12 hours a day at work, you might as well be comfortable. Just like all those people who have started working at home.

The computer industry is nothing if not functional. Like the world of entertainment, it understands that intense performance meshes best with comfy clothes. That's what function over fashion is all about. Where best to impress a visiting client? At the pompous big-bucks restaurant downtown or the little Vietnamese place that serves exotic delicacies and makes you feel cosmopolitan as well as comfortable? Why be boring at great cost when you can be imaginative and have money left over? Again, function over fashion.

Can't We Get Another Couple of Years Out of the Old One?   It's hard to find anyone who wants to buy anything these days that is (a) big, (b) expensive and (c) not really very interesting (washing machines, dryers, televisions, freezers, microwaves, dishwashers, furnaces or family cars). With the exception of home computers, which still carry some novelty, the purchase of so-called big ticket commodities is down sharply. Even computer equipment isn't selling as quickly as the industry had predicted. A 1994 Royal Bank survey detected a new reluctance among Canadian consumers to buy anything bigger than a breadbox unless it was absolutely needed. Clothes? Second-hand clothing stores are thriving, and people who wear "previously owned" clothing actually brag about it. Cars? Alex Drozdow, coordinator for the used car division of the Automotive Retailers Association of B.C., claims that "used cars don't carry the stigma they used to."[4] The most important trend in North American automotive retailing is the used car megastore – places like Driver's Mart, CarMax and AutoNation stock hundreds of cars. Estimates for new car sales in Canada predicted that nearly 1.25 million units would be sold in 1996, an improvement over '95's dismal showing. But less than a quarter into the year optimistic predictions had been pared down as sales were below 1995's level for the same period. Sports equipment? Many Canadian sporting goods stores have gone under, victims of the predatory pricing of American-based chains. But used sports equipment stores are popping up in their place, and it isn't unusual to see CEOs and cabinet ministers taking their children there.

Make It Last. Whatever happened to the throw-away society? In the Spend-and-Share era, disposability was a symbol of a new affluence and the plastics industry thrived. When Dustin Hoffman was told to seek a career in plastics in *The Graduate*, viewers nodded their heads. Nothing to cherish was made out of plastic, but there were lots of plastic things you could buy, use and then throw away. In the Sink-or-Swim era, you may not buy as much, but you'd like to develop some kind of relationship with what you do buy. Disposable products don't have the élan they once had.

Better Safe Than Sorry. In the mid-1950s, responsible corporate citizen that it was, Ford designed seatbelts and the padded dash. Car buyers gagged. Style was everything; safety was a turn-off. Today, car makers rush to launch vehicles with air bags up front, air bags on the doors, crumpling metal that buffers impact – structural cages worthy of space capsules – and other safety devices that Ralph Nader only dreamed of. CBC broadcaster Danny Finkleman, has wondered aloud why people don't just pull on inflated space suits and crash helmets before they climb into their cars. Boomers are beginning to feel fragile.

That's one reason Canadians love banks – despite the annoyance of service charges. The only thing we love more than banks is big banks combined with big government, to make us feel cozy. Financial columnists marching to the drum of the free market sometimes wax indignant that the federal government continues to insure the first $60,000 depositors place in Canadian banks. The suggestion is that consumers should either incur the risk of losing their deposits or assume responsibility for buying deposit insurance themselves. The way we're doing it now might irritate those who believe the private sector should be able to buy the Peace Tower, but it's so safe and secure.

Taking A Stand.   Losing their hard-earned reputation for passivity, consumers are starting to show a penchant for protest and boycotts. Ask the folks at the Sports Authority, the very successful Florida-based mega sporting goods chain. When Sports Authority opened in Toronto, it was greeted with protests, Why? Because among the many sporting goods it sold were guns. Not handguns or AK-47 assault weapons, but run-of-the-mill shotguns and rifles. No matter that Canadian Tire and many other retailers sell similar guns. No matter that guns are legal, and that hunting is still popular in rural Canada. None of this subtracted from the fact that Sports Authority had an image problem. Here was a big American firm invading the Canadian marketplace, featuring a line of merchandise that was exactly what many Canadians don't like about the United States. A survey the Angus Reid Group conducted for the Sports Authority showed that, right or wrong, it stood to lose a huge amount of business at some of its Toronto stores if it didn't change its policy. "Looks like y'all don't like guns up there" came the response from senior Sports Authority executives in Florida. "Well, they're gone." Wise move.

Rogers Cablesystems knows what it's like to be on the wrong side of consumer opinion. Canada's largest cable operator is still scrambling to defuse the ill will it engendered among Ontario and B.C.

consumers with its "negative optioning" approach to selling new packages of cable programming. Customers were furious that the onus was on them to call in to avoid being billed for new channels. Not only did Rogers vow never to do it again but it has since adopted measures to counteract its image of a marketplace bully, primarily by cutting prices on other services.

During the 1990s, Canadian consumers have become increasingly vocal in their complaints about everything from price to quality. Electric, gas and telephone utilities that once breezed big price increases past regulators now have a much tougher time, in part because the number of interventions from customers has been escalating. Just about everyone who deals with the consuming public is finding it tougher sledding. TV networks are forced to reconsider the amount of on-air violence. Food retailers deal with near consumer revolts when advertised specials are out of stock. Automobile manufacturers are forced to recall models because of defects that would have gone unreported a decade ago.

For many retailers and manufacturers, the emergence of more vocal consumers in Canada is more that just a nuisance. Indeed it can be very costly. According to Doug Saunders, writing in the *Globe and Mail* early in 1996, a number of recently successful class action suits "paves the way for a new era of Canadian consumer activism, in which people with relatively small grievances can challenge miscreant companies on behalf of thousands of other consumers, employees or shareholders."[5] Though legal precendents will likely make class actions more prevalent in Canada, the decision to use this means of redress will likely hinge on more than the action of the courts. Changing values may be equally important. As in Canadian politics, the increasing assertiveness of consumers suggests an erosion of trust in established institutions. It may also signal an equally important shift in fundamental values.

As I said earlier, economics isn't everything. Canadians are also thinking of alternate sources of happiness, many of which are likely to curb the shopping addiction we developed during the Spend-and-Share era. We may be seeing the first significant shift in consumer values since the 1960s. Now many people are starting to look for new approaches to contentment. Of course, some consumers don't have much choice about cutting spending because their bank balances won't sustain their previous lifestyle. Others know that they won't always be making the money they are making now, so they're being prudent before it's too late. And some have discovered that trading time and energy for more money and material possessions really *doesn't* buy happiness. These employees are often willing to take government and corporate buyouts; they're people in search of a less-harried outlook on life. Finally, there are idealists who believe that we might be able to build a more sustainable world if more of us pulled back from the material quest. Although the percentage who have cut consumption out of concern for the environment remains small, a genuine desire for ecological renewal is evident in my polls. In the 1990s, after nearly half a century of keeping up with the Joneses, it is no longer unfashionable to be seen cutting back.

Alternatives to Consumption. What are the alternatives to consumption? If Canadians decide to cut back – or are forced to cut back – will we pay more attention to our minds? With the increased emphasis now being placed on the concept of a learning society, I wouldn't be at all surprised. Will we start paying more attention to people and less attention to things? That is already starting to happen, both among young people as well as older Canadians trying to restructure their priorities. It seems a good bet that over the next few decades, an emphasis on emotional growth will overtake the postwar preoccupation with material well-being. One more thing: if our minds, hearts and souls are going to become more important to us, it would be foolish to leave out our bodies. Shopping isn't going to be easy to replace as the national pastime. But there are signs that many Canadians are considering some relatively low-cost physical, intellectual, emotional, and spiritual alternatives.

The Physical. I think it's likely that "ownership" of physical contentment will replace ownership of commodities, at least among large segments of what used to be the middle class. Good health offers two distinct benefits: it feels good, and it's cheap. Booze and cigarettes are expensive. Jogging and its sensible companion, walking, are virtually free. Combine that economy with a new awareness of health risks and a fear that government-funded medical coverage will decline, and you have a lifestyle for frugal times. Sales of inexpensive, nourishing foods – especially in the non-meat, non-dairy categories – should soar. In the U.S., 15,000 low-fat products were launched in 1994 alone. Sales of *Prevention*, a U.S. magazine offering advice on maintaining good health, have climbed steadily since 1990, after remaining flat throughout the 1980s.

The Mental.   Of course there are books, the demise of which I believe is vastly over-stated. Books survived television, and I expect they will survive the computer and the CD-ROM, which are a lot harder to take to bed. But there is no denying that there are increasing alternatives to books, one of which involves putting your head into cyberspace. Some call it escapism and others call it joining the electronic community. Whatever you call it, surfing the Net generally activates more brain cells than sitting in front of a television. Some Canadians are already busy replacing material reality with virtual reality, and not all of them are the guys who carried pen protectors in their pockets in high school.

Soon most households in Canada will have a computer, and the use of modems is increasing rapidly. Cyberspace is not a perfect alternative to materialism because it can be expensive. The better hookups cost money, and browsing can be costly, even before you start shopping on the World Wide Web. Whatever you use it for, the Internet is interactive – an encouraging improvement over television, especially when you consider how many urban Canadians don't know their next-door neighbour.

Finally, we should expect a larger percentage of both young people and adults to take advantage of universities and other schooling opportunities, if they don't get priced into the stratosphere. In the Spend-and-Share era, education ended when you left school; except for life's hard knocks, you were as educated as you were ever going to be. Not any more. Whether you study to improve your situation in the workplace or simply to get a grip on an increasingly complicated world, learning is going to be considered an increasingly valuable commodity. They don't call it the knowledge society for nothing.

The Emotional.   Older Canadians look back to the Great Depression and World War II as tough but communal times. Perhaps tough times will again have their compensations in human relations. Interpersonal values – including "family" values – are being rediscovered and redefined. "Nesting" means more people are spending time in their homes and spending money on their homes. In a topsy-turvy world, we're all looking for security, and the home is a good place to start, for the aged, middle-aged and young alike.

Whom you care for has begun to close the gap on what you own. Most baby boomers have owned their fair share of things. On the other hand, not all of them have been satisfied with their relationships. Young people may be setting an example here: many young Canadians have not enjoyed the same access to material goods that boomers had in their twenties, but seem to find sustenance in people. Consider how many people in their twenties now walk around in groups – not necessarily paired off in couples – eating, walking, talking and generally socializing together. The coffeehouse has emerged as the symbol of sociability. It's estimated that by the year 2000 there will be more than 10,000 specialized coffeehouses in the United States.

In a sense, this sociability is not unique to today's younger generation; after all, many boomers spent much of their adolescence packed into 1960 Fords and Chevys, cruising the drag. But that was a teenage phenomenon; this is a trend of those in their twenties and even thirties, without the cars. Cars and insurance are expensive, particularly for young people. With money tight, young people are staying home longer. According to Statistics Canada, over 65% of 20 to 24 year old Canadians are still living with their parents. And a 1996 Angus Reid Group survey found that one in four Canadian adults expects their parents to be living with them. That's a far different family unit than the stereotype of the nuclear family that predominated during most of the postwar era. Though historical polling data in Canada don't exist on this issue, surveys taken by the National Opinion Research Center in the U.S. show how profoundly attitudes have changed. In 1973, 58% of Americans thought it was a poor idea for old people to share a home with their children. Twenty years later, that number had dropped to 36%.

The Spiritual.   In the spring of 1993, *Maclean's* carried a cover story on a poll we had taken on the religious attitudes and practices of Canadians. "God Is Alive," proclaimed the magazine cover – a claim backed by findings that showed a surprising level of faith among the 25 million Canadians that consider themselves Christians. The most important finding was the surprising level of participation in small churches and unofficial denominations. The established religions are still struggling with declining attendance. But something is simmering in community halls and meeting places beyond the territory of the conventional churches. The *Maclean's* story drew a near-record level of reader mail, much of it from religious Canadians who were thankful to learn that they weren't alone.

Canadians seem to be displaying a renewed interest in spiritual matters. *The Celestine Prophecy,* a book about a journey to South America that becomes a spiritual quest, has dominated the Canadian best-seller lists for almost two years, selling more than 100,000 copies. Pope John Paul II's book, *Crossing the Threshold of Hope,* sold almost as many copies. Over the next two decades, an ageing generation will confront their mortality. This alone suggests increasing levels of spiritual searching and religious practice. But it will be augmented by heightened levels of insecurity about the future and a sense of impotence in the face of the many new forces shaping our lives. It's too early to declare the start of a full-fledged religious revival, but religion may be re-emerging as a central element of daily life for growing numbers of Canadians.

I don't believe that we are returning to an old romantic set of Norman Rockwell values. It's hard to be romantic about the fact that more than 21% of Canadian children – 1.4 million of them – were living in poverty in 1993, *before* many governments started cutting back. The 1991 census showed that there were nearly one million single-parent families in Canada, constituting 13% of all families. Relationships probably mean much more than material goods in most of these families, yet what is more crucial are the commodities not being purchased. Not being able to afford a new snowsuit is quite a bit different from not being able to afford a new snowmobile.

Disciples of Phyllis Schlafly, who organized the successful campaign in the U.S. to defeat the Equal Rights Amendment, may claim that we are starting to recognize more important values than personal liberation, and that it doesn't always pay to have both parents spending most of their time out of the home. But my own view is that two forces are dovetailing here. We are seeing people put relationships before things because relationships are more significant, and because we can no long afford to worship things as we once did.

Are there fewer divorces because we are paying more attention to our marriages? Or because some couples that might have split up a decade ago now recognize that the consequences often involve poverty? The specter of penury – like the specter of being hanged in the morning – has a way of concentrating the mind. Hard-nosed realists will offer one interpretation, romantics another. Whatever the answer, there is little doubt that the family is becoming a more significant bonding agent than it has been since the Second World War. "The State of the Family in Canada," a 1994 Angus Reid survey done in conjunction with *Maclean's*, produced ample evidence to confirm this trend.[7]

The alternative to materialism for young Canadians is more complicated. Some people in their early twenties find decent jobs, but they are the exceptions. Many more have a top-level education – far superior to what boomers graduated with – but either work at two or more low-paying jobs, or none. Leonard Stern, himself of X-age, but with a good job as a reporter at *The Ottawa Citizen*, laments the kiss-off of a generation: "The tenured, or middle-class, is like a bus with no more room for passengers. The over-educated twenty-somethings are trying to elbow a way in before it pulls away. Some have made it, while others are only half-aboard, hanging on with irregular contract work. And some ... feel there's no point in even queuing up."[8]

It is hard to get a fix on what will happen to alienated young people who have "dropped out" of the mainstream. Some provincial governments are trying to prod them into the workplace by cutting back on welfare, but even many of those employed have minimum-wage, no-benefit jobs and regard "the system" as exclusive and unfair. The anti-materialism of the hippies of the 1960s disappeared quickly, swamped in a sea of money and materials. This movement may last longer. What the hippies sold out for is no longer easy to acquire.

Not all young Canadians have turned their backs on society. This group is extremely diversified. Some hardly have time to breathe outside of work. Some luck into good jobs and metamorphose into clones of their parents. Those who can't find any work hang out in coffeeshops, nursing espressos as well as any member of the beat generation. Or they hang out at shopping malls, or at home. This is the generation known for producing MA and PhD students in dead-end jobs, but many sense that an education will pay dividends some day, and, in the meantime, studying is more interesting than mind-less work.

So what does this all add up to? At one extreme, we have become such an individualistic society that according to Robert Putnam even the number of people showing up at bowling alleys on their own has increased. Yet the isolation and loneliness that figured in the works of sociologists such as David Reisman (*The Lonely Crowd*) in the 1950s is giving way to a greater sense of community. It may be that individuality has peaked among some demographic sectors and that the overall trend is actually toward more *togetherness*. Evidence from the Angus Reid Group's Family Study series certainly points in this direction. That's encouraging, because when we look beyond the family to the broader reaches of public life, exactly the opposite seems to be happening.

Eight

THE TRANSFORMATION
OF PUBLIC LIFE

*"One way or another the fate of humanity
in the new millennium [will] depend
on the restoration of public authorities."*

Eric Hobsbawm, AGE OF EXTREMES

My first glimpse of the new Canadian politics came on a warm afternoon in Winnipeg in August 1990. An associate passed me a stack
of computer tables, which contained the results of a survey we had
just completed for the upcoming Ontario election. I took one
glance, shook my head and congratulated myself for having put
extra effort into this one. The 1990 campaign had proven extremely
difficult for pollsters. Newspaper and television networks that are
normally eager consumers had decided to pass this time around.
David Peterson's Liberals held an enormous 20-point advantage in
the polls, prompting several editors to tell me that since the result
was a foregone conclusion, they wouldn't be needing our services.

Pollsters are naturally curious people, so about three weeks before
election day we decided to conduct a poll anyway, even if it cost us
some of our own money. It's hard to pass up an election, even when
it has all the signs of being a boring one. We had predicted the

Liberal minority that brought Peterson to power in 1985, and we had predicted the massive majority that crowned him in 1987, so we were looking for the hat trick. Southam News, our media partner from the early 1980s, threw in some money in exchange for exclusive use of whatever we turned up, as dull as it might be. Except that it turned out to be far from dull. After digesting the numbers, I called Jim Travers, then general manager at Southam News. "Hey, Travers," I said, "hold the front page. It looks like the NDP is finally going to get a shot at running Ontario."

I remember putting the phone down, gazing out at the sweeping vistas of city and prairie that only an office tower in Winnipeg can provide and trying to ponder what all this meant. An NDP government in Ontario was certainly big news. But there was more to it than that. For someone who had a career analyzing the political scene, there was a bigger story here – the death of conventional wisdom in Canadian politics.

Since then, there have been plenty of other political surprises. In 1991, the B.C. Liberals were so weak that party leader Gordon Wilson had to seek a court order to be able to take part in televised debates. Few British Columbians were even able to tell you who the Liberal leader was. Well, he may have been considered a nuisance candidate, but his performance in the debates captivated the voters. He ended up winning 30% of the votes and came within a hair of forming the government.

A year later came the referendum on the Charlottetown accord. I was one of many who felt that Canadian voters would support this agreement, not just because Canada's so-called elite supported it but because (I was convinced) many Canadians simply wanted to put the matter behind them. But that's part of the reason we take polls – to verify or contradict the instincts of those who think they are experts. Sure enough, the Angus Reid Group once again proved itself smarter than Angus Reid: our polls during the referendum campaign proved my instincts dead wrong.

A week before voting day, I went to Washington to give a lecture at the Canadian Embassy. The speech had been booked long before the referendum had been announced, so it was pure coincidence that I found myself speaking to several hundred Americans with news that was not only hot but, for the Canadian government, decidedly unpleasant. Several embassy officials pulled me aside before my lecture to inform me that it would be improper to say anything that would embarrass the prime minister. I ignored their warning; I am simply not very good at muffling the truth. The first question after my lecture came from an American reporter; he was puzzled that the country could reject the accord when so many leading Canadians supported it. The reason, I was compelled to reply, was that "Canadians no longer trust anything initiated by Brian Mulroney – he is the most hated leader in the free world." (For the remainder of Mulroney's term, our Ottawa office was black-balled by the federal government.)

In Alberta, Ralph Klein, formerly the populist mayor of Calgary, swept to victory in the 1992 provincial election with the kind of approach that (not surprisingly) hasn't traditionally produced a winner in Canadian politics: he ran against his own party. He promised tough measures to deal with the fiscal folly of the previous Tory government, even though he had been a senior cabinet member in that government. No matter. Klein won handsomely and proceeded to do exactly what he had promised – cut programs. That his popularity, as recorded by our polls, increased after these measures stunned many veteran observers of Canadian politics.

Klein's victory should have prepared the pundits for Mike Harris's "Common Sense Revolution," but how often do two weird lightning bolts strike so close to each other? Yes, everyone knew that Bob Rae's NDP government would be defeated in the 1995 Ontario election. But few suspected that a former golf pro from North Bay would administer the *coup de grace* to the sophisticated Rae. For the two years leading up to the election, Harris had hovered at around 20% in the polls, dwarfed by Lyn McLeod's Liberals, who spent most of the run-up to the election at 50% or better. McLeod wasn't well known and didn't make much of an impression at public appearances. But most pundits thought she would become Ontario's new premier. Rae was dead, and Ontarians – so conscious of their "world-class" image as cleaner, more upscale Americans – weren't about to vote for what many saw as an ex-jock. Surprise! The polls began to swing halfway through the election, and Harris was suddenly a winner. Why the shift? More than anything, middle-class voters in Ontario, especially those living in the suburban communities around Metro Toronto, saw Harris and his Common Sense Revolution as the answer to their growing anger rooted in declining take home income and increased insecurity about their jobs.

Then there was the 1995 Quebec referendum. At the beginning of the campaign, the Yes side was in such poor shape that sovereignist scholars, learned men who not only studied the science of politics but taught it to students, wrote an open letter pleading with then premier Jacques Parizeau to cancel the vote and avoid humiliation for the separatist cause. That was before Lucien Bouchard was summoned to assume control. Suddenly, this appealing leader was telling Quebeckers that a "magic wand" would change the mood of the province and that the separatists would rally to victory. The federalists laughed, scornfully but nervously. Their anxiety was well grounded. For a few very panicky moments during the final week of the campaign, Bouchard had the Yes forces out front. I recall looking at the computer printout from our final poll, taken a few days before the vote, and seeing the specter of something I never would have thought possible: the death of Canada.

The road from the demise of conventional wisdom to the possible end of a national dream has taken many twists and turns through this turbulent decade. Not every election has been a surprise, but there have been enough of them that it's time to rewrite the rule book on how Canadian politics works and inspect some of the fissures beginning to show in the foundations of our political order.

I have said that the role of politicians in effecting change in society is generally overrated. Nevertheless, our politicians are the people we hire to try to ride the winds of change for us. The political arena is where we watch people representing the winners and losers of any new era paraded into public view. We have already seen people with jarring new viewpoints – including Lucien Bouchard and Mike Harris – assume the reins of power in Quebec and Ontario. Do the beliefs of men like these reflect the thinking that will guide us in the coming decades? Or are they little more than momentary reflections of our confusion and the confusion of our times?

Nobody knows yet. All we can say for sure is that the forces we talked about earlier are producing a new brand of politics. Tough times inevitably lead to less civility, a meaner scramble for diminished spoils of power. In the 1990s, it has sometimes felt as though a sinister fog has descended upon the Canadian landscape. Are we voting in a way that will best enable us to survive in the Sink-or-Swim era? Or in a way that we hope will lift the fog and bring back the sunshine?

Certainly we're feeling anything but sunny. Pollsters have been struggling for new ways to express the sense of anger, pessimism and despair that has dominated the public mood. I myself am not a pessimist. I am, however, a realist, and I am not alone in portraying our current quandary in a way that Bay Street cheerleaders don't like. The reality is this: most Canadians agree that the average person is facing a lot more hardship than our rah-rah economists are willing to concede. Veteran pollster Allan Gregg, in assessing the results of his 1995 year-end poll for *Maclean's*, described the public mood as the worst he had seen in 20 years.

Perhaps it would be better if we shrugged it off and got on with cleaning up the mess. Our gloom certainly isn't helping us. In fact, I would argue that Canadians' disappointment with the way the Spend-and-Share era ended has obscured the country's common vision, disoriented our collective identity and threatens the very essence of the Canadian dream. On the other hand, pretending that our new world is terrific plays into the hands of the minority likely to emerge as winners in the Sink-or-Swim era, many of whom don't seem to care how many others are sinking. The Canadian public is frustrated, angry and restless, and rightfully so. Canadians have little faith in the contradictory signals they are receiving from politicians, although some leaders have managed to sell a simple little message that what Canada needs now is less government and more private initiative.

Not all Canadians are buying the quick fix offered by champions of an unrestrained marketplace. Some of us are still peering through the fog, searching for answers that may be more effective over the long run. We live in a country founded on the principles of peace, order and good government, and our outlook has traditionally reflected those objectives. But as we move toward the end of a century that Sir Wilfrid Laurier predicted would belong to Canada (and which, at many times, *has* been very good to Canada), we are feeling neither peaceful, orderly nor good about ourselves. It is hard to know which is the greater threat to Canada: that it will divide, or that it will disintegrate. We no longer have a strong sense of who we are and what we stand for. These are the threats to nationhood that cry out for leadership from national and provincial governments, but governments at all levels are essentially bankrupt and in decline.

It isn't only Quebec that is hurting us. From British Columbia to Newfoundland, people are looking for guidance and support in adjusting to the restructuring of the workplace. Not only does the gulf between rich and poor Canadians threaten to grow even deeper, but as the advantages held by the "winners" increase, so, seemingly, does their contempt for the "losers." The mounting threats to Canadians' social well-being call for a strong national consensus, but deep regional divisions and political fragmentation are generating less in the way of consensus than Canadians have ever known. Quebec is merely the salt in our national wound, but that doesn't stop it from stinging like a scorpion. As separatist forces in Quebec regroup behind Lucien Bouchard for one final campaign, the hands on Canada's "doomsday" clock tick as close as they ever have toward midnight. Weary and dispirited federalist forces in Quebec and Ottawa find themselves hamstrung by widespread indifference or defiance within their own ranks.

A GLOBAL PROBLEM

Quebec is a distinctly Canadian conundrum, but our other problems are far from ours alone. The emergency wards of contemporary politics are overflowing. To the south, Americans are still shuddering from bombings in Oklahoma City and at the World Trade Center. These are just the most obvious manifestations of a deeply troubled society. America's enemy within may be more potent than all its former overseas adversaries. Hugh Segal, the senior Tory strategist who gets as distressed about simplistic right-wing solutions as he does about simplistic left-wing solutions, has argued that as serious as Canada's problem with Quebec separatism may be, it doesn't rank with festering inner-city problems in the United States.

Americans promote democracy as their proudest attribute, and Americans promote it around the world, but at home it has developed anemia. Newt Gingrich's controversial "Contract with America" emerged from a national election campaign in which fewer than 40% of Americans bothered to vote. Observers are becoming increasingly concerned about the alienation of the U.S. voter, gridlock on Capitol Hill, the agenda of the radical right, the growing gap between rich and poor and the seemingly intractable problems confronting the black underclass. In far-off Hawaii and

Alaska, owning a star on Old Glory no longer holds such overwhelming appeal. Small but apparently serious separatist movements are starting to voice dissatisfaction.

Overseas, Britain seems to have recovered from its loss of imperial power, but its national image has been threatened by a new insult: membership in the European Community. The flap grows worse as the EC grows in influence and authority. Other British difficulties include unemployment, racial antagonism, unproductive industries and the decline of the middle class, whose well-being was supposed to lie at the very heart of Thatcherism. Scottish separatism may not be as dramatic as Quebec separatism, but it continues to stick painful little pins into the shrunken British empire. As for the endless *annus horribilis* of the monarchy, how could what passed for majesty a century ago turn out to have such feet of soap? Even the Australians want out from under the Crown.

The mood in France has been equally contentious. In 1995, Paris was rocked by public demonstrations as politicians attempted to impose cutbacks the protesters felt would dramatically alter what France has meant as a society. Lower subsidies to farmers made sense to the marketplace but were immensely unpopular, partially because they threatened France's fading self-image as a people with their roots in the countryside. The EC makes sense to economists but further encroaches on the staying power of the French language, already staggering from the English domination in commerce and entertainment. Civil service strikes that brought Paris to a standstill in the fall of 1995 would likely have incurred wrath on this side of the Atlantic but won grudging support from a majority of Parisians.

Indeed, anyone looking for evidence of social unrest can point randomly to almost any spot on the globe – the widespread hostility toward foreigners in Germany, the murder of street children in Brazil, the rise of private armies in west Africa, the disillusionment with the "shock treatment" of capitalism in Russia, the civil wars in Sri Lanka, Bosnia and Indonesia.

Where you would not expect to be able to point would be toward "Asian tigers," those countries that are quickly becoming major forces in the new international economy. Yet even here you find signs of discontent. Hong Kong has been rocked by demonstrations and suicides stemming from an unemployment rate that climbed to 2.5%.[2] What would be an insignificant rate of unemployment in Canada is considered a disaster in a nation with a non-existent social safety net, and inconsistent with Hong Kong's self-image of economic success. This self-image will likely require a major makeover in 1997 when Hong Kong again becomes a part of China.

Thailand has won a reputation for new-found prosperity as one of the five Asian tigers, but a 1995 Woodrow Wilson Center study suggests that, after inflation, ordinary Thais have hardly benefited. While Thailand's per-capita income has increased by a multiple of 15 over the past 30 years, the per-capita income of salaried workers has increased only by a multiple of 3, leaving urban workers with income of less than $1.50 a day, and rural workers with about 50 cents. Citing the fact that the top 20% of Thailand's population earns nearly 60% of the country's income, the WWC report said that the quality of life for ordinary people had decreased over the past two decades. And this is a country trumpeted as one of the *beneficiaries* of the new economic order. [3]

Crises confronting societies around the world vary, but there are often common threads. New economic and social pressures are upsetting political orders in many countries, leading to a redefinition of social values, a more difficult process of consensus-building, the rise of new political movements and challenges to the integrity of the nation-state. Globalization and technological advances are clearly building huge fortunes for some and improving the standards of living for others; they are also cutting others adrift from the marketplace and the umbrellas of government, driving them to seek protection and a sense of belonging at a more local and even tribal level.

The suffering in Canada cannot be compared to the suffering in more desperate parts of the world. Furthermore, our political upheavals fall well short of the coups and civil wars that have plagued other places. But Canada is not what it was. It is fair to say that the political, economic and social equilibrium of Canada's Spend-and-Share era has been knocked off its moorings. East of the Ottawa River, Canada is in rough shape economically. Saskatchewan and Manitoba aren't exactly millionaires' row, and the North is iffy at best. That leaves southern British Columbia, southern Alberta and southern Ontario as "have" regions. Does that mean these regions are politically stable? Hardly. The Klein and Harris governments reflect American political ideology more than anything since W.A.C. Bennett, and while British Columbia still sails under the NDP banner, the Liberal Party, which is well to the right of the traditional Tory mainstream, can claim a moral victory in the 1996 election since it captured the largest share of the popular vote.

CHANGING POLITICS IN CANADA

In the 1993 federal election, more political parties competed than at any time in the history of Canada – 14 parties ran for office and 5 captured seats. The NDP and Conservatives, both strong influences during the Spend-and-Share era, were virtually wiped off the political map. Three years later they are still on life support, showing only the flicker of a pulse.

Liberals, Conservatives and New Democrats have always had different philosophies, but Tory governments invented institutions such as the CBC and Ontario Hydro, and New Democrats were close enough to the Trudeau Liberals in the early 1970s to keep that minority government alive, so the gaps between their thinking have never been huge. Moreover, national parties tended to coalesce on issues that clearly required consensus, which in postwar politics has usually involved Quebec. Now, our national parties can't seem to agree on anything – most particularly Quebec. The days of broad agreement on national policy belong to a distant past that many Canadians believe will never return. There was political bickering during the Spend-and-Share era, but there was enough money around to satisfy pretty well everybody. It usually didn't make that much sense to go to the barricades on an issue, particularly since the electorate wasn't likely to go with you.

The Trudeau Liberals and the Mulroney Tories were far less concerned about pursuing ideology than they were about staying in power. While Trudeau was much more adept than Mulroney at portraying himself as a man of deeply held beliefs, he had no compunctions about letting the NDP dictate the terms of most of the legislation passed during his minority government of 1972-74.

Nor did he hesitate in appropriating the Conservatives' wage-and-price control strategy after he won the 1974 election by denouncing it as the work of the devil. This kind of legerdemain embittered some people (particularly Robert Stanfield), but most voters shrugged it off.

Many Quebeckers now look back on the patriation of the Canadian constitution in 1982 and see nothing but the unscrupulous betrayal of René Lévesque by "English Canada." The sad part about this nasty memory is there was consensus on the issue, so much, in fact, that former Alberta premier Peter Lougheed and others wonder whether the skewering of Lévesque was really necessary to get the job done. Even separatist historians concede that most Canadians – including Quebeckers – thought it ludicrous that the British Parliament retained final say on political decisions made in Canada, by Canadians and for Canadians. Trudeau has always insisted that Lévesque was determined to scupper any kind of settlement, but doubts linger. There is a feeling that Lévesque would have paid a huge price for walking away from patriation, because rejecting it would have been the gesture of someone determined to spoil the party if he didn't get his own way.

As much as Lévesque wanted sovereignty for Quebec, he nevertheless thought that Canada was a decent place to live. Canadian politicians used to have to invent problems to disguise the fact that, for the most part – give or take the English-French divide – Canadians lived in relative harmony, according to widely accepted values. Not so in the 1990s, when there is no longer enough money in the economy to make everybody happy.

The rich are sick of sharing. The middle class is desperately trying to cling to the middle of the ladder, despite all the broken rungs. Its members (and many of its former members) spend a lot of time trying to determine who is most responsible for doing them in – corporations, governments, governments in concert with immigrants, governments in concert with the poor, and so on. This is a new mentality in a country whose frontiers were opened up by government and which has been nourished by governments for much of its 129 years. It reflects the viewpoint that much of what Canada has always been *about,* at least in economic and social terms, has been wrong. This allegation captured widespread support in English-speaking Canada just as a majority of French-speaking Quebeckers were voting to support the contention that much of what Canada has always been about, in cultural and political terms, has also been wrong. Needless to say, it is difficult to keep a country's spirits up when two of its three most muscular political movements (Reform and the Bloc) keep hammering home that the essence of Canada's political, social, economic and cultural heritage is fundamentally flawed. Is it any wonder that the spirits of Canadians, already battered by the vicissitudes of massive economic change, are flagging a bit?

There has never been so much rhetoric maintaining that what Canada has been for all these years doesn't make sense any more, nor has there ever been so much disinclination among politicians of different stripes to try to make Canada something better than it has been. It would be easy to condemn Canada's new breed of politicians for being so unconciliatory toward one another, but these are people with distinct points of view, and in the 1990s, these points of view are on a collision course.

Why should the Bloc Québécois forge a common bond with their adversaries in Ottawa? After all, what interest do they have in making Canada a more attractive place to live? And Preston Manning's views on Canada and its relationship to Quebec are so different from those of Jean Chrétien that forging a consensus on a common referendum strategy was out of the question. How different from the 1980 Quebec referendum, when every federal party lined up behind the government to project a united Canadian front. In 1995, mutual disdain replaced mutual support.

During the Spend-and-Share era there was a shift from what political scientist Ken Carty has called the age of "brokerage politics" to a new age of "electronic politics and personal parties." The historic function of political parties as "agents of persuasion," influencing politicians between and during campaigns, was eroded by a new dynamic that more or less shaped the party into the television persona of the leader. Additionally, the role of parties as sources of information and feedback from the regions was diminished by the accelerating influence of private polling. The Liberals of the early 1970s groused that Trudeau didn't listen to the party. He didn't have to. He was in direct contact with his pollsters, who were in direct contact with the electorate. And the message, easy to pass on, was that we wanted more government.

So powerful was that message that it became gospel, even when other messages should have been delivered. Senator Keith (the Rainmaker) Davey was top campaign strategist to the Liberals during most of the Spend-and-Share era. During my brief tenure as an official Liberal pollster during the early 1980s, I made the mistake of telling the good senator that my polling clearly showed that westerners were concerned about the budget deficit. "That may be," I was told, "but no party will ever get elected by running on a deficit platform. What do you want to do, turn the voters off?"

I couldn't argue with Davey. Consider what happened to Robert Stanfield in 1974 and Joe Clark in 1979 when they tried to campaign on platforms of fiscal prudence. The Conservatives turned the tables on the Liberals when Norman Atkins, the senior Tory adviser, urged Brian Mulroney to promise more of everything. John Turner, who hinted that maybe it was time to spend less, was, of course, defeated.

These days, the deficit rule has clearly been stood on its head. Now the rule reads: "If you don't focus on the deficit and promise to do everything in your power to eliminate it, you will be defeated." The indiscriminate shrinking of governments is almost as misguided as the indiscriminate bloating of governments. But then, winning politics has never had much to do with the real needs of society, particularly during election campaigns. Ralph Klein and Roy Romanow won with slice-and-dice, and no Canadian politician who has won an election since has dared to sing another refrain. The exception is B.C., where Glen Clark won with a decidedly activist agenda. But it is worth noting that the only reason Clark won was that the almost 60% of voters who wanted less government split their support among four parties.

The old rules held that a leader must be well educated, good looking (well, actually, sexy), in good health (jogging made for a great photo opportunity) and above all able to articulate a broad vision of politics and society. Some of the most charismatic leaders of the Spend-and-Share era matched this profile: Pierre Trudeau, Ed Schreyer, David Peterson, Bill Bennett, Peter Lougheed and even

Brian Mulroney. Although the most exercise René Lévesque seemed to get involved the two fingers used to hold his cigarettes, he also matched the profile for success in this era.

The formula for successful leadership in the 1990s involves a far different alchemy. Sex appeal has become a handicap (just ask B.C. Liberal leader Gordon Campbell); photo ops at a pool hall are worth more than those at the jogging track and broad visions aimed at building consensus can be political suicide. The "ideal" politician in the 1990s speaks the language of ordinary people and not the bureaucrats, makes concrete promises that will be kept, is more realistic than idealistic and never uses the words "trust me."

Leadership that came to be based on broad values and the charisma of politicians has been transformed into a "contract" with an electorate no longer interested in process, pretty faces or hollow slogans. Both Mike Harris and Jean Chrétien sold themselves as unpretentious, ordinary guys willing to commit themselves to quasi-contractual obligations with the electorate (Harris had his "Common Sense Revolution"; Chrétien cited chapter and verse of "The Red Book"). That's what today's voters seem to be ordering up as leaders: ordinary people who will do what they say they are going to do. And when they don't, the public clamour can be deafening. Sheila Copps was forced to resign because she had promised to do so if the GST wasn't scrapped. A decade ago, resigning for failing to keep an election promise was unheard of.

Politicians whose personal styles would have kept them on the margins of power a generation ago now have a strange appeal. Bob Rae may have been the smartest guy around. He also had a nice sense of humour, and he went out of his way to appeal to everybody, even the business community. But he ended up being clumsy and was in trouble halfway through his mandate. He was replaced by a man who favoured "common sense" over intellect and drew up a contract setting out how he would bludgeon big government into submission. Guts are in, intellectuals are out.

The successful politician of the 1990s is more hard-nosed realist than idealist. Charisma, new spending and grand promises are out. No-nonsense is in, although it must be mixed with optimism because voters still live on hope. Kim Campbell faced tough odds when she took over from Brian Mulroney, but she buried herself forever when she started to sound like a ponderous academic speculating on the inevitability of high unemployment. Voters don't want to hear about things that can't be fixed.

Policy, leaders and parties – the three cornerstones of Canada's political system have all been wracked by the turbulent events associated with the emergence of the Sink-or-Swim era. Why? Globalization and the changing role of communications technology provide part of the answer. The rest concerns the changed mood of the Canadian voter.

THE NEW CANADIAN VOTER

During the Spend-and-Share era, political parties could actually point to their "core" support, a significant part of the electorate that voted according to predictable patterns. For the most part, when the electorate changed its mind the process was steady and predictable. In discussing forecasts for an election campaign on *Canada AM*, pundit Gerry Caplan might say, "The NDP core vote is 20%." Everyone would nod their heads – even spokespersons for the other parties – because they knew he was speaking the truth. In fact, every party could count on core support because most voters were loyal to one of the three main parties. Elections were decided by the 20% or so of "swing" voters, located predominately in trendy and populous southern Ontario and volatile British Columbia.

Regional voting patterns in those days contributed to the stability and predictability of electoral politics. The late sociologist John Porter characterized the Canadian political order as one in which "regional interests far outweigh class interests." This astute observation was consistent with the conventional wisdom at the centre of Canadian politics for several generations: clever Quebeckers will always vote for the party that will end up forming the government in Ottawa. Ontarians will do just about anything *except* elect the NDP. The west will swing to the left (except for Alberta) and swing to the right, but it will never vote Liberal. Election campaigns were really just icing on a cake that had already been baked. The unwritten rule was that the vote would not normally move more than 5% during a campaign. Veteran political types told me that when I got into the polling business, and when I studied the results of Canadian elections during the 1960s and 1970s, they were almost invariably right. But political rules began to change in Canada even before the turmoil of the Sink-or-Swim era.

I was reminded of the 5% "rule" when I was hired by the Liberals to do daily tracking polls for the 1984 federal election. I recall standing in front of John Turner and the back-room boys in a smoke-filled session at the Château Laurier in Ottawa, presenting polls I had taken in anticipation of a possible election. "Prime Minister," I said, "you have a good lead, but a very fragile lead. People are waiting to see whether you represent real change from the style of Pierre Trudeau" (whom most Canadians loathed by then). Turner was an old-school politician who had heard everything he thought he needed to know: that he had a sizable lead. My caveat was ignored. All anybody in that room wanted to hear was that their guy had a 10-point lead on the Tories. The prime minister called a snap election. After that, he watched his support plummet by about 30% over the next 60 days.

Some old pros dismissed the volatility in that election as a freak event. The next year, after decades of Tory rule in Ontario, Frank Miller blew a substantial lead, losing the Ontario election to David Peterson's Liberals. Even the old pros started to get the message that the rules had changed. When you fast forward to the 1990s, you find that the 5% rule is dead and gone. So are all those rules about how various regions will vote, or which party has a lock on a particular sector of the electorate. The only political rule left is that there aren't any hard-and-fast rules any more.

Loyalty ranks second only to power on any politician's list of assets. For the electorate, however, loyalty has all but vanished. How can anybody be loyal to anything when you never know what the party's position will be two years later? Wasn't Brian Mulroney's position on free trade – however inevitable – the exact opposite of the philosophy Sir John A. Macdonald had built the Conservative party on (and the opposite of the position Mulroney himself put forward in the 1983 P.C. leadership race)? Did Bob Rae's social contract – however well reasoned – have anything to do with the beliefs of the labour movement, which thought it finally had a premier it could call its own? What point is there in being loyal when what you've been loyal to is an illusion?

Today's electorate is polygamous and volatile. Of course, there have been volatile electorates throughout Canadian history; otherwise governments would never change. But voters of the 1990s have given the word *chameleon* new meaning. Political scientist Jonathan Lemco accurately describes the situation when he points out that "Canadian voters are now less likely to retain allegiance to any single party and more likely to call themselves 'independents'. And those who do identify with a party are less likely to support their party's candidates than at any time in the postwar era."[1]

A country full of independent-minded voters not only makes it more difficult to project the outcome of an election; it also makes elections much harder to choreograph. Elections used to be like intricate chess games in which grand (spin) masters like Keith Davey and Norman Atkins would dazzle observers with deft moves intended to be timed for an election-day checkmate. While elections may still be as complex as chess games, the rules are now more akin to Snakes and Ladders. Once you roll the dice, anything can happen. The voting intentions of large numbers of Canadians are on a hair trigger, ready to explode at any moment, changing the course of elections and taking our lives into uncharted territory.

And voters, like consumers, have also become more vocal. Peter Newman has chronicled this trend in his recent book, *The Canadian Revolution,* observing that Canadians have become far less deferential, especially in their relationship with politicians. It isn't as if vocal voter protests – even violent voter protests – are new to Canadian politics. Our political landscape is pockmarked with protests involving groups as disparate as farmers, university students, organized labour and Quebec separatists. But the din of *individual* protest has risen in recent years, particularly with the growth of "talk radio" call-in shows. Canadians may not be gathering in the streets to protest as they did in the late 1960s and early 1970s, but they have become much more opinionated in their living rooms.

How often do you hear anyone call to offer congratulations to politicians who may actually have accomplished something in office? Very rarely, and the host is likely to give such a person short shrift, assuming it's a party supporter on the phone. Instead, we phone to vent our spleen against politicians, most of whom we treat with all the reverence reserved for snakes.

When I was growing up, I heard all kinds of adults express opinions. Admittedly, some did so at the top of their lungs, but in those days many Canadians also made their points quietly, after a lot of thought, with the modesty that comes with knowing that while you might be right, you might also be wrong. The decibel level has risen lately. More Canadians are demanding to be heard, on the radio, at microphones in community meetings and in the polling booth. Since 1990, we've had six referenda and plebiscites, equal to the number held during the previous 30 years.

The most famous of these was the referendum on the Charlottetown accord. Rarely had the collective elite of the country been more united in support of a potential solution to a problem. And never have ordinary Canadians taken such delight in telling the elite to stuff it. This was surprising, since most of those who spoke in favour of Charlottetown were respected people. But when the elite falls into disfavour, it doesn't matter how wise or respected they are. The thin strands of trust that linked Canada's elite with ordinary Canadians snapped sometime before that referendum, and the results showed it. People were fed up with fancy formulae that were supposed to deal with what had become a gut issue inside and outside Quebec. What had always been a much more hierarchical country than, say, the United States suddenly seemed more like a free-for-all of individual expression.

Public opinion in Canada had a new, rude energy. Ordinary Canadians had begun to sense that the deal that they had been getting since the Second World War, which had vaulted many of them into lives of comfort and respectability, was vanishing. If that deal was off, one sensed, so was much of the submission to authority that went with it.

In February of 1995, then B.C. Premier Mike Harcourt learned how uncomfortable life can become when politicians think they can harness public feistiness and project themselves as "politicians of the people." On the advice of a Washington-based consultant, the New Democrats staged a televised town hall meeting with a "random" assortment of B.C. voters; party organizers thought they were pretty safe because its own communications people had screened most of them in advance. But not all of them. A very vocal woman named Lynn Mullen berated Harcourt over the difficulties of living on welfare and made a name for herself in front of a huge television audience. The browbeaten Harcourt sent the consultant back to Washington.

Like consumers, voters are also growing more value conscious. The Canadian voter today is extremely sensitive to such issues as government waste and politicians' pensions. Taxation wasn't a huge issue when pay packets were fat, but many Canadians who have started living on less are demanding that governments and politicians do likewise. Government safety nets may be more important than ever during tough times, but a sizable percentage of the population is determined to cut some of those nets adrift before too many more Canadians start depending on them. Reductions in welfare rates and unemployment insurance benefits have significant support among the dwindling middle class and people trying to climb back into the middle class. There is far more willingness to ascribe blame to the poor these days, even though it's getting much easier to sink into poverty than it used to be. In fact, we felt more generous toward people who arguably had more opportunities to escape poverty in the 1970s and '80s than we do to people who are *really* up against it today, when there is less money to go around. People at all levels are feeling threatened and don't want to encourage any more nibbling at their portion of the pie.

That the "winners" are more likely to turn their backs on the "losers" has been interpreted as a sign that Canadian politics is taking a hard swing to the right. I doubt that – or at least I doubt that we are headed down the American road, which is crowded with libertarians convinced that government is their greatest enemy. Yes, I see a backlash against welfare abuse in Canada; one 1994 survey showed that 80% of Canadians thought there had been significant abuse of the welfare system.[2] And yes, I see widespread conviction that all governments must be much more cautious about spending money. But even in Alberta, the most right-wing province in Canada, there has been vehement protest from both the poor and the middle class over health-care cuts. That isn't exactly a sign that we are ready to completely abandon our heritage of social compassion. The truth is that Canadians are more concerned about excessive government spending these days because taxes are higher than ever while service levels are dropping.

I recall meeting with Clark Davey, then publisher of the *Montreal Gazette*, in early 1985, about six months after Brian Mulroney's first landslide. Davey was fuming over the misuse of government jets by Mulroney cabinet ministers, and was convinced that this was the end of the line for the Tories. The electorate, which had grown accustomed to misuse of government jets by ministers such as Eugene Whelan and Otto Lang during the Trudeau years, never got as upset over this issue as did journalists. Today, I think Davey's assessment would be correct, and I am certain that it wouldn't take long for a publisher to whip voters into a frenzy over misuse of jets. You could probably even persuade some Canadians to stand on the runways so the minister's planes couldn't take off, the way Chinese protesters stood in front of tanks at Tiananmen Square. You think Jean Chrétien doesn't know that? Nowadays, it isn't unusual to see ministers flying commercial, even if they are in business class.

GOVERNMENT

During the Spend-and-Share era, as we've seen, governments were recognized for the crucial roles they played in Canada's mixed economy. National and regional policy objectives were served through a myriad of Crown corporations and agencies, which in some cases competed directly with the private sector. Though the idea of the mixed economy was not unique to this era, the number and influence of these bodies accelerated greatly from the early 1960s to the mid-1980s. In 1961 *Maclean's* ran a lead editorial advocating that education, which had been under provincial jurisdiction since Confederation, be placed under federal control. That kind of jurisdictional power play wasn't likely to succeed, but Ottawa did plenty of encroaching in fields that belonged to the provinces, including education, health and urban affairs.

Making ample use of its spending (and borrowing) powers, the federal government became increasingly busy prodding ordinary Canadians to behave in ways deemed beneficial to the national well-being. Then government, unsullied by the profit motive, was there to serve the public. Entering the civil service was considered a noble calling. When I graduated from university in 1969, many of my fellow graduates were recruited by federal agencies and departments. The rest of us were envious. They were going to build a better Canada.

As we move toward the millennium, the golden days of government have clearly come to a close. A few of my friends still work in the federal public service, but the luster is gone. It isn't just the flattened-out wages and disappearing career opportunities that have left the place dispirited. There is also an awareness that most Canadians are down on the public service, and that no matter how hard they work and how much they care about Canada, few people appreciate what they are doing. One civil service friend went to a high-school reunion recently and was accused by the same people who had envied him 25 years ago of now occupying a job that amounted to little more than "welfare with dignity."

We live in an age in which the free market economy and the private sector are lionized and government involvement is treated with contempt. The same private sector that seemed such a threat to civilized society in the 1960s is seen as our last chance at salvation today. Privatization is viewed as the alternative to taxation and bureaucratic lethargy. Forgotten or ignored are the problems that can develop when people operating in nobody's interests but their own secure a stranglehold on the way things are run.

Deregulation and decentralization ooze the intoxicating smell of freedom and limitless possibilities. Power has swung to the private sector, where enthusiasts argue that if the public doesn't like the way companies behave, we can always vote them out by withholding our dollars. Journalist Andrew Coyne and other neo-conservatives would have Canadians believe that the marketplace is a more efficient version of democracy than Parliament. The fatal weakness in the argument, of course, is that in the marketplace, people without money don't get to vote. People with money, on the other hand, get to vote over and over again. Never mind. In the 1990s, we have convinced ourselves that governments have failed us and market forces must decide.

ATTACHMENT TO CANADA

In 1994, I committed a minor act of treason. It happened at a meeting in Ottawa, with a group of politicians and senior civil servants. What I did was refer to myself as a British Columbian. I wasn't trying to make a spectacle of myself. It just happened. The words came out of my mouth during a discussion of the federal role in providing social programs. As I recall, I said something like, "As a British Columbian, I don't think the federal government should be trying to micro-manage social programs like training." I didn't get an immediate reaction, but later someone pulled me aside and said, "That's the problem with you people from B.C. You don't think of yourselves as true Canadians!"

The question of who is a true Canadian has been raised repeatedly since Confederation. Until the Second World War, most of us were "hyphenated" Canadians, drawing our identity from our ancestors, most of them from Europe, and the conviction that whatever Canadians may be, we were something different from

Americans. And we weren't really British either, despite the Queen. It was all a bit vague, but we muddled through. The war gave us a better sense of ourselves, and politicians started trying to clarify the concept of what being a Canadian should mean. Americanism was bound to keep tugging at us, particularly with the new influence of television, ever-increasing trade ties and our cold war NORAD connection, so the time had come for some distinct new symbols.

The maple leaf flag was the most obvious, but that was window dressing compared to some of the social programs introduced during the Spend-and-Share era. Far more persuasive in making the point that we really were a different society was the national medicare system introduced by the federal Liberals during the 1960s, borrowed from the Saskatchewan NDP. Medicare was like a badge that said that Canadians did things differently than Americans did – notably, with more compassion. During the 1970s and '80s, thousands of young Canadians flocked to Europe with maple leaf flags sewn on their jackets and knapsacks. Their symbolic statement was about a country that was in the process of creating a great society.

Unlike Americans, Canadians have never been trained to display patriotic pride. We don't hold our hands over our hearts when we sing the national anthem – in fact, many of us don't sing at all. What matters more to Canadians is that one big plus (medicare) and that one big minus (no handguns or assault weapons). What has excited us about ourselves isn't the RCMP musical ride or even our ability to survive long winters without turning to violence. It's been our capacity to create universally admired social programs that use collective means to address individual needs.

Today, our fondness for this Canadian attribute seems to be

waning. Our attachment to Canada may also be on the wane. It isn't so much that we are increasingly prone to describe ourselves as British Columbians, or Quebeckers, or Newfoundlanders.[3] That's a world-wide phenomenon. The search for identity appears to be leading people to define themselves with more tribal precision, from Texas to Inuvik, from Scotland to Paris and, more disastrously, from Chechnya to Bosnia. Of far greater significance is the damage the new era is doing to the "roots" of attachment to Canada, to the self-image of Canadians as a people with a difference that we all share.

We were proud of being multicultural, proud of our universal health-care system, proud of our compassion for the disadvantaged. We still pay lip service to our multicultural mosaic, but surveys show that we are actually less tolerant of minorities than Americans are. Medicare is starting to look crumbly around the edges. The once overwhelming opposition to user fees – even among better-off Canadians – is beginning to evaporate in the face of underfunding and perceived government neglect. Most Canadians believe that the system will deteriorate over the next decade. It is particularly distressing to hear 20% of Canadian doctors say they would seek care in the U.S. if they became seriously ill. As for the poor, for whom Canadians have always cared, we are starting to turn our backs. Welfare cutbacks, which have their greatest impact on children in poor, single-parent families, are being legislated with enthusiasm. That declining empathy is translating into declining commitment to poorer regions of the country. As political scientist J.F. Conway has observed, "for the first time in our recorded polling history, a majority of Canadians oppose programs of economic support for poorer regions, a key cement binding the federation together."[4]

NATIONAL UNITY AND THE QUESTION OF QUEBEC

One of the Yes side's symbols in the 1995 referendum was the peace symbol. At first, it seemed out of place to me. There was Jacques Parizeau's bus painted in psychedelic colours and adorned with the well-known symbol from the 1960s. Then it hit me: the Quebec sovereignty movement is less about the future than the past. In these times of turbulence, when more than one in 5 Montrealers lives below the poverty line, many Quebeckers are yearning for some kind of certainty. Certainty is easier to find among your own people than it is in the outside world. It's also easier to find in the past than in the uncertain present.

The rise of Quebec nationalism was a direct result of the unique dynamic that created the Spend-and-Share era. Television, neo-Keynesian economics and a new postwar generation of baby boomers helped lead to a definitive value shift in Quebec that manifested itself in many of the same ways it did in English Canada: a redefinition of gender roles, unbounded confidence in government, a new sense of material well-being and endless optimism about the future. In Quebec, these values squared off with church-dominated traditions and an inward-looking culture to produce a historic transformation – the Quiet Revolution.

Quebec society underwent massive changes during the 1960s. Attendance at mass fell from 80% to 20%. The birth rate plummeted from one of the highest in the developed world to one of the lowest. And the state replaced the church as the central institution in Quebec society. Politicians and bureaucrats replaced bishops and priests as moral and political teachers. In a single tumultuous decade, the orientation of Quebec changed from a society resistant to the forces of modernity to one that embraced them with open arms.

Nationalism during this era expressed itself most overtly in Quebec's desire for increased powers and responsibilities. The public sector pie was growing and the federal government was dominating that growth, but Quebec wasn't about to shrink into the background just when its psyche was growing by leaps and bounds. Quebeckers wanted a bigger piece of the action. According to Quebec sociologist Hubert Guindon, the growth of the separatist movement was promoted first and foremost by the emerging political class in Quebec City who fought with Ottawa bureaucrats over their sphere of activity in the new age of government.[5]

The Spend-and-Share era encouraged experimentation and risk taking – that was what Quebec nationalism was all about. A buoyant economy increased confidence, and the increasing powers being ascribed to governments around the world fit right in. Canadians outside Quebec couldn't understand why anyone would want to threaten the nation's economic and social progress, but they neglected to come to grips with Quebec's craving for political and cultural growth. Quebeckers wanted to invest vast quantities of the new energy into strengthening their own society and protecting their own language. Trudeau thought that could best be done in Ottawa, and made considerable progress. René Lévesque and his colleagues wanted to build their fortress closer to home.

For many of my separatist friends in Quebec, the past three decades have marked a steady march from the stirrings of the Quiet Revolution toward the final goal – sovereignty. Like Chairman Mao's Long March, there have been setbacks along the road, but the momentum never disappears and is largely untouched by whatever happens in Ottawa, Toronto or Edmonton. Since the first stirrings of Quebec nationalism in the early 1960s, its supporters have looked to the past with a combination of bitterness and resolve – *Je me souviens* – and to the future with bravado – *gens du pays*. The movement's majestic battleship was the Quebec state and its many appendages, such as Hydro-Québec. Even the emergence of the entrepreneurial class that made up Quebec Inc. in the 1980s spoke with confidence to what could be accomplished in a world in which the energy of Quebeckers worked in tandem with the state. This movement could have been shaken by the chaos and fears of the Sink-or-Swim era; instead, it was strengthened, if altered somewhat. Governments in both Ottawa and Quebec City will inevitably be weakened by the new realities, and the struggle for power between them now seems less relevant. In fact, Ottawa is scurrying to devolve powers in a way that will give *all* provinces more autonomy. The new attitude seems to be: "Take what you want – just pay for it yourselves."

The battle for jurisdiction now seems less important than the battle for the hearts and minds of the people. The implicit question is: "Where do you feel most secure in this nasty, messy world?" If the Canada of the 1990s is starting to feel foreign to many Canadians outside Quebec, imagine how it feels to many of those *inside* Quebec.

Then Bloc leader Lucien Bouchard energized the faltering Oui campaign by warning Quebeckers that Ottawa was preparing to make major cuts in fiscal transfers, unemployment insurance benefits and a host of other programs. Voters in the PQ heartland – a combination of rural regions outside Montreal and the bureaucratic nerve centre of Quebec City – have the most to fear from the new realities. Governments have nourished both of them, and now that government is in retreat there is fear in the air.

Premier Jacques Parizeau blamed the loss of the referendum on "money and the ethnic vote." Again, it was money from outside, foreigners from outside. The No vote was stronger in Montreal, which is marginally better suited to adapting to the Sink-or-Swim era. But even there separatist strength has grown. Montreal has gone into steep decline both as a port and as a financial centre.

Quebec has strong players in the new international marketplace, but they aren't exactly the heroes in Quebec that you might expect. Major private sector operators such as Bombardier and Power Corp., clearly in favour of free trade and maintaining strong ties with the outside world, were perceived as villains by a sizable proportion of the electorate during the referendum campaign. How can you trust institutions whose allegiance is clearly far more closely tied to world markets than to the interests of Quebec society?

This separatist movement is a strange movement: it wants change, but change that goes backward to more secure and comforting times. That such times can ever come again may be an illusion, but how much more of an illusion than the one that exists in the rest of Canada – that our economy can be saved by unrestrained capitalism?

THE FUTURE SHAPE OF CANADIAN POLITICS

The Sink-or-Swim era is straining the soul of Canada. The political equilibrium we once knew has been thrown out of kilter. The party system has become fragmented, governments are in retreat, the foundations of national identity are under assault, and the separation of Quebec is moving steadily from the unthinkable to the very possible. Voters are now poised on a razor's edge, ready to cut one way or another at a moment's notice, looking for something or somebody to blame for their troubles at work and at home.

When I bounce these observations off audiences, I am invariably besieged with an avalanche of questions. Is this a short-term adjustment before we move back to "business as usual" or are these the opening pages of an entirely new chapter in Canadian public life? If it is a new chapter, how different will it be from what has gone before? Are we really moving significantly to the right? Are we becoming Americans who wear toques? Will we end up joining the United States, marching behind our own Newt Gingrich, someone like Conrad Black, perhaps? There are no easy answers. However, this much is clear: forces that shaped our past have been ushered out the back door, and new ones are banging at the front.

Canada has been globalized to the point that we are swimming – or shall I say sinking? – in foreign money. We are no longer *maîtres chez nous* economically, and if you aren't masters of your own house economically, you aren't masters politically either. The smugness of the Spend-and-Share era, when in our giddiest moments we pretended we were running our own show, is gone. So is much of the influence and authority of the federal government. The decline of nation-states is a worldwide phenomenon, but in many cases, such as Canada's, it has been accelerated by growing dependence on outside economic decision-makers. In the candid words of the department of finance, "we have suffered a tangible loss of economic sovereignty." Lester Thurow, one of America's top economists, is even more direct on this subject. Speaking to the Municipal Finance Officers Association in Muskoka in 1995, Thurow said bluntly: "You Canadians are pygmies. If all of Canada were an American state, it would rank fifth or sixth in GDP terms. Yet you think trade decisions will be made in Ottawa. They'll be made in Washington."[6]

Free trade is changing the pattern of Canadian economic activity from east-west to north-south. It is easier for an Ontario-trained physician to locate a practice in Texas than in British Columbia. In the 1960s it was fashionable to lament the level of U.S. investment in Canada. In the '90s, we celebrate every time somebody comes calling, and worry that good multinational head-office jobs might move to the U.S. The craving for jobs has put traditional Canadian nationalism on hold.

Are we really moving inexorably to the right? When the Berlin Wall collapsed in 1989, both democrats and capitalists rejoiced. You can distinguish the two by sorting out what matters most to them. Garry Trudeau, creator of the popular Doonesbury cartoon strip, zeroed in on the distinction the week after the Wall came down. Mark Slackmeyer, one of the main Doonesbury characters, saw its fall as a triumph of the human spirit. His no-nonsense father, on the other hand, saw it as a victory for capitalism and a defeat for government intervention in the marketplace. "Don't you see," said the elder Slackmeyer, his eyes glowing with entrepreneurial conquest, "It's over. We won."

Only seven years after this watershed event, more than communism lies in tatters. Social democracy is in retreat. Traditional

Canadian liberalism, in the tradition of the late Paul Martin Sr., has all but gone into hiding. Even Hugh Segal, intellectual carrier of the Tory grail, keeps insisting that his favourite colour is blue, not pink, as the so-called neo-conservatives keep suggesting. The Canadian political landscape is now dominated by three pillars of conservatism – Ralph Klein, Mike Harris and the man with the biggest set of knuckles in Ottawa, Finance Minister Paul Martin.

Where does that leave us Canadians, in terms of political ideology? The image that dominates is that of a smallish country, inundated by American media and American culture and glutted with the convictions of American politicians. A country joined to Americans by the spiritual bonds of materialism and free trade, following our southern neighbours in an inexorable march to the right. There certainly is evidence to suggest that this is exactly the direction we're taking.

As political scientist Richard Sigurdson has observed, Canadians both young and old feel threatened by what they view as a collapse of traditional values. This has led to a backlash against programs like affirmative action and pay equity as articulated by various conservative groups including REAL Women and the National Citizen's Coalition.[7] The Reform Party of Canada, while not formally linked to any of these organizations, owes part of its success to its ability to provide a political voice to alienated individuals concerned about, among other things, family values and unhyphenated Canadianism.

Whether globalization produces a huge shift to the right remains to be seen. This much is clear, however. Forces of the Spend-and-Share era that encouraged the growth and centralization of government have been overtaken by a new form of globalization that, in the Canadian case, undermine the authority of the central government and encourages a continuing process of downsizing, privatization, decentralization and deregulation.

Nowhere will this process be more evident than in Canadian culture. In the new era, our cultural Maginot Line has been overrun. Cultural spending is much more constrained and cultural control is increasingly difficult to impose. The CBC still plays a valued, if somewhat peripheral, role in gathering issue-oriented Canadians around their radios, but CBC television, at least in English Canada, is becoming increasingly marginalized, to the point of irrelevance. In the world of satellite broadcasting and the Internet, governments are hard-pressed to control the spread of child pornography and hate literature. How can they hope to check the spread of less-pernicious outside influences?

Globalization has also provided a new justification for Quebec separatists who claim that the rest of Canada is less important as trade patterns change and new global opportunities open up. Even on the cultural front Quebec is less threatened by global integration than the rest of the country (at least in the short term), because it truly does have a distinct culture built around the French language. (The observation that Quebec may have an advantage in this respect led a friend of mine to muse during the 1995 referendum that perhaps the whole of Canada should change its name to Quebec and vote yes.) On the other hand, there will always be concern about assimilation, particularly with the increasing penetration of the mainly English Internet and because English has become the dominant language of global trade.

During the Spend-and-Share era television helped build a national consensus. Today, that influence has not been diluted in

Quebec the way it has in the rest of the country, simply because the number of French-language TV stations that can earn sufficient revenue to stay in business is limited. Elsewhere, the number of channels available is proliferating and the era of mass-audience TV networks is drawing to a close. Scores of English-language stations, most of them originating in the United States, are fragmenting the viewing audience across the country.

While Canadians have always had nuanced differences in how they looked at things, their window on the world used to be a shared lens through which anchormen Lloyd Robertson and Knowlton Nash provided a common base of information for understanding events. In the 1960s and '70s, most households only had one television, around which families shared a frame of reference.

Now, different families and different members of families are liable to draw their information from just about any direction. Watching the nightly news may still be a ritual for some, but it doesn't draw entire families together as it once did. Moreover, "new technologies are accelerating a shift of power away from the traditional voices of authority in journalism," according to American analyst Ellen Hume.[8] The line between news and propaganda has become fuzzy. Hard news is increasingly leavened with a mix of infotainment, infomercials, docudramas and other forms of near news. "Localism is the next television frontier," says Moses Znaimer, head of Toronto's successful City-TV. With that kind of fragmentation, consensus on any major issue becomes more and more improbable.[9]

Optimists predict that this new age will unleash an avalanche of information, creating a better-informed electorate and a community-active electorate. But it may also foster narrower outlooks. It may offer fertile ground for the legions of hate-mongers that already spew forth on American TV and radio. Rush Limbaugh may soon seem tame. When Holocaust denier Ernst Zundel wants to send a message that would be illegal under Canada's anti-hate legislation, he merely slips down to Buffalo and buys TV time or goes on the unpoliced Internet.

The emerging technology of the Sink-or-Swim era will transform public life in Canada as dramatically as television did during the transition from print. The new themes are empowerment and fragmentation. The consensus-building magic of mass-audience network television will fade, and Canadians will become increasingly divided as to how to build and maintain a country. Our leaders, who already seem more fallible than during the days of Churchill, Roosevelt and King, will have more trouble leading us. Their detractors will have less trouble dividing us.

Globalization and the new technology carry with them the seeds of loss and gain, optimism and pessimism, hope and despair. They will create opportunities for some, insecurities for others. They will fragment, decentralize, tribalize and privatize. Some analysts, including the respected John Ralston Saul, say the effects will be empowering. Saul, author of the thought-provoking *Voltaire's Bastards,* believes that empowered individuals, less reliant on the state, will come together and help build strong communities as never before. Perhaps he's right. On the other hand, the country could disintegrate, and it will be hard to forget the haunting perception that Canada was a very special place.

Canada's political future will largely depend on the economic fallout of the current transformation. If globalization and new technology yield the gains in standard of living that many economists predict, there is a good chance of establishing a new equilibrium, one that won't shatter our national identity or produce long-term political strife. One can imagine an exciting future – empowered individuals, thinking and acting at a new level of awareness, freed from the drudgery of repetitive work.

But if that's the future, why are the early signs so fraught with problems? Why are there so many nagging doubts? Middle-class Canadians with decent and secure jobs enjoyed being middle class a lot more than many are now enjoying being lower class, with two second-rate jobs or no jobs at all. Anybody whose world seems relatively stable – and who thinks life is business as usual – isn't paying attention. If people are going to be relieved of the drudgery of work by the new technology, who will take care of them? The state? The state is essentially bankrupt, and under attack for having tried to take care of too many people in easier times.

Changing times are changing voting patterns. Some of the new patterns constitute a reflection of the anxiety and bitterness of a dispossessed middle class. These voters, many of whom live in the suburbs of Canada's largest cities, have seen their dream of middle-class prosperity evaporate. They paid most of the taxes that helped carry the less fortunate during the good days. If their lives have changed for the worse, for many of them it's because they've been carrying the poor on their backs. If their dreams are shattered, the poor are going to pay.

These are the voters most ready to buy into the arguments of the upper classes that the poor get in the way of prosperity – arguments that most Canadians used to dismiss as the self-interested sermons of the rich. In English-speaking Canada, these are the voters demanding change in the Mike Harris mold. In B.C., our polls indicated that these are precisely the voters who were most likely to abandon the NDP and switch to the deficit-cutting Liberals. A sense of impotence and frustration prompts people to seize any opportunity to increase control over their own destiny, even if their hopes end up being dashed. The volatility of these voters signals more than just a break with tradition; it demonstrates a willingness to opt for radical alternatives to the political status quo.

Inevitably, the future of economic security in Canada will be critical to the political future of Canada. Canada's political traditions are now swirling around in the wind, and it is still too early to tell whether they will land upright or face down. Just as the inventors of the nuclear bomb came to question the implications of their creation, so the people who inspired the technologically driven economy are starting to worry about what they have done. Gordon Moore, the wealthy founder of Intel, the world's leading computer chip manufacturer, has expressed concern that new technology and globalization are not only producing a growing gap between rich and poor but are sowing the seeds of political instability.

Even market analysts are starting to worry. Stephen Roach, head of Wall Street's investment giant Morgan Stanley, is distressed that "the once tight linkage between trends in productivity and real wages in the U.S. economy appears to have broken down."[10] In other words, workers who used to share in the benefits of better production no longer do.

The flow of income out of the pockets of workers and into the pockets of entrepreneurs and investors will lead to more frustration at the polls, and elsewhere. At the moment it is government bureaucrats who are taking the flack for having spent and wasted taxpayers' money in recent years. But corporate attitudes may also start reaping the whirlwind. Social commentator Edward Luttwak senses an ugliness in the soul of modern business executives that may backfire. "The seventies fashion of 'human resources management' ... is entirely passé", Lutwak says, "having given way to a new kind of fashion – a suitably desexed North American version of machismo: the cult of the 'tough' executive who fires his subordinates without sentiment or hesitation."[11]

Luttwak points to a series of danger signals in America – rising support for more and speedier executions, the return of chain gangs and similar types of scapegoat thinking that tends to blame everybody's problems on one simple cause, in this case a breakdown in law and order. He sees an insecure and shrunken middle class looking for blood. In Canada, the level of public insecurity has reached record proportions. Support for a return to capital punishment stands at over 70%. The quest for rehabilitation has given way to a thirst for punishment and revenge. Immigrants and people on welfare, never popular at the best of times, become objects of increased hostility when things start going wrong.

Centrifugal forces are at work. As J.F. Conway has observed, "the daily political ties that bind individual loyalties to the distinctiveness of the Canadian experiment are weakened. As individuals – especially the middle class, whose access to social programs is increasingly under attack even as their tax rates remain high – begin to see that they are in the rat race alone and unprotected, the law of the jungle will begin to prevail and commitment to Canada as a society and as a political experiment will wither and die. And who can be proud of such a Canada?"[12]

Can we find a way to reap the benefits of this new age? Or will it end up costing us not only our pay packets but our country and our souls? The answer clearly depends on how we adjust. If we are intelligent, we have a chance. If we lash out blindly, we have much less chance. It is time to sink or swim. At moments like this, it's important to remember one thing: people who swim alone are far more likely to drown.

Nine

STAYING AFLOAT IN
THE NEW ECONOMY

"This, above all, to refuse to be a victim.
Unless I can do that I can do nothing."
Margaret Atwood, SURFACING

Early in 1996, I spent a morning with about a hundred high-school teachers and guidance counselors in the interior of B.C. Although I noticed many heads nodding in agreement as I discussed the problems Canadians were experiencing, I was not prepared for the protest that erupted when I had finished. "We believe all your statistics and what you say about the trends," said one of the teachers, "but we have 10,000 students in our high schools and they need hope. Without hope, they are lost."

There are currently about one and a half million Canadians aged 14 to 17, and the teachers were right: the situation isn't very hopeful for them right now, at least in the job market. Youth unemployment rates are as high as 30% for those with only a high-school education. Costs for attending post-secondary schools are shooting up. And there's a net decline in full-time jobs. So, it isn't easy for these kids to get excited about building a career. Their parents are no less fearful. Earlier this year, Gallup reported that about two-thirds of Canadians expect the next generation will be worse off than they are.[1] Among respondents in 17 countries participating in this survey, Canadians were tied for third place on this measure of pessimism about the future.

Rekindling a sense of hope and optimism is our most important challenge. And although it may be most acute for Canada's young people, it doesn't stop there. As I have tried to demonstrate, the new economy has become like white water churning through our lives – drowning job security, dampening consumer spending, eroding the political foundations of Canada and washing out paths that once led to stability and prosperity. Everywhere we look, the way ahead seems ill defined, the terrain strange and, for many, even hostile.

Only six or seven years ago, there was optimism that a new era, then in its infancy, would provide Canadians with an improved quality of life and a secure path to the future. The equation was simple and alluring: globalization and new technology would bring higher productivity, cheaper consumer prices, good jobs in the expanding "knowledge industry" and would allow Canadian companies to grow beyond the confines of our limited market.

The only catch, we were told, was the need to shed a few pounds, to rid ourselves of some of the inefficiencies and dead weight that had been allowed to accumulate in our public institutions and many corporations. And why not? In the late 1980s, the Canadian economy seemed to be running at full tilt. Even better, the world was becoming a much friendlier place, as Soviet-style communism and the cold war receded into the history books. For anyone reluctant to step into this brave new world came a stern warning, "There is no going back," cautioned Harvard professor Michael Porter in his 1991 report on the new competitive environment facing Canada. "Instead of looking longingly at the past, Canadians must adopt the new paradigm for what will determine future Canadian competitiveness."[2] The elements of Porter's new paradigm? Productivity enhancement, a greater emphasis on exports, less government, more investment in technology. It might be tough, but the discipline of the Sink-or-Swim era would make us all better swimmers in the economic Olympics.

So far, the best we can do is tread water, and too many Canadians are drifting toward the bottom of the pool. Half a decade after Porter's report, the realities of his new paradigm are increasingly evident: exports are up but exporting companies are not producing many new jobs; productivity is rising, but most workers aren't sharing in the benefits[3]; profits are buoyant, but some of the most profitable companies have celebrated by laying workers off rather than hiring new ones. CEOs in Canada are earning so much money that a recent *Globe and Mail* listing of the top 50 didn't have room for many of those earning more than $1 million a year. No wonder Canadians are starting to ask if the real agenda for corporations is "do more, better, for less – *and pocket the difference.*"

The attack on waste and duplication in government has turned into an all-out assault on public programs at every level. A combination of privatization, budget cutbacks and steep user fees is eroding the foundations of Canada's public infrastructure. There is no longer a cost-benefit analysis when it comes to providing public services – only a cost analysis. Money has always talked; now it dominates every conversation dealing with the commonweal. As for the much-vaunted knowledge society, thousands of university graduates are waiting tables, delivering pizzas and scrounging for other low-end jobs. When Wall Street and Bay Street talk about a knowledge society, they're really talking about an economic information society. In fact, it often seems that much of the wisdom accumulated over the centuries is irrelevant in this era of cutthroat economic warfare. What are we to make of the new knowledge-based economy when a Vancouver hospital announces it is cutting nursing positions so it can hire less-trained and lower-paid nursing assistants to do their jobs? What are we to make of the knowledge-based economy when thousands of trained workers now worry about being declared redundant in their fifties and forced to find self-employment?

Whom do we blame for this turn of events? We should probably begin with ourselves – for listening seriously to anyone who uses a word like *paradigm*. We are in danger of surrendering our future to a form of management pseudo-science that is devoid of morality and meaning. Forget the past? If there's any reason for optimism about the future, it comes from the past – from our record as survivors. This was a harsh country before the days of central heating. And since our ancestors first hacked an existence out of the land, we've survived several major depressions and two major wars. None of this makes today's anxiety and despair less real. But when people are tempted to treat history as a frivolous extra in our school systems, it helps to remember that Canadians have weathered tough times before. The past is one of our greatest treasures. It has provided Canada with a unique and much-envied culture that may prove to be our most important asset.

I suppose we should also blame economists at places like the department of finance and the Bank of Canada who continue to demonstrate how little understanding they have about what is happening in this country. As journalist Linda McQuaig has demonstrated, the obsession with a zero-interest rate policy at the Bank of Canada in the late 1980s contributed far more to the present debt crisis than program spending. McQuaig's argument has recently been echoed by Dalhousie University economists Lars Osberg and Pierre Fortin of the Université du Québec à Montréal.

They blame the central bank for "inducing the most severe recession in fifty years, destabilizing the national debt and forcing momentous political and social changes on the entire country."[4] John McCallum, the chief economist of the Royal Bank, echoes this critique: "The primary explanation for declining per-capita incomes in the first half of the 1990s lies in the exceptional length and depth of Canada's recession, which was itself due in large measure to the highly restrictive stance of Canadian monetary policy."[5] If the guardians of our economy at Finance or the Bank of Canada had looked around, they might have seen the decline in consumer demand that came with the death of the Spend-and-Share era. John Ralston Saul, curt and insightful, has observed that "if economists were doctors, they would today be mired in malpractice suits."[6]

And then there is big business. Canada's captains of industry have been ardent exponents of the new economy. And why wouldn't they be? They have been the winners. The average income of the CEOs running publicly traded companies that form the governing council of the Business Council on National Issues was more than $1 million in 1995. The average income of the typical Canadian worker is less than $30,000 and falling. Who really benefits from this new economy?

Although words like *crisis* and *tragedy* are overused, they accurately describe our current situation. The *crisis* of Canada today is the combination of economic problems facing us and the increasing impotency of governments that lack either the will or the resources to do much about it. The *tragedy* of Canada today is that just when we need a country that's pulling together in common cause, we have one that keeps finding new ways to pull itself apart.

Can we turn this thing around? Beyond all the feel-good bluster that many economists and business leaders throw at us, is there really any hope? I hazard to say yes, not just because I'm an optimist but because I believe that Canada has some important resources it can draw upon during this period of dislocation. These resources aren't the ones most people usually think of when the subject of Canada's future is raised. They come not out of our forests and mines but from our values and minds. Let me mention three that I believe will be critical to our survival, not just economically but as a nation. To use them, we must snap out of the trance induced by the slick hypnotists of the global economy.

It's time to recognize that we have significant social resources that offer grounds for hope. First, we must understand that our ability to survive and compete in the new economy is not constrained but is strengthened by our heritage of mutual trust, civility and fairness. Second, Canadians' belief in self-reliance provides a powerful basis for a new entrepreneurship, which is already gathering force and holds the promise of new jobs. Finally, while we may despair over the differences that divide us, there are important core values that continue to unite us, values that provide a foundation for building a new Canada.

CANADA'S EDGE IN THE NEW ECONOMY

Did you know that Canada has slipped from twenty-sixth place to thirty-fifth on the "Global Competitiveness Report"? I learned this late in 1995 in *The Vancouver Sun*, in a story filled with the usual warnings that Canada is losing out to more-competitive countries. Apparently Singapore is number one in competitiveness. I've been to Singapore. It's about the size of Edmonton, and resembles the West Edmonton Mall. But it does have some interesting points. For instance, the Singapore government hangs people caught with drugs and imposes heavy fines on those caught spitting chewing gum on the street. In 1992, as part of a special project on world public opinion, the Angus Reid Group commissioned a survey of Singapore residents. The results showed clearly that Singaporeans love their government and their leaders dearly. However, when asked whether they really feel free to express their feelings about their government, two-thirds said no. Enough said about that brand of freedom. I'm sure there are many good things to be said about Singapore, but there are many good things to be said about Canada as well, and I don't think being thirty-fifth on the competitiveness chart is much of a reflection on how good a society we have, which is, after all, the bottom line.

The big scare, of course, is that we will forfeit that goodness if we don't make life easier for big business to locate here. Eleven business-oriented think-tanks got together in January 1996 to rate countries on the amount of "economic freedom" they provide. Vancouver's Fraser Institute announced that Canada tied for sixth with the U.K. Hong Kong, where government spending is only 6.9% of GDP and the top marginal tax rate is only 25%, ranked first, followed by that neo-con beacon, New Zealand, followed by Singapore, the United States and Switzerland. Ireland and Australia tied for seventh, followed by those inveterate losers, the Japanese. In their final report, the authors interpreted the results as proof that economic liberalism guarantees prosperity. But the survey made no attempt to concern itself with issues such as lifespan, ecology, division of wealth or political freedom. Hong Kong, for example, was deemed "the freest nation in the world," although it is about to pass from a non-democratic system of British rule to a non-democratic system of Chinese rule.

The think-tank report illustrates one of the chief problems with how we think about "progress" in the global free market economy. Our measures of progress are almost solely economic. Productivity, growth, investment in technology, the size of a nation's debt – these have become the new standards of advancement. They are relatively easy to measure and to place on graphs. For ordinary Canadians, this process serves to underscore the idea of the economy as "something out there," a mathematical representation of a reality removed from their day-to-day lives. Certainly removed from many of the values and traditions that are part of meaningful daily life for most Canadians – having self-respect, caring for others, helping friends and family, expressing religious values, respecting, or at least tolerating, the views of others, and being involved in the community.

Talk to any Canadian who has been out of the country for an extended period and they will probably tell you how good it felt to come "home." Apart from reuniting with friends and family, they will point to all of the "little things" they missed while away: the relative safety of our cities, the politeness that pervades social interactions, the wide open spaces and, yes, even the quality of our beer. These all contribute to the "quality of life" in Canada. They're not as easily measurable as the things bean counters look at, but they do make a difference. Early in 1996, American journalist Susan Kaplan provided a glowing portrait of what many of us take for granted. "Canada has a flourishing social contract," she wrote in *Newsweek*, "and it shows in ways both large and small. Civility and thoughtfulness create a livability that contrasts markedly with many American cities. Here, we often lack the sense that each person is part of a larger collective, with rights and responsibilities. While Americans may ridicule Canadians for their politeness, it improves the quality of daily life."[7] Economic indicators and models fail to reflect those elements of our culture, traditions and social arrangements that are deeply treasured by most Canadians. Even worse, some of the rhetoric on the new economy argues that we should abandon these arrangements in favour of economic progress.

David Frum, the son of the late Barbara Frum, a highly respected Canadian broadcaster, is a sad case in point. When Alberta Premier Ralph Klein announced plans to scale back cutbacks to kindergarten and health-care funding, Frum was livid. "Despite the vaunted 'Alberta Advantage,'" Frum noted, "a petroleum engineer earning $65,000 a year who quits his job in Alberta to start an independent company is permitted to keep only 54 cents of every dollar he earns. If, on the other hand, he decides to abandon his province and relocate to Idaho, the money he earns above his old salary will net him 72 cents until he hits the top American rate of 36% at more than $175,000."[8] Frum wants to turn Canada into the U.S.A. – and Alberta into Idaho. Like other neo-cons, he is motivated solely by economic considerations. The fact that his petroleum engineer might prefer to live in Alberta with its obvious advantages in health-care and lower crime rates doesn't matter. All that matters, it would seem, is personal greed. All that matters is unrestrained free market economics. If anything gets in the way, throw it overboard. This is individualism run amok. Frum would turn us into Americans, with walled communities and a conviction that anyone on the outside is there because they chose to be – or because they deserve it.

I therefore see that the greatest risk inherent in the Sink-or-Swim era is that its central proposition – unrestrained self-interest – will drown some of the most important attributes of Canadian society. I'm not a sentimentalist here. I am convinced that these attributes are more than cushions to soften the impact of economic decline. They are actually something quite different, important ammunition to a society looking for a fighting chance in the world economy. Canada isn't going to come out on top by offering the cheapest labour and the lowest taxes. More desperate societies have an edge on us there. Canada has much more to offer.

Most of us have been conditioned to think that compassion and fairness can exist only where economic conditions are favourable. It has been drummed into us that during a period of transition, it may be necessary, in the interest of economic performance, to sacrifice programs and policies conducive to broader social objectives. The formula is simple: the only way to build a great society is through a strong economy.

I believe the time has arrived to balance this argument with an alternative proposition: the path to a strong economy is through a great society. Rather than thinking of the economy as something that operates independently of our culture, history and community values, think of them all as interwoven. Instead of thinking only about how much our national debt is dragging us down, we should redefine what we mean by the Canadian balance sheet. We may be surprised to discover assets we aren't aware of, assets critical to our task of creating jobs and reforming government.

The assets I'm referring to are characteristics of our society, in particular, trust, civility and fairness, that make up what the late sociologist James Coleman referred to as "social capital." If Canada is to have any chance for success in the global economy, we must do more than promote unrestrained self-interest. Societies with strong reserves of social capital have more than just a good quality of life; they're also able to develop healthier, more resilient economies. "Social capital," says American economist Francis Fukuyama, "is critical to prosperity and to what has come to be called competitiveness."[9]

TRUST

We all cherish trust. We want to live with people we trust, work with people we trust, walk down the street and trust that no one will mug or malign us. But what most of us often forget is that trust is more than a social treasure. It is also a critical factor in creating a healthy economy. Contrary to the popular assumption that economic organization operates at optimal efficiency when people care about nothing except their own self-interest, considerable evidence shows that the ability of people to cooperate is more important to making an economy work. Too much greed, too much individualism can erode the capacity of people to work together, to solve common problems and achieve shared goals, even when those goals are profits.

Harvard sociologist Robert Putnam has spent a career examining the consequences of varying levels of social capital. "Trust," he concludes, "lubricates cooperation. The greater level of trust within a community, the greater likelihood of cooperation. And cooperation itself breeds trust. The steady accumulation is a crucial part of the story behind the various cycles of civic society."[10] This sentiment is echoed by economist Gilbert Fairholm, who has argued that "trust is a key to productivity and to organizational effectiveness. The key element of a trust culture ... is that effectiveness is based on a willingness of participants to rely on another person for some or all of their individual success." [11]

Without high levels of trust, a society will be mired in excessive legalism and lose the ability to quickly adapt to changing circumstances. The United States, according to Putnam, has dwindling stocks of trust. About 1% of its adult population is in jail. The dominant urban form in many parts of middle and wealthy America is the gated community. Lawyers are everywhere, looking for business

– especially in personal injury and malpractice law. Over the past 10 years, mistrust among elected officials has caused legislative grid-lock, making it difficult, if not impossible, to reach consensus and implement change.

Francis Fukuyama presents a convincing argument that strong economic performance is closely linked to high levels of trust. Some countries, he claims, have the potential for high levels of "sponta-neous sociability," which give them the ability to develop new prod-ucts quickly. Trust springs from the culture, religion and traditions of these societies. It is these sociological and cultural features that "will be key to the success of modern societies in a global economy."[12]

Although it's difficult to measure a society's stock of trust, several indicators suggest that Canada may be well placed in this important area, especially when we compare ourselves to our southern neigh-bours. Canadians are not nearly as litigious as Americans (we have half the number of lawyers per capita) and express far greater trust in those people occupying positions of authority. For example, almost 60% of Americans feel that police corruption is a major problem; only 20% of Canadians hold this view. A similar pattern is evident with respect to levels of trust in public schools. I'm not saying that Canadians are saints in the trust department. But at a time when we are berated for our lack of competitiveness it's worth remembering that we have important advantages which shouldn't be ignored. It's also necessary to ask whether the forces of the new economy are undermining this vital asset.

CIVILITY

Not long ago, I found the following anonymous quote on the Inter-net: "People in Japan are proud that there are many vending machines of soft-drinks along the street, because it's a barometer of public peace." If you've ever been to Japan, you'll know that in their day-to-day behaviour, the Japanese strictly adhere to social conventions that reaffirm their responsibilities to others and the importance of their membership in a society they are proud of. They bow when greeting each other not just to be polite but as a sign that their individuality must bend to the broader interests of others. Vending machines that haven't been vandalized provide a daily reminder of the civility of Japanese society.

Civility is a two-way street. It involves an ethic that seeks to include all members of society *and* expects that each has a responsibility to adapt individual actions in the interest of the wider community. According to sociologist Seymour Martin Lipset, whose book *Continental Divide* charts the key differences between Canada and the U.S., our Canadian heritage has involved generous quantities of inclusiveness and civic responsibility. Canada is a society in which collective institutions have sought to embrace all residents. Health care, public education, voter registration procedures and universal social programs have all contributed to a sense of inclusiveness among Canadians. "Our core ethic," says *Toronto Star* columnist Richard Gwyn, "is that everyone should be included fully in the community by the community itself, rather than being required . . . to hack out their own space in the jungle."[13]

Most Canadians have historically had a deep belief in their civic responsibilities. Canada has one of the highest levels of voter participation in the developed world. Crime rates in our cities are among the lowest on the continent. Participation in voluntary associations is also high. The level of civility found here is a source of comment from visitors, especially Americans. "What I love about Canada is its civility," says American urban studies expert

Jane Harbottle. "There's always a willingness to talk things out with reasonable politeness . . . When you step on a Canadian's toes *he* apologizes. No doubt the public politeness of Canadians is exaggerated in foreign eyes, but the fact remains that it has helped them make the compromises necessary to build an enviable nation out of competing regional and cultural interests with a minimum of rancor and strife."[14]

In fact, despite all the infighting we've done over the Quebec issue – or perhaps *because* of all that non-violent infighting – we have gained a certain international fame for our ability to look at all sides of cultural issues. Peter Shwartz, whose book *The Art of the Long View* has served as a bible for many futurists, looks into the next century and sees a critical role for Canada, especially in the Pacific Rim. He sees Canada "as the glue that binds the Pacific Bloc together." Why? Because we "are adept at the skills required to manage a fiercely multicultural political entity." [15]

Canadians aren't nearly as meek as Americans make us out to be. But we do respect civility. Take negative political advertising. It works in the United States – American politicians wouldn't hammer one another with their vicious TV ads if the tactic didn't win votes. Negative advertising doesn't work in Canada. Kim Campbell's brain trust was desperate enough to turn to mean-spirited advertising near the end of the 1993 federal election campaign, holding Jean Chrétien up to ridicule for the way he looks and the way he speaks. The backfire was predictable. Canadians were outraged, and Campbell ordered the ads yanked almost immediately. In *Going Negative: How Political Advertisements Shrink and Polarize the Electorate,* Stephen Ansolabehere and Shanto Iyenger document how demeaning ads demean what people like Thomas Jefferson and Abraham Lincoln dreamed would be the most noble society humanity could ever create: "negative politics generates disillusionment and distrust among the public. Attack advertisements resonate with the popular beliefs that government fails, that elected officials are out of touch and quite corrupt, and that voting is a hollow act."[16]

Once voting becomes a hollow act, democracy becomes meaningless. That's not only bad for society, it's also bad for business. Like trust, civility is more than just a social virtue; it's an essential precondition to effective economic performance. Poet and writer Vaclav Havel, the president of the Czech Republic, claims that "improving the civility of everyday life can accelerate economic development – from the culture of supply and demand, of trading and enterprise, right down to the culture of values and lifestyle."[17] Declining levels of civility, on the other hand, can severely hamper economic growth. In comparing the booming economy of northern Italy with the sluggish performance of the south, Robert Putnam found that the latter is constrained by a lack of civic community, marked by vertically structured politics, a social life of fragmentation and isolation, and a culture of distrust.[18]

Again, however, the dynamic of the new economy is exerting pressure on the culture and traditions of civility in Canada. The "public" territory in Canadian life has been shrinking over the past decade with the growth of user fees, privatization and deregulation. Measures of attachment to Canada show a marked downturn. Increasing numbers of Canadians, especially those on the economic margins, do not feel part of the civic community. They have been largely excluded. It should come as no surprise that the two groups most alienated from Canadian society – young males (because they can't find work) and Quebeckers (because they fear loss of identity) are also the two groups most likely to report that they don't pay the GST. The decline in civility concerns more than the marginalization of the poor. The percentage of their profits that corporations donate to charities has declined throughout the 1990s. Wealthy Canadians (those in the top 8% of income earners) are the most likely to support an abandonment of universal social programs in the interest of tax cuts.

Civility in Canada is endangered by the excessive celebration of the individual. *Globe and Mail* columnist Michael Valpy asks an important question: "We have all these accumulating privileges: Human rights codes, constitutional charters, laws that protect children and their parents from state-sponsored therapeutic intervention, increasingly deregulated commerce markets and so on, all contributing to a philosophy of individual and corporate freedom. But what has happened to individual and corporate obligations?"[19] Exactly. They're on the wane, and if we don't get them back we will not only be abandoning what makes one of the best societies in the world tick, we will be abandoning something crucial to whatever competitive advantage Canada holds in the world marketplace. I know it's hard to squeeze civility on to a flowchart, but without it "bottom lines" will suffer.

FAIRNESS

In the new economy, the prize for individual achievement and corporate success is high incomes and vast wealth. Egalitarian principles, it would seem, belong to a different age in which mushy values like fairness had widespread sentimental appeal. A leveling of differences between economic classes gets in the way of productivity because, we are told, it drains the incentive to achieve. It is an obstacle to economic progress.

In other parts of the world, there is growing concern about exactly the opposite – that the global economy is creating a rapidly growing gap between rich and poor that, unchecked, could destabilize the social order. The *Economist* warned in 1994 that, "Concerns about growing inequality should not be dismissed or sneered at." Why? "In recent years the economic forces of international competition and (above all) new technology have gathered strength. In relatively unregulated economies, they have driven down the incomes of losers and driven up the incomes of winners." [20] Alan Greenspan, head of the U.S. Federal Reserve Bank, has voiced similar concerns: he warned Congress in the summer of 1995, that growing income inequality in the U.S. would become a major threat to "our society."

Concern about growing inequality is not limited to worries about the destabilization of society. Indeed, evidence indicates that fairness facilitates, rather than impedes, economic growth. April Lindgren, writing in the *Ottawa Citizen,* in 1995, noted that "a growing number of studies suggest that more egalitarian societies are better at producing the healthy, educated people needed to fuel the new brain-powered economy."[21] Her argument is economic: Japan, Spain, Belgium and other industrial countries with a narrower gap between rich and poor grew faster from 1980 to 1992 than countries with greater disparities, such as the U.S., New Zealand, Australia and Switzerland. On the other hand, economic greed may do considerable harm. According to Robert Frank and Phillip Cook, we are living in a "winner takes all" society in which "rising inequality is more likely to curtail than to stimulate economic growth."[22]

Fairness is a fundamental ingredient in the cement of social capital that provides a country with a chance to survive and even succeed in the new era. Without fairness, civility becomes compromised and trust erodes. In Canada, an aggressive program of fiscal transfers including UIC, CPP and welfare has served to check the tendencies toward greater income inequality that seems, everywhere, to be a consequence of the new economy. The result is that declines in the relative position of middle and lower-class Canadians have not been nearly as great as in other countries. The Centre for the Study of Living Standards shows that Canada, unlike the U.S.A., has so far not experienced the growing polarization of total income between high and low income workers. [23] As in the U.S., the actual wage gap has expanded, but this has been muted by transfer payments.

That's likely to change with the coming reduction of transfers. Although official statistics still haven't caught the trend, a majority of Canadians feel that the gap between the rich and poor has widened since the start of the decade. Poor and middle-income Canadians report a decline in their standard of living.

Canada's reserves of social capital are at risk of being quickly depleted by the mean-spirited individualism of the new economy and undermined by one-dimensional arguments that focus solely on the need for greater economic freedom. Moving silently and insidiously through public and private life, new economic values threaten to destroy those very elements of our national character that have produced a balance of livability and prosperity that is the envy of the world.

Everything, now, must bow to narrow economic considerations. Take the arguments for two-tiered medicine. "Why not build private hospitals?" say promoters of this scheme. "It will take some of the pressure off the existing health-care system." On the surface, this looks like one of those neat win-win situations: rich people pay for their own health care, thereby leaving middle-income and poorer Canadians greater access to existing "public" services. Sounds great – until you're driving little Johnny, bleeding half to death in the backseat because he fell off his skateboard, to hospital and realizing that you can't stop at the Executive Hospital on your left because that's for the rich people. You've got to get to the Grunge Hospital, where with any luck they'll treat Johnny within a couple of hours. Mind you, the equipment isn't great; the rich don't want their money pumped into public hospitals any more since they've got their own. Does that sound like Canada?

Again, we must think of the Canadian balance sheet in more than solely economic terms. In a January 1995 issue, the *Economist* argued that when it comes to long-term investment, Canada still has an edge. It pointed to Philips Electronics' decision to move some product lines from Mexico to London, Ontario, and Chrysler's decision to set up a research unit in Windsor. "These firms have discovered that the lure of low wages in southern United States and Mexico can be outweighed by the productivity of a loyal, well educated, albeit highly paid, workforce." The Canadian experiment has not been the disaster that some commentators make it out to be. "The next time Moody's and Standard and Poor's sit down in their American offices to scrutinize Canada's economic health," says Sherri Torjman, an analyst with the Caledon Institute on Social Policy, "they may want to consider our social health as well. Next time the credit raters on Wall Street set out to calculate the pluses and minuses of the Canadian economy, they may want to take into account the quality-of-life factors for which we never get credit – but which are crucial to good business and to the well-being of the country as a whole."[24] Maybe our department of finance should do the same. We need a balanced budget, one that includes consideration for economic *and* social capital.

In 1995, the World Bank issued a report in which it ranked 192 countries on the basis of their overall wealth. Canada finished second, just behind Australia. Rather than restricting itself to GDP comparisons, the survey examined resources – both natural and human. Countries with huge natural assets, such as Russia and Canada, had a clear advantage. But that didn't necessarily mean they would score well. Russia finished forty-fourth. The difference between second and forty-fourth was mainly social capital. Luxembourg, Switzerland and Japan, countries not exactly laden with natural resources, finished third, fourth and fifth. Note that no other country in the western hemisphere finished in the top 10. Now is the time to call on our social capital, not treat it as some kind of economic burden. It is time to stand up to the small-minded thinking that can't see the intangibles so important to successful enterprise.

Though a full listing of all the steps that can be taken to shore up Canada's reserves of social capital is beyond the scope of this book, three measures deserve consideration. The first concerns the need to place a stronger emphasis on fiscal programs aimed at providing all Canadians with access to basic services and an income they can live on. I'm not saying we should abandon efforts to reduce deficits and reform the social safety net but that these efforts should not take place in a sociological vacuum. Tax cuts, user fees and the wholesale privatization of public services may look good to the accountants, but what effect will they have on our reserves of social capital? We must be cautious when considering proposals for further downsizing in the name of deficit cutting and distinguish between those that are absolutely necessary and those that are little more than Trojan horses aimed at undermining the essential character of Canadian society.

A second measure concerns what many Canadians see as increasingly irresponsible behaviour on the part of corporations – an obsession with maximizing shareholder values to the detriment of employee and community interests. An Angus Reid poll conducted in 1996 shows that 60% of Canadians feel that corporations are becoming more irresponsible. Several proposals have been brought forward to deal with this issue. In the U.S., two leading Senate Democrats released a proposal in 1996 that reopened the debate about the corporation's social purpose. Minority Leader Thomas A. Daschele and Jeff Bingaman, who heads Daschele's Task Force on Living Standards, proposed a new kind of federally chartered corporation. The proposed legislation calls for a new class of corporation – the "R" corp, with the "R" for responsible. The idea is to reward corporations that invest in employees and communities. An "R" corp would receive lower taxes and streamlined regulatory treatment.

In Canada the emphasis so far has been on voluntary action in the corporate sector. Early in 1996, for example, a workshop on business ethics at the University of Toronto was devoted to the need for ethics codes which spell out the responsibility of employers to employees and vice versa. Sensing growing levels of public concern, Yves Desjardins-Siciliano, vice-president of law and external relations at Bell Mobility, warned participants that Canadians "are sophisticated consumers and citizens" who have "high expectations of businesses beyond their products and services."[25] Whether through regulation or consumer pressure, companies in Canada must come to understand that they have special responsibilities to protect and enlarge Canada's store of social capital.

Finally, we must remember that families are the foundation of civility. The fiscal attack on welfare recipients threatens to create a new generation of Canadians, raised in poverty, and with little attachment to the broader values that sustain the social order. In a CBC *Morningside* interview in 1996, Frazer Mustard, president of the Canadian Institute of Advanced Research, made a convincing argument that an extra dollar spent on a program to help children, especially those living in poverty, could earn a return of seven dollars from a combination of savings from expensive programs aimed at treating the damage of child poverty and reducing the social disruption that is often associated with a lack of civil values.

Already there is evidence that the values of the new economy threaten to deplete our social capital just at a time when its ingredients are more desperately needed than ever. Self-interest is replacing collective responsibility, mistrust is unseating confidence in public institutions and optimism about our collective future is declining. The most important challenge facing Canada's leaders and policy-makers is to foster a climate of sharing, mutual trust and civility. In the rush to set our economic accounts in order, let's not forget the fundamental values that have kept us together in the past and will help us secure the future. The restructured global economy presents a major challenge to every society in the world. Why would a country like Canada, with a clear advantage in the area of social capital, want to throw that advantage away? This isn't just a question for philosophers. It's a question that the Canadian business community should be asking itself as well.

THE FUTURE OF WORK

When my children were younger we used to go to the Shrine circus every year. Our favourite act was always the last one on the program. It involved Aldo the Human Cannonball being fired from a cannon mounted at one end of the Winnipeg Arena into a net at the other end. It was hard not to be captivated by Aldo, who defied gravity and risked personal injury to provide the audience with a dramatic finale to an afternoon filled with magicians, clowns and animal acts. What made Aldo's act work wasn't just the cannon or his training or even his bravery, but the net. Indeed, without the net, the act couldn't take place. There's a link between risk taking and security that exists not just for circus acts but in many other areas of human endeavour. This link may prove especially important as a key to resolving one of the greatest challenges of our current age – the creation of jobs.

I'm not suggesting that we should sign up to become human cannonballs, but we're going to have to start thinking in innovative ways about our jobs. We're going to have to become more entrepreneurial and take more risks. And we must begin by recognizing that there is no guarantee that the new economy will produce good, well-paying and secure jobs. Commenting on the widely held belief that restructuring will create more jobs than it destroys, former Molson's CEO and deputy minister of finance Marshall Cohen noted, "It is time to start questioning that faith. If we are destroying jobs faster than we create them, the implications for social policy are profound."[26] No longer does a strong economy necessarily mean more jobs. It could even mean fewer, especially if we are talking about what most of us think of as a good job: full-time work for a decent salary.

We need to recognize that there's not much chance that many jobs will be created in areas dependent on government funding. And we need to be careful when listening to people like Nuala Beck, whose "five star" employers in the new economy include universities and hospitals. Anyone who reads the papers or works at these places will tell you that these institutions are working feverishly to cut staff, or to replace well-paying jobs, such as professors and nurses, with poorer-paying jobs, such as contract lecturers and nursing assistants. The same holds for most large corporations. With some notable exceptions in high technology and computer services, most large companies will probably continue to shed rather than create full-time jobs. Big business in Canada, like the U.S., is increasingly "nation-less," and even under conditions of favourable markets, it is as likely to use its profits to expand outside of Canada as to invest in this country.

Northern Telecom is a good example. In spite of strong revenue growth that all Canadians can be proud of, Nortel is creating most of its new jobs outside Canada. The *Financial Post's* 1986 best-seller, *100 Best Companies to Work for in Canada,* is an interesting historical read, but not many of these employers are hiring. Some have even experienced spectacular de-hiring. Others are following the pattern evident across Canada of hiring increasing numbers of part-time and temporary workers. Consider, for example, Calgary's Nova Corporation. In 1990, it hired 554 new employees of which 509 (92%) were placed in permanent full-time jobs. Four years later, 776 new employees were hired but only 65 positions (8%) were permanent full-time; the rest were either temporary or part-time. The sad reality is that large companies, even those whose management would dearly love to hire more Canadians, are being boxed in.

Competitive pressures and mobile capital make it difficult for many to resist restructuring and downsizing.

We also need to confront the training myth. There's no doubt that people with specialized skills will have a much better chance obtaining good, high-paying jobs. There's also no question that basic skills in keyboarding and the use of computers are now essential for almost every job. But will more training alone translate into more jobs? According to the U.S. Labor Secretary Robert Reich, there's a "field of dreams" element to many of the arguments about training and jobs: "if you train the workforce," the myth goes, "jobs will come." I remain skeptical that training and skills upgrading can cure the current malaise in job creation. For many large employers, the advent of new technology coupled with re-engineering has actually reduced skill needs. "At the middle and lower echelons, more and more workers rely on skills that are easier to learn than those of their predecessors," says labour specialist Simon Head, whose analysis of the changing American workforce has challenged the training myth. He cites the bitter strike in the U.S. between the United Auto Workers and Caterpillar, which ended in part "because the company found it could rely on temporary help agencies to replace virtually all of its striking shop floor employees."[27] I believe we need to focus on more than just skills training. The digital age has produced an explosion in the volume of information at our fingertips. We need more people who are able to convert this information into knowledge, people who feel confident about taking risks and assessing opportunities. We need this talent because it's time to face the ultimate truth about jobs in the new economy: we're going to have to generate them ourselves.

There are two paths along which this will occur, and both begin at the same point: entrepreneurship. This is, of course, one of the decade's sexier words. Many people assume it means a desire to get rich in a climate of unrestrained capitalism. But nothing could be further from the truth. Entrepreneurship is about taking responsibility and creating bold new initiatives. It involves a refusal to listen to the naysayers standing on the sidelines shouting, "It can't be done!" Entrepreneurship isn't about personal greed but is about ambitious ideas tackled with others in a spirit of cooperation and sharing. Finally, and perhaps most important, entrepreneurs, like human cannonballs, perform best when there's a net.

Entrepreneurship is critical to job creation because only through the creative thinking and risk taking of hundreds of thousands are we going to extricate ourselves from the corner the new economy has painted us into. We can resist globalization and new technology to some extent, but we can't defeat them. We can legislate companies to become more responsible, but we must eventually recognize that they are faced with the choice between sinking or swimming. The challenge is to exploit the resources and new markets at our disposal and allow the plans and schemes of many Canadian entrepreneurs to flourish. We must create conditions favourable to entrepreneurship.

So the first path involves small business and the creation of privately owned enterprises. The second, though less well known, is equally important. It involves the application of entrepreneurial thinking in existing companies and, yes, even government agencies. In both cases, our challenge is to foster the kind of bold, innovative thinking – risk-taking behaviour – that will make a difference in the new economy.

The fastest-growing category of employment in this decade has been self-employment. Nearly 350,000 Canadians have started a business in the 1990s. Some 2.1 million workers are now self-employed; that's about 15% of the labour force. Maybe it's time to recognize that this is not a momentary shift but where the future really lies. If we're going to have any success in creating jobs, it will depend on the energy and creativity of thousands of Canadians. It will also depend on governments becoming more serious about developing programs to help small businesses get launched and grow. First, we must dispense with the myth that new small businesses usually fail. According to Walter Good, who heads the University of Manitoba's marketing department and is an expert in small business, the real rate of small business failures is between 25 and 40% – not the 80% number that "has become folklore."[28] Because of this myth, small business has been "long shunned" as the poor cousin in the commercial family. The perception may be starting to change. "The ground is more fertile than it used to be," says University of Toronto professor Michael Bliss, who has written extensively on business history. "More people are talking about founding their own business. You see more business springing up. This is the way we have to grow if we are to compete in the world."[29]

In a big world, we should increasingly think *small?* I know this sounds contradictory, but the more you think about it, the more sense it makes. The big companies, with all their re-engineering and technology, have become efficient at producing relatively standardized products. What they often lack, however, is the personal touch, and customized features demanded by local and niche markets. Take the micro-brewing industry. While the major players in the Canadian brewing sector are consolidating their operations and closing plants, local micro-brewers are thriving. In Winnipeg, where Labatts recently closed its plant and shed about 200 jobs, Richard Hoeschen has gained an increasing market share with his Fort Garry Brewing Company. By offering a product substantially different than the major brewers and a name heavily linked to Winnipeg's history and tradition, Hoeschen now presides over a thriving, expanding operation.

Thousands of jobs need doing – and inventive people are anticipating needs and fulfilling them, often outside the formal economy. They have the advantage of knowing their local markets and are prepared to work hard to realize their dreams of independence. But they also need help, especially if we're going to produce the jobs that are necessary. The biggest misconception about entrepreneurship is that it flourishes best in an environment of unrestrained self-interest. I'm not saying there aren't nasty little self-centered people in the business world – you'll find plenty. What I am saying is that most successful business people have a sense of mutual advantage and community responsibility. The dictionary defines entrepreneurship, more than anything else, as a taking of responsibility. And Canadians are willing: according to a 1996 survey, an astonishing 60% said that, given a chance, they would rather run their own business than work for someone else. That's a lot of energy and creativity waiting to be unleashed.

When I talked about Canada's social capital, I talked about trust, civility and fairness. Believe it or not, these qualities not only apply to the world of business, they nourish it. Ask any entrepreneur about the business person they respect most; it's usually the guy with whom they can make a deal over a handshake, rather than in a room full of lawyers. Few businesses get beyond the start-up phase without the cooperation of co-workers, and it's hard to win that cooperation if those people aren't treated fairly. Small-minded business people express contempt for the state, but smart operators know that for a business, the society it operates in is like the air it breathes. Good air produces healthy organisms. Entrepreneurs may resent bureaucratic restrictions, but they do want good roads, safe streets, reliable utilities and all the other pluses that good governments provide. Look at medicare. The Canadian medicare system gives Canadian entrepreneurs an edge over Americans, who often must bear the extra expense of private health-care coverage. Individual responsibility is important to entrepreneurs. So is social responsibility.

If business people are going to show the proper respect for good government, governments need to show more understanding of the nourishing environment that needs to be created for small entrepreneurs. Stimulating jobs in the small business sector will require more than the elimination of bureaucratic red tape and more than social capital. It's going to require some kind of intervention to assure better access to capital. In this case, I mean the kind of capital they keep in banks. And I do mean *keep*.

You can't pursue an entrepreneurial dream without money, and nobody but the very rich can bring a viable enterprise to fruition without access to credit. Yes, one-person companies are beginning to proliferate, often operated out of the home. And many of these can be bankrolled out of savings, or out of a buy-out package from a company or government. But, by definition, one-person companies create only one job. Canada needs thousands of new companies that each create at least a handful of jobs and, with determination and any kind of luck, more. Those kinds of companies need cash. When I started my company in the late 1970s, I became painfully aware of this constraint – the first time I was turned down for a loan. My bank manager told me that tight money was good for small business because it forced budding entrepreneurs like me to run profitable operations – or die. His last name was Coffin.

I'm not an expert on business financing, but I do know that it takes money to start a business and even more to help it grow. I also know that the banks have been progressively tougher in granting credit to small business. They want entrepreneurs to put up more and more of their own assets before they use the bank's money. The banks' logic is that this practice will produce better small businesses, because owners will be more prudent when spending their own money. Unfortunately, it also means that a lot of entrepreneurs with good ideas – but no money to invest – will not be starting ventures any time soon.

A 1995 Canadian Federation of Independent Business survey revealed that access to capital is a major problem facing new entrepreneurs, especially women.[30] Loan rejection rates, according to the CFIB, are particularly acute for smaller, high-risk start-ups. Overall, small firms reporting problems with financing availability have nearly doubled from 20% in 1990 to almost 40% by 1996. The capital needs of small business must be addressed if we're going to get serious about job creation.

One option that should be explored was recently proposed by David Bond, chief economist at the Hong Kong Bank of Canada. It involves the use of RRSP funds. Suppose that regulations were changed so that a portion of annual tax-deductible RRSP contributions over, say, $10,000, could be invested only in special funds aimed at business start-ups. I know this won't be popular for free market zealots who already resent that several provinces have given tax breaks to investors who make RRSP contributions to capital funds aimed at financing local companies. But we're facing a crisis that will never be resolved if we rely only on market forces.

The needs of small business aren't restricted to access to capital. New business owners require market research, management advice and help with legal and many other services. More than anything, we must understand that small business needs a fertile ground in which to take root and grow. We must create the conditions to make this happen.

Small business, though critically important, will solve only part of the jobs problem. Not everyone can run his or her own business, and though many would like to give it a try, most will probably not fulfill their dream. But should that be the end of entrepreneurship? I don't think so. Entrepreneurship can be applied everywhere. My friend Paul is a senior administrator at a post-secondary institution, where he and his colleagues have recently formed a partnership with a Canadian housing manufacturer and several Japanese companies to train Japanese workers in Canadian home-building techniques. This venture will provide more teaching jobs, help sell our lumber and create additional revenue for my friend's college. This example nicely illustrates what entrepreneurship is really all about in the new economy: new partnerships, a constant search for new opportunities, using the resources available and people willing to take risks, be creative, sense opportunity and pull together. In short, thinking big and small at the same time.

Looking outward for opportunity is the *big* thinking part. The small part is equally important, because it involves looking in a mirror and asking: How can I make a difference? Although downsizing and delayering are unfortunate consequences of the new economy, they have the potential of making this question more relevant than ever. Not so many years ago, someone like my friend Paul would have suffered the derision of his colleagues for "selling out" to the private sector. Now, it's called partnership. Some might even call it survival.

David Osborne and Ted Gaebler created an international bestseller when they coined the term *entrepreneurial government* to describe the central proposition behind their idea of re-inventing government.[31] The problem, they claim, isn't whether to have more or less government but how to develop "better" government. More than anything, better government is about taking responsibility, giving better service, engaging in the new enterprises and channeling the forces of change. I know that many people in government agencies and departments work hard – as much in the interests of their organizations as in their own narrow self-interest – to dream big ideas and take at least small steps to realize them. They are the unsung heroes of the entrepreneurial revolution of the new economy.

Equally important are their counterparts in large corporations. Ironically, despite their profit goals, large-scale commercial enterprises often find it difficult to generate entrepreneurial thinking, especially in their middle and lower ranks. Forty years ago, according to David Halberstam, many questioned whether America was "losing its entrepreneurial class to cautious, grey managers, men afraid to make mistakes and take chances." Though the conformity of the 1950s may seem like ancient history, the uncertainty of the 1990s threatens to produce the same results. Such prophets of entrepreneurship as Tom Peters and Stephen Covey have made many converts among senior management, but the sad fact is that many companies are saddled with fierce internal politics and in many cases a rhetoric of empowerment that stands in sharp contrast to a reality of declining autonomy, increased surveillance and heightened insecurity. Why take chances when you could be the next victim? Yet entrepreneurship is precisely what large companies need, especially if they are to create and produce the new goods and services that will appeal to rapidly changing global and local markets.

Today, there are lots of awards and rewards for people who start their own businesses and are successful. Every city stages celebrations to honour entrepreneurs; I know because I was delighted to receive just such an award in Vancouver. But what about these other, less visible heroes, people working in the public sector and large corporations who have had the vision or creativity to build their companies or at least contribute in a meaningful way? This is the other side of entrepreneurship that we must recognize and nurture.

The greatest danger in the present age is that we will stand transfixed, like a deer in the headlights, as the forces of the new economy overwhelm us. An equal risk is that we will be immobilized by a sense of impotence as we wait for the political fixers and economic experts to make things better. We're in the midst of a difficult transition and it will take a combination of personal initiative and mutual support to survive this dangerous crossing. Social capital, money and recognition are all necessary for survival. But the most important of all is our ability to think independently, since without independent thinking, entrepreneurship is not possible.

I say this because there's a mechanistic school of thought that our learning institutions should simply crank out graduates who can fit right into the workplace. Some critics of our education system argue that less attention should be paid to such subjects as history, philosophy, languages, literature and geometry and that more attention should be paid to assembling people with hard, practical skills. This argument ignores the fact that the workplace is changing so quickly that it's virtually impossible to package skills tailored to specific situations without on-the-job training (not one of the Canadian private sector's great strengths). It also ignores the reality that corporations are dismissing droves of people who have precisely the training and experience required for specific jobs. Unfortunately, many of those jobs aren't there any more.

The challenge for Canada's schools is not so much to prepare people for the workplace. Capitalism prides itself on being quick on its feet, and if companies need people to fill particular slots, it shouldn't take long to train them. The challenge for our schools is to stimulate the minds of people from all levels of society. Those minds must be able to wrap themselves around both scientific and social changes, now storming out of the trenches.

Are our young people equipped with the knowledge and confidence in their ability to think that private and public sector entrepreneurs need? In the January 1996 edition of *Harper's*, Lewis Lapham lamented that a 1995 study by the U.S. Department of Education amounted to a "coroner's report" on American education. The study showed that 50% of U.S. high-school seniors aren't even aware that there was something called the cold war. Furthermore, he said, it showed that nearly 6 in 10 are "bereft of even a primitive understanding of where America came from."

Canadian high-school seniors may be somewhat more aware, but "somewhat" is a thin word.[32] We need something more substantial if we are going to restructure our society to cope with new realities. How will young Canadians know that the utter reliance on the private sector helped lead to the Great Depression if they don't even know that there *was* a Great Depression? How will they know how dangerous it is to blame minority groups for society's problems if they don't know the events that created the Third Reich? How will they know that the erosion of democratic principles in the interests of political efficiency was just what Mussolini had in mind when he said he wanted the trains to run on time?

If ordinary people are going to show the flexibility and resilience Canada needs, their minds are going to have to be open to *all* measures that might improve their lives. The kind of mindless pluck that saw 15,000 people line up for work at General Motors in 1995 is commendable. But the jobs GM was talking about really didn't exist, so a lot of people wasted time demonstrating pluck, didn't they? There must be better ways of rejuvenating the Canadian entrepreneurial spirit.

Canadians are going to have to get much more serious about both learning and thinking. At the moment, both the left and the right are content to offer us what Michael J. Sandel calls "an impoverished vision of citizenship." Writing in *Atlantic Monthly,* Sandel said both sides have become accustomed to focusing on individual self interest rather than on the capacity of citizens to share in shaping the forces that govern their collective lives.[33] Canada is 10 steps ahead of the U.S. in this regard, because we have always cared more about our social resources. But the current preoccupation with fiscal restraint – and the imported U.S.-style libertarian thinking that goes well beyond deficit fighting – means that Canada is imperiled as well.

Canada's young people must be educated in a way that keeps them open to all possibilities. Simplistic thinking isn't going to cut it, either in terms of revamping Canada's economy or reinvigorating what has been one of the world's most admired social systems. The simplistic pursuit of material wealth has dominated our lives since the Second World War. Clearly, our post-1989 economy will not be able to provide most Canadians with the material options they've enjoyed over the past quarter century. But we will also have to find alternatives to happiness that involve more than consumption.

We have shrunk our governments and corporations; it is time to start expanding our minds. Our machines are becoming much more sophisticated – and so must we. It is time for another Age of Enlightenment that will take us further than we have ever gone before. Thomas Homer-Dixon, director of the Peace and Conflict Studies Program at the University of Toronto, warns, "We are seeing the emergence of an economic environment in which the winners are relentlessly entrepreneurial, forever on the edges of their seats, watching and waiting to seize new opportunities before others seize them."[34] We should be entrepreneurial about seizing *all kinds* of opportunities, economic and otherwise.

BUILDING A NEW CANADA

There is an almost unanimous desire to rethink government in Canada. Electing governments that will act in the common good is one of the most exciting concepts of modern civilization, and the mindless anti-government fanaticism that poisons right-wing thinking in the United States is both puerile and dangerous. Most Canadians believe, however, that our governments had grown bloated and stale by the late 1980s, and increasing numbers of Quebeckers convinced themselves that government reform was worthless unless Quebec had more civic space to call its own – a separate nation, if push came to shove.

Nothing Quebeckers design, or that Ottawa designs in conjunction with provincial premiers, or that various Canadian interest groups propose, seems to quite hit the mark. Which isn't surprising, given the fragmentation of attitudes across the land. So where are we? We have begun by stripping down federal, provincial and municipal governments to the point that they can no longer deliver much of what we demanded during the past three decades. Where do we go from here? We had better figure that out pretty quickly, because Canada's political foundations may be starting to give way. Never have the two pressures hounding us since Confederation – Quebec separation and U.S. political domination – posed more of a threat. And the two reinforce each other. The more the prospect of separation threatens English Canada, the more futile the quest to strengthen Canadian identity becomes. And the more Canadian governments run on American ideas, the more Quebeckers become convinced that the concept of Canada is largely meaningless.

For all the confusion and distress we are feeling about how we govern ourselves, two things are worth remembering: anti-government backlashes are occurring all over the world right now, and Canadians have always been exceptionally good at making governments work in a way that strengthens society.

Yes, our health-care system let costs spiral out of control before we took a scalpel to it. But we can fix it. We must never forget that we spend about 9% of GDP to produce a first-rate system that provides access to all Canadians. Americans spend 13% of GDP on a system that leaves 30 million people without coverage. That, to me, speaks to a wonderful marriage of compassion and efficiency. And it's a marriage we can make even stronger, if we don't bow to the privileged and private sector interests and dismantle it.

Canadians don't need *less* government at this point. The days of waste and lethargy have largely come to an end in the public service. There is room for more reform, to build governments that are both intelligent and responsive, and we must be willing to sit down and thrash out our priorities in this regard. That's not nearly as simple and sexy as denouncing governments as the mortal enemy of the people and the taxpayers' bank accounts, but it will lead to a more civil society.

So far, I concede, we haven't made much progress in pursuing a new national blueprint. We've invested enormous energy debating every detail of what the new Canada should look like, but few results have been achieved. In the meantime, the old Canada is being battered from all sides, and too many people seem ready to throw up their hands and walk away. This may be an enervating debate, but the prize is priceless.

If we're going to survive as a country, we must move quickly. I say this not only because the Quebec clock is ticking but because the present indecision is chipping away at our core values and draining our reserves of social capital. I've been conducting polls on French-English relations in Canada for more than 15 years. Although attitudes toward the many constitutional issues that divide us have changed with each passing chapter in the saga, one constant has been the good relations between ordinary English and French Canadians. Even through the worst of the Meech Lake debacle and the Charlottetown accord episode, our two founding language groups didn't start hating each other. Now that's starting

to change. Polling in the wake of the 1995 referendum shows that
hostility levels are rising, especially among English Canadians
(almost a quarter describe their feelings towards Quebeckers as
hostile).[35] Trust is eroding.

Fairness is also taking a beating, especially with the emergence of
voting preferences and policy attitudes based on social class.
Throughout my career as a pollster, I have seen deep divisions in
Canadians' attitudes based on gender, age and geography. But never
have I seen those that have emerged in recent years – divisions
based on income. Canada, especially at the provincial level, is beginning to show signs of a mean-spirited class-based politics our
cousins to the south know so well. Whether Ontarians buy Mike
Harris's Common Sense Revolution depends less on their age, sex or
where they live than on how much money they make. Even nationally, there's a deep dividing line between rich and poor: the former
demand that more attention be given to deficit cutting and tax
reduction; the latter are more concerned about cuts to social
programs and inattention on job creation.[36] The Quebec issue may
dominate, but a potentially more important division is growing,
one that threatens our common purpose as surely as the menace
that lurks in Quebec City.

We need to build a new Canada before it's too late. I'm not a
constitutional expert, nor do I have strong views on many issues,
like Senate reform, that are part of our ongoing debate. But I do feel
strongly about the foundation on which the new Canada should
rest – the values of its citizens. I agree with writer Rick Salutin, who
has argued: "In the end, I believe our national crisis is about this
matter of values; it's about whether we truly value the kind of
community Canada is, and could become. If the answer is yes, then

our future won't be determined by the trends or even laws of currently fashionable economics. We'll gather our resources as a nation and find a way to continue."[37]

A foundation built on the beliefs and values of Canadians may at first glance appear awkward and unstable. On many issues, public opinion seems a study in contradiction. We want the federal government to vacate vast program areas including regional development, employment training, social welfare and health care. We want the provinces to run the show, but don't want a patchwork of programs across the country – we want national standards and federal funding. While we support the *concept* of protecting Quebec's language and culture, we remain deeply divided when these guarantees are placed under the label "distinct society." We support the concept of fiscal restraint in general, but back off on many specifics. Clearly, the public is often confused. But on some issues it is not – and this is where we must begin.

There are four enduring beliefs, common to the vast majority of Canadians, that should serve as cornerstones of a new Canada. The first is a deeply held desire to be unique, to create a society fundamentally different from the one to the south of us, or from any other that we or our ancestors may have emigrated from. Putting it more positively, we recognize that compared with *any* other place in the world, we have something special. Although we often have difficulty articulating what that something is, it's there. In many ways, we are a haven, and we would be fools not to continue to take pride in Canada's unique niche in the global community.

Second, beneath all the grumbling, nearly all of us (85%) believe that English and French Canadians can live harmoniously under one flag. This is a crucial belief, because it means that Canadians haven't given up hope. Despite its flaws and its fatigue with the cultural conflict that has dominated Canadian politics for several decades, Canada is not Bosnia, Northern Ireland, the Middle East or many of the other areas of the world in which deep-seated ethnic or religious differences seem so indelible, so insoluble. That bond of hope is fraying at the edges, but it's still intact.

My third building block is a core belief in the importance of a civil society. Canadians' faith in the importance of reason and diplomacy – and their distaste for using violence to solve problems – is the envy of the world. Look around: the bitterness left by violent, arbitrary solutions, some of them imposed centuries ago, still smolders virtually everywhere that peace keeps breaking down. We Canadians have our own passions, but when they threaten to consume us, some kind of safety valve usually kicks in, demanding that sanity, sensitivity and fairness prevail. The Paul Bernardo trial dealt with an ugly, volatile issue in a Canadian way, both in its procedures and in the way the news media covered it. Many Canadians still weren't completely satisfied with the outcome, but most prefer the approach we took to the circus that surrounded the O.J. Simpson trial. Again, you will get arguments that our law enforcement officers might have handled the 1995 confrontation with Native Canadians at Gustavson Lake in a more judicious way. But compare it to how the FBI handled similar conflicts in Waco and elsewhere.

Even on our most contentious national issue – Quebec separation – the vast majority is desperate to reach a fair and civilized solution. There are Canadians who insist that the army be ready to move in and use force if English-speaking Canadians don't get the settlement they want. But that's a distinctly minority view. The specter of violence appalls most Canadians. Even in Quebec, there is a growing belief that groups such as Aboriginals in the North should have something to say about their own self-determination if Quebeckers vote to secede. You can call civility boring if you want. But there are people all over this planet who live in constant fear of physical violence, and they don't call civility boring.

Finally, while the concept of fairness has taken a pounding as class divisions have deepened, a core belief persists among most Canadians that we must try to build a society based on that principle. Premier Ralph Klein lists proudly to the right, as does his province, Alberta. But Klein isn't quite the libertarian ideologue he sometimes seems. His government made severe cuts to kindergarten education, cuts that would have denied early access to education for lower-income children, who need it most. When large sectors of the country's most right-wing province protested vehemently, Klein responded by reinstating full-time kindergarten for all. Canadians grumble about taxes and try to avoid them at every turn, but no one seriously suggests an end to the principle of progressive taxation. Even some of the furore over the GST is based on its regressive nature – it doesn't give lower-income Canadians the break that income tax does. In short, if there's a more fair-minded society in the world, I don't know of it.

These beliefs alone won't solve the quandary of how to reform government in Canada. At best, they're a starting point. But it is important to recognize that there is at least *some* common ground. The forces of change sweeping through Canada have not yet uprooted every element of our common heritage. There is a resiliency to the Canadian character, even in these times of change. Political party attitudes may come and go. Our views on the monarchy may change with the latest royal scandal. Our feelings toward the banks shift with the latest news on their profits. But on some matters, our resolve is so firm that they are part of our core identity. This is the foundation on which we must build the new Canada.

There is, of course, a sense of urgency. And that pressure presents both a risk and an opportunity. The risk is that the complexity of our task requires more time than is available. The opportunity is that the shortness of time, especially on the Quebec issue, will force us to confront the changes that Quebec – and the new economy – demand. Other countries dither about what to change and when, while changing tides slowly erode their social, political and economic foundations. We no longer have the luxury to dither. We must act, move resolutely to a redefinition of Canada – not to appease Quebec, but to save ourselves.

As we approach the new millenium, it is difficult to avoid the sense of apocalypse that grips humanity. "The world," according to Ethan Kapstein, director of studies at the U.S. Council on Foreign Affairs, "may be moving inexorably toward one of those tragic moments that will lead historians to ask, why was nothing done in time?" [38] The tragic moment that Kapstein refers to is precisely the one that lies at the center of my analysis: the problems confronting workers in the global economy. These issues are part of a world-wide phenomenon that Kapstein compares to that which occurred in the 1930s: economic dislocation and the unwillingness of leaders to recognize the profound problems confronting their citizens. I don't pretend to have all the answers, but I know this: we must move quickly – individually and collectively – or historians will ask the same of Canada: "Why was nothing done in time?"

Several chapters ago, I argued that recent Canadian history – from the end of the war, and certainly from the 1960s to the '80s

– cannot be fully understood without recognizing the role that core societal values played in facilitating the transformation of Canada during the Spend-and-Share era. We now stand at another turning point. Many of the values of the 1960s have been worn away. Yet beneath them lies a set of core beliefs that provide a path to the future.

I began this book by stating the obvious: there are powerful new forces arrayed against us. Let me conclude by observing that we can swim against them if we see the opportunity, but as so often when facing powerful forces, opportunities for true confrontation will be scarce. In most cases, we are likely to have more luck if we can ride these current forces the way a canoeist navigates a stream, accepting the inevitability of their strength without letting them gain complete ascendancy. And whatever we do, we must do everything in our power to resist becoming victims.

To achieve this, Canadians are going to have to look inside themselves for entrepreneurial spirit, and outside themselves for the communal spirit that has sustained this country through its most difficult times. We can get through this if we are determined to grow, rather than shrink, as a people. We must change. But, no matter how dark the clouds, we cannot abandon who we are.

NOTES

PREFACE

1. National Angus Reid Poll, July 1993; Canadian Food Study (Angus Reid Group), February/March 1992.

INTRODUCTION

1. Please see Appendix for all Statistics Canada data sources.

2. Naisbitt, John, and Patricia Aburdene. *Megatrends 2000: Ten New Directions for the 1990s* (New York: Avon Books, 1990), p. 1.

3. Rubin, Jeffrey, "Two Futures for Canada," *Globe and Mail*, May 23, 1992.

4. "Middle Marches Back," *Globe and Mail*, June 28, 1994; Howes, Carol, "Bosses Going, Says Futurist," *Calgary Herald*, April 27, 1995; and "Monkeys in the Middle," *Globe and Mail*, May 9, 1995.

5. "National Angus Reid Poll," *Angus Reid Report*, November/December 1995.

CHAPTER I

1. Reuber, Grant L., "The Impact of Government Policies on the Distribution of Income in Canada: A Review," *Canadian Public Policy/Analyse de Politiques* 9, no. 4 (Autumn 1978), p. 505–29.

2. Boroughs, Don, et al., "Winter of Discontent," *U.S. News and World Report*, January 22, 1996.

3. *Canadian Medical Education Statistics* (Association of Canadian Medical Colleges), 1994; *Enrollment in Programs of Study* (Association of Canadian Medical Colleges Forum), 1996; Wong, Jan, "Flouride Has Dentists Frowning," *Globe and Mail*, March 21, 1996; Makin, Kirk, "Law Graduates Starving for Work," *Globe and Mail*, March 9, 1996; and Duvall, Mel, "Globe Trotters," *Calgary Herald*, February 12, 1994.

4. National Angus Reid Poll, August 1986; National Angus Reid Poll, October/November 1995.

5. Valpy, Michael, "Yours Sincerely, Your Soothing Bank," *Globe and Mail,* March 7, 1996.

6. Galt, Virginia, "Musical Chairs a Crying Game," *Globe and Mail*, November 13, 1993.

7. National Angus Reid Poll, October/November 1995.

8. Courchene, Thomas J., "Celebrating Flexibility: An Interpretive Essay on the Evolution of Canadian Federalism" (C.D. Howe Institute Benefactors Lecture, 1995), p. 58.

9. In Nowotny, Helga, *Time: The Modern and Postmodern Experience* (Cambridge: Polity Press/Blackwell, 1994), p. 16.

10. Horsman, Mathew, and Andrew Marshall, *After the Nation-State: Citizens, Tribalism and the New World Order* (London: HarperCollins, 1994), p. xiv.

11. *Report on Business Magazine,* July 1990, p. 137.

CHAPTER 2

1. *Report of the Royal Commission on the Status of Women,* (Ottawa: Supply and Services Canada, 1970), p. 34.

2. *1966 Census of Canada* (Dominion Bureau Of Statistics, Cat. No. 93-610).

3. Ruddy, Jon, "Stop the World—They Want to Get Off," *Maclean's*, November 1, 1965, p. 21.

4. Galarneau, Diane, *"Female Baby Boomers: A Generation at Work"* (Statistics Canada, Cat. No. 96-315E, 1994), p. 43.

5. *Royal Commission on the Status of Women,* p. 8, n. 24.

6. Jackson, Toby, and Harry Bredemeier, *Social Problems in America* (New York: John Wiley, 1963).

7. Lichter, S. Robert, Linda Lichter, and Stanley Rothman, *Watching America* (New York: Prentice-Hall, 1991).

8. Vickers, Jill, "Women in Universities," in Gwen Matheson, (ed), *Women in the Canadian Mosaic* (Toronto: Peter Martin Associates, 1976), p. 206.

9. Vickers, "Women in Universities", p. 203.

10. Hobsbawm, Eric, *Age of Extremes: The Short Twentieth Century 1914–1991* (London: Abacus, 1995), p. 334.

11. Yankelovich, Daniel, "How Changes in the Economy Are Reshaping American Values," in Henry Aaron, , et al. (eds), *Values and Public Policy* (Washington: The Brookings Institute, 1994), p. 18.

12. Postman, Neil. *The End of Education: Redefining the Value of School* (New York: Knopf, 1995), p. 33.

13. Marchand, Philip, *Marshall McLuhan: The Medium and the Messenger* (Toronto: Random House, 1986), p. 177.

14. Galbraith, John Kenneth, *The New Industrial State*, 2nd edition (Boston: Houghton Mifflin, 1971), p. 208–9.

15. "U.S. Business in 1965," *Time*, December 31, 1965, p. 52.

16. Kostash, Myrna, *Long Way from Home: The Story of the Sixties Generation in Canada* (Toronto: Lorimer, 1980), p. xxvi.

CHAPTER 3

1. Crane, David, *The Next Canadian Century: Building a Competitive Economy* (Toronto: Stoddart Publishing, 1992), p. 50.

2. Little, Bruce, "Spending Some Time on Spending," *Globe and Mail*, August 8, 1994.

3. Galbraith, John Kenneth, "Blame History, Not the Liberals," *Globe and Mail*, September 21, 1995.

4. Drucker, Peter, *Post-Capitalist Society* (New York: HarperCollins, 1993), p. 38–49.

5. Paepke, C. Owen, *The Evolution of Progress: The End of Economic Growth and the Beginning of Human Transformation* (New York: Random House, 1993), p. 93.

6. *The State of the Family in Canada* (Angus Reid Group Family Study), April/May 1994.

7. National Angus Reid Group Poll, July/August 1993.

8. *Canada and the World* (Angus Reid Group), March 1992.

9. National Angus Reid Group Polls, September/October 1989, October/November 1992, November, 1995.

CHAPTER 4

1. National Angus Reid Group Poll, March 1996.

2. "The Accidental Superhighway," *Economist,* July 1, 1995, p. 4.

3. Gilder, George, "The Death of Telephony," *Economist,* September 11, 1993, p. 76.

4. "The Revolution Begins at Last," *Economist,* September 30, 1995, p. 15.

5. Tapscott, Don, *The Digital Economy: Promise and Peril in the Age of Networked Intelligence* (New York: McGraw-Hill, 1995), p. xiii.

6. "The Accidental Superhighway," *Economist,* p. 3.

7. Boyle, James, "Sold Out," *New York Times,* March 31, 1996.

8. Stoll, Clifford, *Silicon Snake Oil, Second Thoughts on the Information Highway* (Toronto: Anchor Books, 1995), p. 24.

9. Stoll, Clifford. *Silicon Snake Oil*, p. 24.

10. Head, Simon, "The New Ruthless Economy," *The New York Review of Books*, February 29, 1996, p. 47.

11. Ehrenreich, Barbara, "Surfing the Third Wave," *New York Times Book Review*, May 7, 1995, p. 9.

12. Barnet, Richard, J., and John Cavanagh, *Global Dreams: Imperial Corporations and the New World Order* (New York: Simon and Schuster, 1994), p. 13.

13. McLuhan, Marshall, *Understanding Media* (New York: Mentor/Penguin, 1964), p. 298.

14. Barnet and Cavanagh, *Global Dreams,* p. 16.

15. Bezanson, Keith, *Imperatives for Investment through Economic Cooperation* (Speech to the forum on the Greater Mekong Subregion: Investment Opportunities through Economic Cooperation), November 1994.

16. Grant, George, *Lament for a Nation: The Defeat of Canadian Nationalism* (Ottawa: Carleton University Press, 1986), p. ix, 85.

17. Grant, *Lament for a Nation,* p. x, 2.

18. Cook, Peter, "Why Pink Slips Go with Record Profits," *Globe and Mail,* February 7, 1996.

19. *op. cit.* "Celebrating Flexibility: An Interpretive Essay on the Evolution of Canadian Federalism" (C.D. Howe Institute Benefactors Lecture), 1995, p. 36.

20. Platt, Gordon. "Let 'Eagle' Fly as Single Currency, Economists Urge," and Reza, H.G, "U.S. Open Border with Canada," *Toronto Star,* August 27, 1995.

CHAPTER 5

1. McQueen, Rod, "Jobless in Recovery," *Financial Post,* October 14, 1995.

2. Krahn, Harvey, "Non-Standard Work on the Rise," *Perspectives on Labour and Income* (Statistics Canada, Cat. No. 75-001, 1995), p. 39.

3. Marshall, Ray,"The Global Jobs Crisis," *Foreign Policy* (Fall 1995), p. 50.

4. Aronowitz, Stanley, and William DiFazio, *The Jobless Future: Sci-Tech and the Dogma of Work* (Minneapolis: University of Minnesota Press, 1994), p. 3.

5. "After Work: A Blueprint for Social Harmony in a World without Jobs," *Utne Reader,* May-June 1995, p. 54.

6. Rifkin, Jeremy, *The End of Work* (New York: Putnam, 1995), p. xv.

7. Drucker, Peter, *Post-Capitalist Society* (New York: HarperCollins, 1993), p. 33–5.

8. Snyder, David Pearce, "The Revolution in the Workplace: What's Happening To Our Jobs," *The Futurist,* March-April 1996, p. 10.

9. Rifkin, *The End of Work,* p. 174.

10. Rifkin, *The End of Work,* p. 159.

11. Snyder, "The Revolution in the Workplace," p. 8–13.

CHAPTER 6

1. Employment statistics for the period 1967–1989 cited in this chapter are taken from *Good Jobs, Bad Jobs* (Ottawa: Economic Council of Canada, 1990).

2. Canadian Truckers Association, June 1996.

3. *Aviation in Canada: Historical and Statistical Perspectives on Civil Aviation* (Ottawa: Ministry of Industry, Science and Technology, 1993).

4. McQueen, Rod, "Big Six Face Onslaught by U.S. Banks," *Financial Post,* July 29-31, 1995.

5. Shortell, Ann, *Money Has No Country: Behind the Crisis in Canadian Business* (Toronto: Macmillan, 1991), p. 15.

6. Hagerman, Mary, "Creativity Major Asset for Hopefuls," *Financial Post,* October 6, 1993.

7. Cited in McFarland, Janet, "Insurance Shakeup Forecast," *Financial Post,* April 25, 1995.

8. Crawford, Trish, "Thousands of Agents Sent Packing in the GTA," *Toronto Star,* July 16, 1995.

9. Mulroney, Catherine, "Selling Property Will Test Your Mettle," *Financial Post,* October 6, 1993.

10. Gundi, Jeffrey, "Profession Reinventing Itself," *Financial Post,* June 28, 1995.

11. Lee, Jenny, "Enterprise in the Electronic Shopping Mall," *Vancouver Sun,* June 27, 1995.

12. Hodge, A. Trevor, "Why Tenure Is Just a Myth," *Globe and Mail,* September 5, 1995.

13. In McKendry, J.R., et al., "Factors Influencing the Emigration of Physicians from Canada to the U.S.," *Canadian Medical Association Journal* (January 15, 1996), p. 171.

14. Monsebratten, Laurie, "Work-For-Welfare Scheme Isn't Working," *Toronto Star,* July 15, 1995.

15. Lindgren, April, "Job Insecurity: It's Here to Stay," *Ottawa Citizen,* April 23, 1995.

16. Mitchell, Alanna, "Middle Class Cleft Into Haves, Have Nots," *Globe and Mail,* April 24, 1996.

17. In a 1995 year-end poll, 48% of middle-class respondents and 60% of those who defined themselves as "poor" said they were either "disappointed" or "really upset" over the trend toward government cutbacks to programs. On the other hand, 72% of wealthy and 61% of upper-middle-class respondents either "accepted" or "enthusiastically supported" these cutbacks. (1995 Angus Reid Year-End Poll conducted on behalf of CTV News and Southam News.)

CHAPTER 7

1. Carrick, Rob, "Rising Credit-Card Use Sets Off Debt Alarms," *Ottawa Citizen,* January 17, 1996.

2. A 1993 study published by the Grocery Manufacturers of Canada noted that "the battle of the brands is fought millions of times each day on grocery shelves across Canada. 'Which one to buy?' is a key decision that consumers make over and over again on every shopping trip, with store control brands having a strong significant presence in a growing number of

categories." Evidently, "the aggregate probability of a 'brand switch' on any single grocery store purchase is now 50%. That is, just 50% of consumers purchased the brand they bought 'last time' when they select that product again from the shelf."

3. Kosich, George, quoted in *Canadian Business Leaders Speak* (Business Council on National Issues, 1995.)

4. Cited in McMartin, Patrick, "Prices Put New Cars Out of Reach," *Vancouver Sun*, February 21, 1996, p. A2.

5. Saunders, Doug, "Class Actions Signal New Consumer Activism," *Globe and Mail*, February 17, 1996.

6. 3rd Annual Royal Bank Home Ownership Survey, February 1996.

7. The *Family in Canada* study carried out in 1994 with a sample of 2,000 Canadians underscored the centrality of the family in the lives of most Canadians; 89% of those polled described their family life as "full of love," 84% said that it is where they go for "support and comfort," and 83% felt that it was "their greatest joy in life."

8. Stern, Leonard, "Generations," *Ottawa Citizen*, September 11, 1995.

CHAPTER 8

1. Lemco, Jonathan, "Canada: The Year of the Volatile Voter," *Current History*, (March 1995), p. 118.

2. 1994 Angus Reid Group Poll for Human Resources Development Canada.

3. In an Angus Reid Group survey of 3,600 Canadians carried out in February 1996, respondents were asked whether they feel more "attached" to their province or to Canada. Those most likely to name their province rather than the country were not Quebeckers but Newfoundlanders: 72% chose their

province. Two-thirds of Quebeckers responded this way, as did
50% of British Columbians and Albertans. Ontario residents
were the least likely to display provincial affinity, with only
30% naming their province. (*Renewing Canada: Public Opinion
and the New Agenda for Canada,* Angus Reid Group and
Createc, 1996.)

4. Conway, J.F., "Reflections on Canada in the Year 1994,"
Journal of Canadian Studies (Fall 1994), p. 152.

5. Guindon, Hubert, "Social Unrest, Social Class and Quebec's
Bureaucratic Revolution," *Queen's Quarterly* 71, no. 2 (Summer
1964), p. 150–62.

6. Coxe, Donald, "Lester Thurow's Unsettling Outlook," *Globe
and Mail,* October 14, 1995.

7. Sigurdson, Richard, "Preston Manning and the Politics of
Postmodernism," *Candian Journal of Political Science* 27, no. 2
(June 1994), p. 249–76.

8. From the Internet (*Netscape*), January 1996.

9. *Communiqué* (Media Studies Centre), New York, 1994.

10. Roach, Stephen, "Backlash: The View From Wall Street,"
Harper's, January 1996, p. 16.

11. Luttwak, Edward, "The Middle Class Backlash," *Harper's,*
January 1996, p. 14.

12. Conway, "Reflections on Canada," p. 152.

CHAPTER 9

1. Moore, David W., and Frank Newport, "People Throughout
the World Largely Satisfied with Personal Lives," *The Gallup
Organization International Newsletter* (March 1996).

2. Porter, Michael, *Canada at the Crossroads: The Reality of a New
Competitive Environment* (Ottawa: Michael Porter and the
Monitor Company; Business Council on National Issues; and
the Ministry of Supply and Services, 1991), p. 391.

3. In 1994, businesses posted their best productivity performance in 10 years. Business restructuring coupled with only moderate wage increases contributed to a second consecutive decrease in unit labour cost (cost per unit of output calculated as the ratio between labour compensation and real GDP. It is also equivalent to the ratio between labour productivity and hourly compensation). Labour productivity within the business sector increased by 2.4% in 1994 (multifactor productivity measure). Compensation per-person hour increased by 1.6%; this was mainly a result of increased overtime and was the second-lowest rise since 1947. ("Productivity, Hourly Compensation and Unit Labour Cost," *Statistics Canada Daily,* April 21, 1995, p. 5–6.

4. Osberg, Lars, and Pierre Fortin, "Credibility Mountain," in *Unnecessary Debts* (Toronto: Lorimer, 1996), p. 168.

5. Phip, Margaret, "Royal Bank Rips into the Bank of Canada," *Globe and Mail,* May 27, 1995.

6. Saul, John Ralston, *The Unconscious Civilization* (Concord, Ontario: House of Anansi, 1995), p. 4.

7. Kaplan, Susan, "Northern Composure: Americans Could Learn Some Valuable Lessons in Civility from Our Canadian Neighbors," *Newsweek,* February 12, 1996, p. 17.

8. Frum, David, "What's Right," *Financial Post,* February 3, 1996.

9. Fukuyama, Francis, *Trust: The Social Virtues and the Creation of Prosperity* (Toronto: Penguin, 1995), p. 355.

10. Putnam, Robert, D., *Making Democracy Work: Civic Traditions in Modern Italy* (Princeton University Press, 1993), p. 169.

11. Fairholm, Gilbert, *Leadership and the Culture of Trust* (Westport, Connecticut: Praeger, 1994), p. 118.

12. Fukuyama, Francis, "Social Capital and the Global Economy," *Foreign Affairs* (September/October 1995), p. 89–103.

13. Gwyn, Richard, *Nationalism Without Walls: The Unbearable Lightness of Being Canadian* (Toronto: McClelland and Stewart, 1995), p. 256.

14. "The Duty of Civility," *Royal Bank Letter*, May/June 1995.

15. Shwartz, Peter, *The Art of the Long View: Planning for the Future in an Uncertain World* (New York: Doubleday, 1991), p. 183, 184.

16. Ansolabehere, Stephen and Shanto Iyenger, *Going Negative: How Political Advertisements Shrink and Polarize the Electorate* (New York: The Free Press, 1995), p. 47.

17. Havel, Vaclav, *Summer Meditations* (Toronto: Knopf Canada, 1992), p. 15.

18. Putnam, *Making Democracy Work*, p. 15–16.

19. Valpy, Michael, "I Wash My Hands of Him," *Globe and Mail*, February 16, 1996.

20. "Slicing the Cake,"*Economist*, November 5–11, 1994, p. 13, 14.

21. Lindgren, April, "Social Programs: Can We Afford to Let the Poor Get Poorer?" *Ottawa Citizen*, October 2, 1995.

22. Frank, Robert H., and Philip J. Cook, *The Winner-Take-All Society* (New York: Martin Kessler Books/The Free Press, 1995), p. viii.

23. *Centre for the Study of Living Standards Newsletter*, January 1996.

24. Torjman, Sherri, *Investing in People Is Good Business* (Caledon Institute on Social Policy, 1995).

25. Livingston, Gillian, "Businesses Urged to Build Staff Trust with Ethics Code," *Financial Post*, June 1, 1996.

26. *The Link Between Social Policy and Economic Performance* (Ottawa: Human Resources Development Canada, 1996), p. 1.

27. Head, Simon, "The New Ruthless Economy," *The New York Review of Books*, February 19, 1996, p. 50.

28. McNeil, Murray, "Small Doesn't Mean Fat Chance," *Winnipeg Free Press,* October 28, 1995.

29. Spence, Rick, "Entrepreneurial Nation," *Profit: The Magazine for Canadian Entrepreneurs,* September 1995, p. 22.

30. Marleau, Martine, "Double Standard: Financing Problems Faced by Women Business Owners" (Canadian Federation of Independent Business, 1995).

31. Osborne, David, and Ted Gaebler, *Reinventing Government: How the Entrepreneurial Spirit Is Transforming the Public Sector* (New York: Penguin, 1992).

32. A recent report by Susan Crompton reveals that over one-third of Canadian workers have only marginal literary skills. This proportion is higher in Canada than in both Germany and the United States. (Crompton, "The Marginally Literate Workforce," *Perspectives on Labour and Income,* Statistics Canada, Cat. No.75-00, 1996, p. 14–21).

33. Sandel, Michael, "America's Search for a New Profile," *Atlantic Monthly*, March 1996, p. 57.

34. Homer-Dixon, Thomas, "What to Do with a 'Soft' Degree in a Hard Job Market," *Globe and Mail,* April 1, 1996.

35. Angus Reid Group Year-End Poll, December 1995.

36. Angus Reid Group Year-End Poll, December 1995.

37. Salutin, Rick, "A Plea For Canada," *Maclean's*, July 1, 1995, p. 43.

38. Kapstein, Ethan B., "Workers and the World Economy," *Foreign Affairs* (May/June 1996), p. 18.

APPENDIX:
STATISTICS CANADA DATA SOURCES

THE ECONOMY

Canadian Economic Observer (Statistics Canada Cat. No. 11-010-XPB), December 1994, February 1996, April 1996.

Canadian Economic Observer: Historical Supplement 1993/1994, 1994/1995 (No. 11-210).

Capacity Utilization Rates in Canadian Manufacturing (No. 31-03), Fourth Quarter 1985.

Consumer Price Index (No. 13-207), May 1993, December 1993.

Financial and Taxation Statistics for Enterprises 1993 (No. 61-219).

National Economic and Financial Accounts (No. 13-001), Fourth Quarter, 1993–1995.

National Income and Expenditure Accounts 1981–1992 (No. 13-201).

National Income and Expenditure Accounts Annual Estimates 1926–1986 (No. 13-531).

"Productivity, Hourly Compensation and Unit Labour Cost," *Statistics Canada Daily* (No. 11-00IE), April 21, 1995.

Public Sector Finance 1995–1996 (No. 68-212).

Summary of Foreign Trade (Dominion Bureau of Statistics, No. 65-001), 1970.

Survey of Consumer Finances 1981–1991 (No. 13-207).

EDUCATION

Education in Canada: A Statistical Review 1990–1991 (No. 81-229).

Service Bulletin, Education Statistics (No. 81-002), 1980, 1992.

THE FAMILY

Boyd, Monica, and Doug Norris, "Leaving the Nest? The Impact of Family Structure," *Canadian Social Trends* (No. 11-008E), Autumn 1995, p. 15–17.

Chawla, Raj K., "The Changing Profile of Dual-Earner Families," *Perspectives on Labour and Income* (No. 75-001), Summer 1992, p. 22–29.

Divorces 1991 (No. 84-213), 1994.

Families: Number, Type and Structure (No. 93-312), 1991 Census data.

Families: Social and Economic Characteristics (No. 93-320), 1991 Census data.

La Novara, Pina, *A Portrait of Families in Canada* (Target Groups Project, No. 89-523E), 1994.

Lindsay, Colin, *Lone-Parent Families* (Target Groups Project, No. 89-522E), 1992.

Moore, Maureen, "Women Parenting Alone," *Canadian Social Trends* (No. 11-008E), Winter 1987, p. 31–36.

Vital Statistics: Marriages and Divorces 1974, 1981 (No. 84-205).

INCOME AND EARNINGS

Earnings of Canadians (No. 96-317E), 1994.

Income After Tax: Distributions by Size in Canada (No. 13-210-XPB), 1994.

Income Distributions by Size (No. 13-207), 1989, 1994.

Low Income Persons (No. 13-569) 1995.

Public Sector Employment and Wages and Salaries (No. 72-209), 1992–1994.

Rashid, Abdul, "Seven Decades of Wage Earners," *Perspectives on Labour and Income* (No. 75-001), Summer 1993, p. 9–21.

THE LABOUR FORCE

Akyeampong, Ernest, and Jennifer Winters, "International Employment Trends in Industry – A Note," *Perspectives on Labour and Income* (No. 75-001), Summer 1993, p. 33–37.

Bernier, Rachel, "The Labour Force Survey: 50 Years Old!" *Canadian Economic Observer* (No. 11-010-XPB), March 1996, p. 3.1–3.8.

Credit Unions 1983–1994 (*CANSIM* data base, Statistics Canada Time Series).

Employment Change Based on Average Labour Units by Industry Aggregate, Business Size and Life Status (Small Business and Special Survey Division), January 1996.

Labour Force Annual Averages 1989–1994 (No. 71-529).

The Labour Force (No. 71-001), December 1989, April 1990–1996, November 1995, December 1995, February 1996.

MISCELLANEOUS

Electric Power Statistics (No. 57-202), 1989.

Computer Use in the Workplace, 1994 General Social Survey (No. 12-FOO52XPE).

Household Facilities by Income and Other Characteristics 1968 (No. 13-540), 1972.

Leacy, F.H. (ed), *Historical Statistics of Canada*, 2nd edition (Ottawa: Social Science Federation of Canada and Statistics Canada, 1983).

SHAKEDOWN

Market Research Handbook (No. 63-224), 1990.

Touriscope (No. 66-001-PPB), March 1996.

POPULATION AND DEMOGRAPHICS

Galarneau, Diane, *Female Baby Boomers: A Generation at Work* (No. 96-315E), 1994.

Grindstaff, Carl F., "Canadian Fertility 1951–1993)," *Canadian Social Trends* (No. 11-008E), Winter 1995, p. 13–16.

McKie, Craig, "Population Aging: Baby Boomers into the 21st Century," *Canadian Social Trends* (No. 11-008), Summer 1993. p. 2–6.

1966 Census of Canada (Dominion Bureau of Statistics, No. 93-610), June 1968.

Population Projections for Canada, Provinces and Territories 1993–2016 (No. 91-520), January 1995.

Postcensal Annual Estimates of Population 1967–1992. (No. 91-210).

Postcensal Annual Estimates of Population by Marital Status, Age, Sex and Components of Growth for Canada, Provinces and Territories (No. 91-210), 1992.

Report on the Demographic Situation in Canada (No. 91-209E), 1995.

Revised Intercensal Population and Family Estimates, July 1971–1991 (No. 91-537).

Selected Birth and Fertility Statistics, 1921–1990 (No. 82-533).

Silins, J. and W. Zayachkowski, *Canadian Abridged Life Tables 1961–1963* (Dominion Bureau of Statistics, Health and Welfare Division) (No. 84-00-501), 1966.

INDEX

THANKS TO THE 2,000,000 CANADIANS WHO HAVE GIVEN OUR COMPANY THEIR MOST PRECIOUS ASSET:

THEIR TIME.

Over the past decade, more and more Canadians have talked with our interviewers about what they really think of our clients.

Which hamburger, car, diaper or donut is better? How strongly do they feel about crime and punishment, employment insurance, or user fees for doctors' visits? Where will they take their next vacation, what radio station do they listen to, when will they buy their RRSP and which pill do they reach for to cure a headache or ease a cold?

That's quite a list. And, it's only some of the almost 50,000,000 questions we've asked in all.

Also, 20,000 entrepreneurs talked to us, either face-to-face or over the phone. So did 40,000 doctors, 1,100 CEOs, 22,500 business flyers, an astounding 90,000 agricultural producers, and 35,000 credit card users. Just to name a few.

Thanks to these people and thousands more, the Angus Reid Group now conducts $25 million in research annually, and employs over 120 full-time researchers and 400 part-time interviewers using some of the world's most sophisticated person-to-person telephone interviewing systems.

In 1979, we opened our doors above a 7-Eleven store in Winnipeg. Since then, we've grown into a truly nation-wide research company with full service offices in six major Canadian cities.

And now, thanks to the people we've interviewed and the clients we've gained, we've expanded into the U.S. to manage projects ranging from a joint venture with CNN to assignments for many Canadian and American companies with market research interests in the U.S. and in over 20 countries throughout the world.

So if you need insight into your business, talk to the people who are already talking to more Canadians – and more people around the world – than ever.

Sincerely,

Angus Reid